Action in Late Ming Thought

Joanna F. Handlin

Action in Late Ming Thought

The Reorientation of Lü K'un and Other Scholar-Officials

University of California Press
Berkeley • Los Angeles • London

University of California Press
Berkeley and Los Angeles, California
University of California Press, Ltd.
London, England

Printed in the United States of America

Library of Congress Cataloging in Publication Data
Handlin, Joanna F.
Action in late Ming thought.

Bibliography: p.
Includes index.
1. Lü, K'un, 1536–1618. 2. Philosophy, Chinese—960-1644. I. Title.
B128.L854H36 181'.11 82-2762
ISBN 0-520-04380-4 AACR2

1 2 3 4 5 6 7 8 9

For my father and to the memory of my mother

Contents

Preface ix
List of Abbreviations xiv

PART I
Sages and Average Men

1 The Official as Scholar during the Ming Dynasty 3

2 Sages 33
Lo Ju-fang, Educator 41
Hai Jui, Administrator 54

3 Yang Tung-ming: In His Hometown 65

4 Feng Ts'ung-wu: In the Academy 84

PART II
Lü K'un: New Avenues to Sagehood

5 As Doctor to Society 103

6 By Writing for Women, Children, and the Poor 143

7 In Search of Crises 161

8 By Correcting Faults 186

Conclusion 213

Glossary 219
Bibliography 231
Index 247

Preface

The outermost context into which this work falls concerns the tantalizing resemblances between the views of Lü K'un (1536–1618) and those of nineteenth and twentieth century Chinese, which historians have interpreted as responses to the challenge of the West. Among the many points of resemblance are: the willingness to write in a vernacular language that even "the common man and woman" could understand, a softening of attitudes towards women, an unabashed endorsement of the value of expediency, guidelines by which the common people could take the initiative in community projects, and meetings for mutual self-criticism. Foreshadowing Hu Shih (1891–1962), Lü K'un defined values according to pragmatic principles; and foreshadowing T'ao Hsing-chih (1892–1946), he tried to spread literacy by training the barely literate to teach the illiterate.

Whether these similarities stem from a repetition of circumstances (which may be roughly summarized as "dynastic decline") or whether they result from the continuation of a subsidiary Confucian tradition associated with the statecraft of local officials must await further study. For the moment it is sufficient to say that the strands of continuity, however dimly defined at present, are indicated by the frequent republication of Lü's works during the eighteenth and nineteenth centuries, and that Lü therefore deserves our attention.

As the experience of China's confrontation with the West, culminating in the Communist revolution, rolls away from us, our perspective on Chinese history broadens and shifts. The question "Why did China fail to respond adequately to the West?" had before the mid-1960s predisposed writers to look only for obstacles to change and to dismiss the Ming dynasty as a mere dry run for a presumably stagnant Ch'ing. Now, with an expanded perspective it has become completely plausible and contemplable that study of the late Ming will offer a key to recent Chinese history.

The inner context of this work concerns Lü's similarities to the so-called radical followers of Wang Shou-jen (1472–1529), in particular the members of the T'ai-chou school, which included such colorful figures as the son of a salt merchant who roamed the countryside to teach artisans and peasants, or a disaffected scholar who organized his lineage to resist unfair taxes. Lü resembled the T'ai-chou school in democratizing education, using records of merit and demerit, appealing to the emotions, and maintaining that learning should be easy and even pleasurable. Like the T'ai-chou school, Lü responded to the dramatic changes that were occurring in late Ming society and thought: the commercialization of rural areas, the proliferation of intermediate market towns, the spread of literacy, and the rise of vernacular fiction. Also like the T'ai-chou school, Lü was frustrated with court politics and skeptical about classical learning.

That Lü escaped censure while the T'ai-chou school earned condemnation for its teachings, and was even blamed for the fall of the Ming in 1644, demands an explanation. Lü's good reputation points to his unusually creative imagination in finding acceptable ways to react to the very changes that had also stimulated the T'ai-chou movement. It moreover suggests that the Confucian tradition allowed far more flexibility than historians have commonly believed. Others suffered for speaking out; Lü found a voice that would serve his times. He drew strength from the realistic details of everyday life to which all could relate; he placed those details in provocative contexts that involved life and death; and he used metaphors, most often of illness and battle, where conventional modes of discourse had failed. Lü thus drew readers into his vividly realistic world and moved them to think.

The search for a pattern behind Lü's responsiveness to social change gave this book shape. To define that pattern it was necessary to answer such questions as: How did Lü impose order on the vast array of concrete details on subjects ranging from running soup kitchens for the destitute to committing a petty faux pas in entertaining? Why did concerns to which his predecessors had devoted only a few terse sentences unfold into numerous detailed categories in Lü's writings? Why did he write up elaborate administrative plans while others who also coped with problems in local government did not? And what enabled him to write with equal success on both self-cultivation and administration?

To answer these questions and to characterize Lü's outlook, it was helpful to compare and contrast him with four other late Ming thinkers: Lo Ju-fang (1515–88), Hai Jui (1515–87), Feng Ts'ung-wu (1556–1627 [?]), and Yang Tung-ming (1548–1624). Through this process, commonly associated ingredients or correlations could be identified.

Several similarities between Lu and Hai suggest a possible correlation between preoccupation with rules and regulations and pessimism about human nature. But an explanation in terms of personality alone will not explain why writing about administrative matters—writings for which I use the rough label "statecraft"—intensified during the late Ming.

To some extent, the late Ming concern with statecraft can be understood as a response to bureaucratic inefficiency, to frustration with court politics, and to deepening social problems, of which banditry and widespread famine were but two signs. But above all, the study of Lü K'un led to the conclusion that his interest in writing about statecraft was part of a general reorientation, of a change in outlook, and not simply a response to worsening social and political problems. Even in the area of moral self-cultivation, far removed from the tasks of bandit control and tax collection, Lü took not the Classics but his experience of specific events as his point of departure. And even in self-cultivation, Lü organized his thoughts in terms of crises—an approach that also suited writing about military and medical matters. Examples of statecraft writings can be found long before Lü's day. However, Lü's outlook brought concrete facts and personal experiences into the foreground of his writings and gave statecraft an acceptable centrality. Likewise Lü's outlook, not simply the spread of literacy among the common people, stimulated him to write numerous didactic works and handbooks for women, children, and the poor. The importance of Lü's outlook to his productivity in this area will emerge from a contrast with Lo Ju-fang. Also specifically related to Lü's outlook rather than to objective social problems was his impulse to prepare against banditry, to sponsor medicine, and to teach beggars to become self-reliant. In these and numerous other ways, Lü K'un's reorientation shaped his plans for social action.

Many have generously given their time to comment on and criticize my work during its many stages. Above all, I would like to thank Professor Frederic Wakeman, Jr. for going far beyond his responsibilities as a graduate adviser to offer perceptive editorial comments on and cheering encouragement throughout numerous drafts of this work; Professor Wei-ming Tu both for informative and lively discussions about Neo-Confucianism and for guidance through my early confrontations with several extremely difficult texts by Lü K'un; and Professor Wing-tsit Chan for painstakingly checking my translations of passages from Lü K'un's *Shen-yin yü* [Groaning Words]. Others who have commented on the manuscript in one or several of its many versions include Professors Cyril Birch, Paul A. Cohen, Stanley Engerman, Philip A. Kuhn, Ruth Handlin Manley, Frederick W. Mote, Susan Naquin, Willard J. Peterson, Henry Rosemont, Laurence Schneider, Benjamin Schwartz, and John E. Wills, Jr. In addition Professors Patrick Hanan and Maureen Robertson both promptly responded to my pleas for help in translating several sticky passages. For any errors that remain, I alone am, of course, responsible.

I would also like to thank several institutions for providing environments for stimulating "learned discussions": the Fairbank Center for East Asian Research at Harvard University for its hospitality and office space for several stretches of time from 1976 on; the University Seminar on Neo-Confucianism at Columbia University both for an affiliation that dates from 1973 and for two opportunities to discuss my work on Lü K'un; the Bunting Institute for a stimulating affiliation in 1976–77; and the Ming History Project at Princeton for its hospitality during the summer of 1980.

I am also indebted to the staffs of many libraries. I would like specifically to thank: those at the East Asiatic Library at Berkeley who responded with great alacrity to my seemingly whimsical requests when I began work on my doctoral dissertation; and those at the Harvard-Yenching Library, in particular, the late K'ai-ming Ch'iu, George Potter, Deborah White, and Eugene Wu, who have over many years facilitated in every way possible my use of that very fine library. It is with the permission of the Harvard-Yenching Library that Lü's chart of his teacher and six friends is reproduced here.

For this work I have gratefully received support from numerous sources: from the American Association of University Women during 1972–73 to write the doctoral dissertation on Lü K'un that subsequently became the point of departure for this book; from the National Endowment for the Humanities during 1976–77 to expand that dissertation into a manuscript; and from the American Council of Learned Societies (which in turn was partly funded by the National Endowment for the Humanities) during 1980–81 for a new project from which I stole some time to revise the manuscript.

It would be misleading to say that this book grew out of a doctoral dissertation, as if to suggest that it grew like a plant whose shape was formed early on, the change taking place thereafter only in size. Facts, like multifaceted tiles, can be selected and rejected, shuffled and reshuffled, to form numerous distinct mosaics. Accordingly, the process by which this book was formed can best be described as a sequence of efforts to recombine into a coherent view pieces of pictures that my own rude questions had repeatedly shattered. That I forsook the easy for the difficult, the biographical treatment of Lü for the thematic, can in part be traced to my parents who had frequently claimed that in writing one must above all have something significant to say. That I persisted in my endeavor was also largely made possible by their encouragement and by the moral support of David and Holly Handlin, Ruth (Handlin) and Larry Manley, and numerous steadfast friends.

Abbreviations

CWCWC Lü K'un, *Ch'ü-wei chai wen-chi*.

DMB L. Carrington Goodrich and Chaoying Fang, eds., *Dictionary of Ming Biography*.

ECCP Arthur W. Hummel, *Eminent Chinese of the Ch'ing Period*.

FSHC Feng Ts'ung-wu, *Feng Shao hsü chi*.

HJC Hai Jui, *Hai Jui chi*, ed., Ch'en I-chung.

HTCC Lo Ju-fang, *Hsü-t'an chih-ch'üan*.

MJHA Huang Tsung-hsi, *Ming-ju hsüeh-an*.

SCKK Yang Tung-ming, *Shan-chü kung-k'o*.

SCL Lü K'un, *Shih-cheng lu*.

SYY Lü K'un, *Shen-yin yü*, ed., Kōda Rentarō.

I

Sages and Average Men

1

The Official as Scholar During the Ming Dynasty

That the rise of evidential studies was one sign of a significant change in orientation sometime during the late Ming and early Ch'ing dynasties has been accepted as an incontrovertible fact by most historians.[1] Differences of opinion occur not over whether an important change took place but over how to evaluate and explain that change. Historians continue to puzzle over why the change took place, what role the Ch'ing takeover in 1644 played in bringing it about, who the protagonists of the new outlook were, and how enduring the new outlook was in the Ch'ing. In answering these ques-

1. Liang Ch'i-ch'ao, for example, called attention to the early Ch'ing interest in "practical statesmanship" and empirical research, which he interpreted as a "reaction against the Neo-Confucianism of the Sung and Ming." He further interpreted the various Ch'ing methods of learning as "fundamentally different from those of the Ming thinkers." Liang Ch'i-ch'ao, *Intellectual Trends in the Ch'ing Period*, in particular pp. 21–22. For a critical evaluation of various interpretations of early Ch'ing thought, see Yü Ying-shih, "Some Preliminary Observations on the Rise of Ch'ing Confucian Intellectualism." Yü notes a sharp rise in philological studies during the Ch'ing, but in contrast to Liang, argues for continuity between the Sung-Ming and early Ch'ing trends. Willard Peterson also comments on the reorientation. He notes that several outstanding early Ch'ing scholars, Huang Tsung-hsi, Ku Yen-wu, and Fang I-chih, "by emphasizing the plethora of phenomena, their complexity and multiplicity, manifest a disinclination or even resistance to the dominant view that there is an underlying overarching, or unchanging unity that could and should be revealed to men's minds." Willard J. Peterson, *The Bitter Gourd*, p. 12. Also illuminating aspects of the reorientation are the many fine essays collected in Wm. Theodore de Bary et al., eds., *The Unfolding of Neo-Confucianism*. Particularly useful have been: Edward T. Ch'ien, "Chiao Hung and the Revolt against Ch'eng-Chu Orthodoxy"; Wei-ming Tu, "Yen Yuan: From Inner Experience to Lived Concreteness"; and Willard J. Peterson, "Fang I-chih: Western Learning and the 'Investigation of Things.'"

tions, in deciding on precisely how to weigh and assemble the pieces of the puzzle, historians may strongly disagree. Concerning what the basic pieces are, however, most historians have arrived at a consensus.

Characterizing this reorientation was, first, an intense interest in writing about matters of statecraft, or "managing the world" (*ching-shih*)—such as water conservation, agronomy, and military defense. Second, many scholars during that time turned from metaphysics to "practical" or "solid learning" (*shih-hsüeh*) and expressed a concern that learning be useful. Third, personal experience supplemented, if not superseded, received opinions as a source of authority for knowledge. Often accompanying this—but not always, for the leanings of specific scholars varied widely—was an objectification of learning. Classical texts became objects of study as much as sources of authority. Consequently, the field of evidential studies blossomed. No longer awed by the sanctity of texts, scholars felt free to examine them in their historical contexts. Books until then revered as timeless embodiments of "truth" were by the end of the Ming subjected to analysis as historical objects, analyzed philologically, and even exposed as forgeries.[2]

In addition to these ingredients, this book will consider two others. Many scholars of the new outlook stressed that language should be simple and "easy to understand." Some even forsook opportunities to display their facility with refined classical allusions and experimented instead with writ-

2. For a discussion of Chiao Hung as a precursor of Ch'ing evidential studies, see Edward T. Ch'ien, "Chiao Hung and the Revolt against Ch'eng-Chu Orthodoxy." For a discussion of evidential studies and Ch'en Ti (1541–1617), who was a friend of Chiao Hung, see Jung Chao-tsu, *Ming-tai ssu-hsiang shih*, pp. 270–83. In reaction to learned discussions, Ch'en stressed practicality and personal experience, argued that ideas change with the times, and even claimed that had Confucius been alive during the Ming he would not be engaging in learned discussions. See also the biography of Ch'en Ti by Fang Chaoying in *Dictionary of Ming Biography* (hereafter *DMB*), pp. 180–84. Early Ch'ing figures interested in the study of phonetics include Ku Yen-wu and Fu Shan (1607–84). For a discussion of Ku's thought, see Hou Wai-lu, *Chung-kuo ssu-hsiang t'ung-shih*, 5:204–252. For a discussion of Fu's thought, see ibid., 5:266–288. For Yen Jo-chü (1636–1704), who exposed as forgeries sections of the *Book of History*, see Liang, *Intellectual Trends*, p. 33.

ing in the vernacular. Finally, the assumptions of how man related to his environment and to others, and consequently the very definition of community—or the characteristics that men shared most consciously—changed. This book will also discuss numerous fine points of the reorientation, but for the moment, a long list, dangling in space without explanatory context, can do little more than hint at the magnitude of the change.

Taken individually, none of the ingredients was entirely unprecedented. Long before the Ming, some scholar-officials had written about statecraft, or had debated over whether one should build wisdom on books or on intuition. Ever since the Sung dynasty, scholars had gradually turned away from metaphysical speculation to practical learning. But only during the late Ming did these ingredients, which had formerly merely flickered on the periphery of the scholarly world, coalesce to assume an unprecedented centrality so that even those who persistently engaged in speculative learning could not ignore the challenge of the new outlook. Although some Ch'ing scholars continued to examine metaphysical questions in detail, the center of gravity of intellectual life had changed. No longer confident that there existed a universal principle that every enlightened person would understand, scholars concentrated instead on the phenomena of the external world and on the personal experiences through which those phenomena could be grasped.[3]

Past studies of the reorientation have generally concentrated on the evolution or transmission of ideas among the great thinkers.[4] However, the problem of uniting office and learning, service to society and cultivation of self, was in fact one that all thoughtful and conscientious officials—not simply the great philosophers—faced. During the Ming, the

3. Willard J. Peterson goes so far as to observe, "The hegemony of Neo-Confucianism (*Tao-hsueh*) was broken" (*Bitter Gourd*, p. 166).

4. Especially useful for understanding the background of popular culture against which the reorientation took place was Tadao Sakai, *Chūgoku zensho no kenkyū*. Several works that probe into the relationship between late Ming Neo-Confucianism and popular religion have also contributed to a fuller understanding of the reorientation. See in particular Judith A. Berling, *The Syncretic Religion of Lin Chao-en*; and Chün-fang Yü, *The Renewal of Buddhism in China*.

spread of printing enabled educators and administrators of diverse talents in areas other than Neo-Confucian philosophy to display their efforts to seek guidance from Confucianism for their actions. Their writings are no less important than those by the leading Neo-Confucian synthesizers in illuminating the vitality and power of Confucian ideas. To understand the late Ming reorientation in particular, it is necessary to abandon the standards of philosophical depth conventionally held by intellectual historians and to look instead at the forms Confucianism took in action.

The reorientation can to some extent be traced to specific economic, social, and political changes, in particular to the commercialization, the spread of literacy, and the political chaos of that period. A section of this chapter will outline these trends, and later chapters will often refer to them. The change in orientation can also to some extent be explained as a reaction to the intellectual relativism and speculative thinking to which mid-sixteenth-century scholar-officials had fallen prey.[5] This explanation is correct in its broad outlines and will also receive some attention. However this book is less concerned with interpreting the reorientation as a reaction to past attitudes, or tracing it to specific events, than in describing how scholar-officials interpreted the available opportunities to fulfill their responsibilities to cultivate themselves and serve society. Viewing new trends as reactions to past events and attitudes, after all, only partially helps to define the specific direction of the new trends. Crises prompted the changes, to be sure; but why were certain responses chosen over others? The call for foresight can be traced to the atmosphere of crisis surrounding the late Ming court; but such a reductionist explanation neither suggests the limits of the scholar-official's foresight nor why a particular definition of community accompanied the foresighted outlook. Not specific causes for the change in orientation, then, but how men interpreted their opportunities is the main subject of this book. Therefore the chapters that follow will address such questions as how scholar-officials translated their un-

5. See, for example, Liang, *Intellectual Trends*, p. 27. In addition, numerous seventeenth-century writers explicitly criticized the speculative thinking of the late Ming (see note 78 below).

derstanding of Confucianism into plans for action, whence they derived authority for their ideas, what was the reach of their imagination, what were the social implications of their ideas, and why certain solutions worked better than others.

Great thinkers were involved in the reorientation, but they were not necessarily central to it. Indeed many characteristics of the reorientation—the use of vernacular language, the rejection of high-flown talk for practical matters, and the emphasis on personal experiences—required little sophisticated thought and may even have represented an adjustment of thinking to the expanding audience of the semi-educated.

As the standards for what was important in learning changed, skills other than the capacity to formulate landmark syntheses in the development of Neo-Confucianism came to be appreciated. Philosophical depth and erudition continued to win some praise, to be sure, but so did the ability to draw up practical plans for efficient administration, to convey personal experiences forcefully, and to write in simple, direct language. Hence the reorientation made room for men of mediocre scholarly and literary gifts to leave their mark.

One illuminating example of the numerous facets of the late Ming reorientation is Lü K'un (1536–1618).[6] Lü's writings, sweeping in scope, enable us to penetrate many remote corners of late Ming society as well as the deep recesses of Lü's mind. Lü's writings include memorials to the throne, correspondence with numerous prominent scholars and officials, and administrative guides for the bureaucracy, at one end of the spectrum, and, at the other, didactic works for women and children, and an intimate record of his activities and reflections. Thus they offer invaluable clues to both his public affairs and private thoughts. Moreover, Lü treated these areas vividly and realistically, for he believed that the truth, even if unflattering, should be recorded.[7] Even as a

6. Biography of Lü by Chaoying Fang in *DMB*, pp. 1006–10. For a list of sources for biographical information on Lü, see ch. 5, n. 1 below.

7. Li K'un, "Colophon," *Ning-ling hsien chih* (1693), p. 18a. At the beginning of the dynasty, Lü K'un's family had been incorrectly registered under the name of Li. After passing the *chin-shih* examination, Lü petitioned that the original surname, Lü, be restored. Lü K'un, "Lü Li hsing yüan pei" in *Ch'ü-wei chai wen-chi* (hereafter *CWCWC*), 8:64b–65a.

young man, he had taken to heart Confucius's warning that ornament should not supersede content.[8] "Just as a portrait painter will retain sunken eyes and a high nose," so should the historian, Lü noted in his colophon to a gazetteer, include the bad as well as the good points.[9] Lü's writings are so replete with concrete and intimate details that they provide an unusual opportunity to explore the anxieties of a scholar-official who lived during a period of political and social upheaval.

Lü alone of all the thinkers of the Wan-li period (1573–1620) won a respectable place in the Confucian temple. In 1826, an official serving in Lü's native province of Honan sent a memorial to the Board of Rites to request that Lü be placed alongside Liu Tsung-chou (1578–1645), T'ang Pin (1627–87), and Huang Tao-chou (1585–1646), all of whom had just been canonized in the preceding few years.[10] The memorial specifically praised Lü for his practical learning and for his avoidance of high-flown superficial language, as did prefaces written when Lü's collected writings were published in 1827. The canonization of Lü, along with the publication of his collected writings, coincided with the resurgence of interest in statecraft during the nineteenth century.

Lü by choice did not establish a school of thought. In fact, his outlook, as later chapters will reveal, simply did not leave room for the expression of student-teacher relationships. Nonetheless, the list of famous officials of the next dynasty

8. Li K'un, "Colophon," *Ning-ling hsien chih*, p. 18a. The passage to which Lü refers is: "When ornamentation prevails over natural substance, you get the pedantry of the scribe" (*The Analects of Confucius*, tr., Arthur Waley, p. 119).

9. Li K'un, "Colophon," *Ning-ling hsien chih*, p. 18a.

10. See Ch'eng Tsu-lo, "Memorial," in *Lü tzu i-shu*, pp. 1a–4a. Ch'eng served as governor of Lü's province, Honan. According to Ch'eng, Liu, Huang, and T'ang had been canonized in 1822, 1823, and 1825 respectively. See also Yang Kuo-chen (1782–1849), "Preface," *Lü tzu i-shu*, pp. 1a–2b. Yang also served as governor of Honan from 1827 to 1834. For Yang, see the biography of his father, Yang Yü-ch'un, by Fang Chao-ying in Arthur W. Hummel, ed., *Eminent Chinese of the Ch'ing Period* (hereafter *ECCP*), p. 897. For Lü K'un, see T. Watters, *A Guide to the Tablets in a Temple of Confucius*, pp. 218–20. For Liu, see ibid., pp. 220–23. For Huang, see ibid., pp. 224–27. For T'ang, see ibid., pp. 237–39.

who admired Lü and sponsored the republication of his works is impressive.

Lu Lung-ch'i (1630–93), a well-loved magistrate—who both edited a Sung handbook on local administration and wrote an intimate record of his own thoughts—commissioned the republication of Lü's *Shen-yin yü* [Groaning Words].[11] Chu Shih (1665–1736), a highly successful official, who had addressed such practical problems as famine relief and whose interest in the practice rather than the contemplation of Confucian concepts led him to the study of ritual, published an annotated edition of Lü's *Ssu-li i* [Supplement to the Four Categories of Rituals].[12] Ch'en Hung-mou (1696–1771), able governor of many provinces and active local ad-

11. Biography of Lu Lung-ch'i by Rufus O. Suter in *ECCP*, pp. 547–48. Numerous works by Lu Lung-ch'i, replete with colorful, critical, and detailed comments about late Ming thought and his own times, are available and deserve a full-length study. Lu found inspiration in many aspects of Lü K'un's works. For example, when he wished to promulgate the K'ang-hsi emperor's maxims through rural lectures (*hsiang-yüeh*) but found no guidelines in the official statutes, Lu consulted Lü K'un's writing on the subject (*Lu Ch'ing-hsien kung nien-p'u*, p. 15b). See also Lu Lung-ch'i, *San-yü-t'ang jih-chi*, 2:57b. For a discussion of K'ang-hsi's maxims and *hsiang-yüeh*, see Kung-chuan Hsiao, *Rural China*, pp. 184–88. Lu Lung-ch'i also commissioned the republication of Lü K'un's *Shen-yin yü* and wrote a laudatory preface to the work in 1687 (*San-yü-t'ang wen-chi*, 8:12a–13a). For Lü's work on self-cultivation, see *Shen-yin yü*, ed. Kōda Rentarō (hereafter *SYY*). Lu edited a Sung dynasty guide for local administration, *Li-cheng chai-yao*, and read widely in statecraft writings (*San-yü-t'ang jih-chi*, 2:8b). Lu's record of self-cultivation in the form of a diary resembles the preoccupation with daily affairs of *SYY*. For a discussion of why self-cultivation based on the scrutiny of daily affairs suited those who also wished to write about administrative matters, see chapter 8, below. Although Lu Lung-ch'i admired Lü K'un, his writings reveal a partial retreat from some of Lü K'un's views, in particular, from Lü K'un's strong preoccupation with the amoral, institutional dimension of local government, which chapter 5 of this book will discuss below. In fact, Lu explicitly opposed Lü K'un's view that such legalistic thinkers as Shen Pu-hai and Han Fei Tzu had conformed to the Kingly Way ("Tu Shen-yin yü i," in *San-yü-t'ang wen-chi*, 4:23a; also *SYY*, 5:752). This is one of seventeen criticisms which Lu Lung-ch'i expressed about *SYY*, his overall admiration for the work notwithstanding. *San-yü-t'ang*, 4:18b–25a. In addition, Lu Lung-ch'i criticized Lü K'un's categorical criticisms of all Sung scholars. Ibid., 4:19b–20a. See also *San-yü-t'ang jih-chi*, 2:73a. For a reprint of Lu Lung-ch'i's criticisms, see *Lü tzu i-shu*.

12. Biography by Rufus O. Suter in *ECCP*, pp. 188–89. Chu wrote his preface to Lü's *Ssu-li i* in 1719. The annotated work was republished several times.

ministrator and educator, included excerpts from several of Lü's works in his *Wu-chung i-kuei* [Five Types of Transmitted Guidelines]. In addition Ch'en edited and published an edition of Lü's *Groaning Words* under the title *Lü-tzu chieh-lu.*[13] Hung Liang-chi (1630–93), known for his interest in local history and famous for his Malthusian observations on population growth, also edited an edition of Lü's *Groaning Words.*[14] Finally during the K'ang-hsi period (1661–1722),

13. Biography by Rufus O. Suter in *ECCP*, pp. 86–87. Ch'en Hung-mou anthologized sections of the following works by Lü K'un: *Hsü Hsiao-erh yü* in *Yang-cheng i-kuei*, 2:10a–18a; *Hao-jen ko* in *Hsün-su i-kuei*, 2:16a–b; *Ming chih*, which is drawn from Lü's *Shih-cheng lu, chüan* 1, in *Ts'ung-cheng i-kuei*, 1:34b–50a; *Hsing-chieh*, in *Ts'ung-cheng i-kuei*, 1:50a–52b; *Nü hsiao-erh yü* in *Chiao-nü i-kuei*, 2:1a–4a; and *Kuei-fan*, in *Chiao-nü i-kuei*, 2:4a–38b. The four collections edited by Ch'en Hung-mou are included in Ch'en's *Wu-chung i-kuei*. Ch'en also republished sections of Lü's *Shen-yin yü* as *Lü tzu chieh-lu*, in 4 *chüan* with a supplement in 2 *chüan*. Ch'en published the first part in 1736; he later obtained a copy of the original edition, realized his edition was incomplete, and published the supplement in 1738 (*Ssu-k'u ch'üan-shu tsung-mu, ch'in-ting* 96:26b). In his work on the charitable schools of Yunnan province, Ch'en includes among books that should be reprinted and distributed both his edition of *Lü tzu chieh-lu* and Lü's *Ssu-li i* (Ch'en Hung-mou, *Ch'üan Tien i-hsüeh hui chi*, 1st *ts'e*, 24b).

14. Biography by Lien-che Tu in *ECCP*, pp. 373–75. In his preface of 1748 to the republication of *SYY*, Hung comments that the book can be used like medicine to cure the ills of both men and society (reprinted in Kuang-i shu-chü, typeset ed. [Shanghai, 1935], p. 9). The list presented here of Ch'ing scholars who took an interest in Lü K'un is by no means complete. Li Yung (1627–1705) lists Lü's *SYY* among books to be consulted judiciously for the understanding of "essence" (*t'i*) ("T'i-yung ch'üan hsüeh" in *Erh-ch'ü chi*, 7:5b). Li also lists Lü's *Shih-cheng lu* (hereafter *SCL*) as indispensable daily reading for those committed to practical matters, or "function" (ibid., 7:6b–7a). Li Yung shares with Lü K'un and some of his contemporaries the preoccupation with correcting faults which chapter 8 discusses ("Hui-kuo tzu-hsin" in *Erh-ch'ü chi, chüan* 1). Li Yung also includes excerpts from Lü's *SCL* in his own anthology on local administration ("Ssu-mu pao-chien" in *Erh-ch'ü chi*, 28:10a). See the biography of Li Yung by Dean R. Wickes in *ECCP*, pp. 498–99. For a discussion of Li Yung's thought, see Hou Wai-lu, *Chung-kuo ssu-hsiang t'ung shih*, 5:289–300. Liang Chang-chü (1775–1849), a close friend of Lin Tse-hsü, also frequently read and referred to Lü K'un. He cited numerous passages from *SYY* (Liang Chang-chü, *T'ui-an sui-pi*, 1:4a; 1:8b; 2:1a; 2:3b–4b; 4:6b; 4:10b). He also referred to Lü's *SCL*, which, with *SYY*, he believed to be indispensable reading for provincial officials (ibid., 5:6a). Liang was also familiar with Lü's less well-known work, *Chiu-ming shu* (ibid., 13:13a). A preface to Liang's work mentions that Liang Chang-chü took special inspiration from Ku Yen-wu's *Jih-chih lu* and Lü's *SYY*. Ku Yen-wu's work has received far more attention than Lü's by historians but it is important to

four of Lü's didactic works for children and women were jointly reprinted for distribution to charitable or community schools.[15]

That Lü's works were frequently republished during the Ch'ing dynasty testifies to his importance. That men who were engaged in practical administration not only looked to Lü's *Shih-cheng lu* [Records of Practical Government] but also to his work on self-cultivation hints at the special quality of his outlook. As later chapters will show, Lü integrated the areas of local administration and self-cultivation through a framework that gave equal weight to Confucian ideals and the harsh social realities of his time.

By analyzing the internal structure and the mosaic of themes in Lü's rich and prolific writings, one can explain—in terms of his own statements—why he believed, for example, that beggars should become self-reliant or that vernacular songs should be written for his clan. By examining which themes cluster together and which dominate the foreground of Lü's writings, one can further characterize the conceptual framework through which Lü imposed order on his world and gave shape to his social plans.

An internal analysis will thus reveal the complexity of Lü's writings and the thoroughness with which he integrated his diverse experiences. But to appreciate fully what was engaging and exceptional about Lü K'un, one must step out of the maze of themes to view with some perspective the whole Lü K'un. For this, comparisons between Lü and four other late Ming figures proved useful. Yang Tung-ming (1548–1624)[16] and Feng Ts'ung-wu (1556–1627)[17] were chosen after surveying the extant writings of Lü's acquaintances for those that

---

note that in one context at least Lü's work was given equal weight. See the biography of Liang by Gussie Esther Gaskill in *ECCP*, pp. 499–500. I would like to thank James Polachek for bringing Liang's interest in Lü to my attention.

15. Su Yu-mei, "Preface" (1827), *Lü shu ssu-chung ho-k'o* in *Lü tzu i-shu*, 1a. The four works were *Hsiao-erh yü*, *Hao-jen ko*, *Tsung-yüeh ko*, and *Kuei chieh*, all to be discussed in chap. 6 below.

16. Biography by Huang P'ei and Julia Ching in *DMB*, pp. 1546–47. For further bibliographic information, chap. 3, n. 1 below.

17. Biography by Charles O. Hucker in *DMB*, pp. 458–59. For further bibliographic information, chap. 4, n. 3 below.

were sufficiently interesting to justify the special attention of whole chapters. Lo Ju-fang (1515–88)[18] and Hai Jui (1513–87)[19] were chosen because they were important points of reference for Lü K'un's generation.

The four contrasting examples leaned markedly either toward self-cultivation and education, as was the case of Lo Ju-fang and Feng Ts'ung-wu, or toward active service to society, as was the case with Hai Jui and Yang Tung-ming. Through studies of these men one can sort out the specific problems, assumptions, and personal traits associated with the pursuit of one avenue or the other. The contrasts will permit an appraisal of Lü K'un's achievements that won praise for reuniting office and learning.

The comparisons will also illuminate significant differences between the two generations. Lo and Hai enjoyed opportunities to exert their energies individualistically and self-confidently. Yang, Feng and Lü of the next generation were aware of criticisms that Lo and Hai had provoked. Lo Ju-fang's euphoric confidence that everyone could become a sage inevitably gave way to disillusionment as Lü's generation began to ask just where all the sages were. Feng, Yang, Lü, and even those of their generation who acted heroically in the Tung-lin movement, were acutely aware that limits to permissible scholarly activity had narrowed. Finally, because Lü K'un, Yang, and Feng shared the same milieu and discussed the same problems, each illuminates the implications of the choices made by the others. Examining how Lü resolved problems that Yang and Feng faced inadequately will help to define the significance of the reorientation.

The small sample of five men by no means exhausts the range of personalities and intellectual positions of the late Ming. However several features of the Chinese scholar-officialdom make it possible to use a carefully selected small sample as a key to defining the late Ming reorientation. First, however different their personalities and geographic origins, these five men shared a common culture. They had studied

18. Biography by Julia Ching in *DMB*, pp. 875–78. For further bibliographic information, chap. 2, n. 10 below.

19. See biography by Chaoying Fang in *DMB*, 474–79. For further bibliographic information, chapter 2, note 3.

the very same classical texts in order to pass the civil service examinations. These texts, which they cited often to express their views, remained constant points of reference. For example, virtually all scholar-officials believed in—or at least paid lip service to—the dictate of *Ta hsüeh* [The Great Learning] that one should strive both to cultivate the self and serve society.[20] They differed only in how they translated that belief into action. Second, each generation of scholar-officials shared certain issues. For all the diversity in their views, for all the idiosyncracies in their personalities, the scholar-officials belonged to a social world that was actually remarkably small. Through the capital newspaper, officials scattered throughout the empire kept abreast of important affairs. Just how frequently the newspaper was printed and how widely it circulated cannot be determined. But its importance in keeping officials informed is clear; numerous references to items in the capital newspaper can be found even in the small portion of Ming writings surveyed for this study. Yang Tung-ming commented that he and his companions read the newspaper from time to time.[21] Keng Ting-hsiang (1524–96), a close friend of Lo Ju-fang and political supporter of Hai Jui, referred to it frequently.[22] It was in the capital newspaper that Tsou Yüan-piao (1551–1624)—who was an acquaintance of Yang, Feng, and Lü—read criticisms of Lü's *Groaning Words*.[23] And it was also in the capital newspaper that Feng Ts'ung-wu and several of his companions read an essay, "On being an official and being a man."[24]

Scholar-officials also kept in touch with one another by writing frequent letters, sometimes even to those whom they

20. "The ancients who wished to illustrate illustrious virtue throughout the kingdom first ordered well their own States. Wishing to order well their States, they first regulated their families. Wishing to regulate their families, they first cultivated their persons. Wishing to cultivate their persons, they first rectified their hearts." James Legge, tr., *The Chinese Classics* 1:357.

21. Yang Tung-ming, *Shan-chü kung-k'o* (hereafter *SCKK*), 7:70b.

22. Keng Ting-hsiang, *Keng T'ien-t'ai hsien-sheng wen-chi*, 2:18b; 2:22b; 3:54a. Biography of Keng by Julia Ching in *DMB*, pp. 718–21.

23. Tsou Yüan-piao, *Yüan-hsüeh chi*. Biography of Tsou by Charles O. Hucker in *DMB*, pp. 1312–14.

24. Feng Ts'ung-wu, [*Feng*] *Shao-hsü chi* (hereafter *FSHC*), 14:1a; also 18:1a.

knew only by reputation or through the reports of friends. In the sections of letters represented in the collected writings of many noted scholars, certain names—such as those of Keng Ting-hsiang and Tsou Yüan-piao—repeatedly occur. Undoubtedly social prestige and political power often determined whose letters were preserved in these collections. Nonetheless, the repeated appearance of certain names is a sign of the vast networks through which information was exchanged.

In addition to the circulation of information through letter-writing and the capital newspaper, much intelligence must also have spread by word of mouth as officials, lecturers, and prosperous merchants who hobnobbed with officials, moved about the country. Surely an official who served in the government for ten or more years was quite thoroughly informed about the major issues, not to mention scandals, of his day.

That members of a generation belonging to different philosophical schools shared common concerns has been obscured in most discussions of Ming thought because historians have taken as their guide Huang Tsung-hsi's famous *Ming-ju hsüeh-an* [Records of Ming Philosophers].[25] In this work Huang categorized the vast array of roughly two hundred Ming thinkers primarily according to student-teacher affiliations and geographical ties. But friendships in fact often crisscrossed the various schools he defined. Consequently the affiliations that distinguished one member from another within a generation may in fact have been less important than the issues they all shared. This is particularly true for the seventeenth century when the growing emphasis on personal experiences loosened the bonds between some students and teachers.[26]

25. Biography of Huang Tsung-hsi by Lien-che Tu in *ECCP*, pp. 351–54. For a discussion of Huang's thought, see Hou Wai-lu, *Chung-kuo ssu-hsiang*, 5:144–203. For a discussion of Huang's political thought, see Wm. Theodore de Bary, "Chinese Despotism and the Confucian Ideal: A Seventeenth-Century View." Huang Tsung-hsi, *Ming-ju hsüeh-an* (hereafter *MJHA*).

26. Willard Peterson comments on Ku Yen-wu and Fang I-chih as "masterless" men who "did not portray themselves as continuing the teachings of a particular mentor" (*Bitter Gourd*, p. 12). Further discussion in chap. 8 below.

Lü K'un, who affiliated with no school and whom Huang therefore placed in the category of "miscellaneous scholars," was acquainted with and in some respects resembled: Chang Yüan-pien (1538–88) of the central Che branch of the Wang Yang-ming school;[27] Tsou Yüan-piao of the western branch of the Wang school;[28] Meng Ch'iu (1525–89), Meng Hua-li (1545–97), and Yang Tung-ming of the northern branch of the Wang school;[29] Yang Ch'i-yüan (1547–99), Keng Ting-hsiang, and Chiao Hung (1541–1620) of the T'ai-chou school;[30] Feng Ts'ung-wu of the Kan-ch'üan school; and Ku

27. For Lü, see *MJHA*, 54:5a–b. For Chang, see *MJHA*, 15:4b–5a. For a letter debating several points with Lü K'un, see Chang Yüan-pien, *Chang Yang-ho wen-hsüan*, p. 29. Biography of Chang by L. Carrington Goodrich and C. N. Tay in *DMB*, pp. 110–11.

28. *MJHA*, 23:1a–2b. For four letters Tsou wrote to Lü, see Tsou, *Yüan-hsüeh chi*, 2:12b–16b. Tsou also wrote a preface to Lü K'un's *SCL*, then bearing the title of [*Hsin-k'o Lü Shu-chien hsien-sheng*] *Chü-kuan pi-yao* (Wan-li edition). In that preface, after blaming social turmoil—in particular the financial difficulties faced by merchants and tenants—on lax laws and sleazy clerks, Tsou praised Lü's work for analyzing the advantages and disadvantages of various aspects of local government and for his clear exposition of regulations. All those responsible for caring for the people, Tsou concluded, must heed this work (ibid., 4b–6b). In a preface to writings by Feng Ts'ung-wu, Tsou ranked Lü along with Meng Ch'iu and Meng Hua-li (see note 29 below) among five great scholars of his time (Tsou, *Yüan-hsüeh chi*, 4:74a). For five letters from Lü to Tsou, see *CWCWC*, 4:49a–60a. Biography of Tsou by Charles O. Hucker in *DMB*, 1312–14.

29. For Meng Ch'iu, see *MJHA*, 29:2b–3a; *Ming shih*, 283:3191–92; and *Ch'ang-li hsien chih* (1866), 5:32a–b. For letters Meng wrote to Lü K'un, see Meng Ch'iu, *Meng Wo-chiang chi*, 1:27a–29a. Lü mentions Meng Ch'iu admiringly in a letter to Tsou Yüan-piao, *CWCWC*, 4:49a–50b. Meng also corresponded with or addressed poems to Chang Yüan-pien, Hsü Fu-yüan, Tsou Yüan-piao, Ku Hsien-ch'eng (Meng, *Meng Wo-chiang chi, passim*). Meng hailed from Hsin-an, Honan, and was a close friend of his fellow townsman, Meng Hua-li. For Meng Hua-li, see *MJHA*, 29:8a; *Ming shih*, 283:3191. For letters from Meng Hua-li to Lü, see *Meng Yün-p'u hsien-sheng chi* (preface, 1597), 3:3a–4a. Meng Hua-li also corresponded with Chang Yüan-pien, Yang Tung-ming, Hsü Fu-yüan, Ku Hsien-ch'eng, Feng Ts'ung-wu and Tsou Yüan-piao (*ibid., passim*). For Yang Tung-ming, see *MJHA*, 29:8b–9a; Huang Tsung-hsi notes that Yang's friends included Tsou Yüan-piao, Feng Ts'ung-wu, Lü K'un, Meng Ch'iu, Keng Ting-hsiang, Chang Yüan-pien, and Yang Ch'i-yüan (ibid., 29:8b). Biography by Huang P'ei and Julia Ching in *DMB*, pp. 1546–47; and chap. 3 below. For nine letters from Yang to Lü, see *SCKK*, 7:44a–55a. For a letter from Lü to Yang, see *CWCWC*, 4:13b–14a.

30. For Yang, see *MJHA*, 34:22a–b, and the biography by Julia Ching and Huang P'ei in *DMB*, pp. 1505–6. For Keng, see *MJHA*, 35:1a–b and

Hsien-ch'eng (1550–1612) of the Tung-lin Academy, which fervently opposed the radical ideas of the T'ai-chou school.[31] If Lü K'un was somewhat exceptional in refusing to affiliate with a particular school, he was by no means unique in enjoying relationships with friends who represented a broad range of philosophical positions. With this in mind, this work will draw attention to those issues shared by Lü K'un's generation.

Before examining the attitudes of these men in detail, it will be necessary first to describe more fully just what were the scholar-official's responsibilities to moral self-cultivation and service to society, and then to outline in broad terms the late Ming context in which the change in orientation took place.

The official as scholar

In China, the official was also a scholar; he was both practical administrator, and moral leader. He drew inspiration from Confucius, who saw moral perfection, the cultivation

---

the biography by Julia Ching in *DMB*, pp. 718–21. For Chiao Hung, see *MJHA*, 35:8b–9a. For analyses of Chiao's thought, see Edward T. Ch'ien, "Chiao Hung and the Revolt against Ch'eng-Chu Orthodoxy," and Jung Chao-tsu, *Ming-tai ssu-hsiang shih*, pp. 256–69. In his concern for practicality and for evidential studies, Chiao has more in common with Lü K'un than his mentor, Keng Ting-hsiang. For similarities between Lü and other members of the T'ai-chou school, see chap. 6 below.

31. Lü was acquainted with and corresponded with Feng Ts'ung-wu, whom Huang Tsung-hsi placed in the Kan-ch'üan school (*MJHA*, 41:6b–7a). Feng recognized Hsü Fu-yüan (1535–1604) as his teacher (*FSHC*, 4:2a). But Feng also joined forces with Yang Tung-ming and Tsou Yüan-piao in sponsoring the Shou-shan Academy in 1622 (*DMB*, pp. 1313, 1546). And Hsü corresponded with Tsou Yüan-piao, Meng Ch'iu, and Keng Ting-hsiang as well as Feng (Hsü Fu-yüan, *Ching-ho t'ang-chi*, 3:32a; 4:19a–21b; 4:47a–48a; 2:34a). Clearly Huang Tsung-hsi's classification did not accurately reflect social realities. This Hsü Fu-yüan should be distinguished from Hsü Fu-yüan (1599–1665). The two men are incorrectly crosslisted in *DMB*, p. 1506. For Ku, see *MJHA*, 60:1a–2a, and biography by Heinrich Busch in *DMB*, pp. 736–44. For a discussion of Ku's thought, Jung Chao-tsu, *Ming-tai ssu-hsiang shih*, pp. 284–301. Ku defended Lü K'un against slanders in 1587 (*Ku Tuan-wen kung nien-p'u*, 16a). For a letter from Lü to Ku condoning Ku's activities with the Tung-lin Academy, see *CWCWC*, 5:6a–8a.

The importation of large quantities of silver to supplement the limited yields from China's own mines further stimulated economic development. During the 1530s silver began to trickle into China from Japan, where rich deposits had just been uncovered. After 1571, with the Spanish establishment of an administrative center in Manila, silver from Mexico and South America poured into China through trade with the Philippines.[36] How much silver circulated in China during the last decades of the Ming cannot be determined; but it is clear that silver had an enormous impact on the Chinese economy and society, the manifold dimensions of which historians are only slowly sorting out. The penetration of ample amounts of silver even into remote rural areas made possible, for example, a tax reform called the Single-Whip method. Introduced experimentally in the 1530s and then applied more vigorously around the 1580s, taxes were collected in silver rather than grain, the tax base was changed from household to land, and payments for land taxes and labor services were unified.[37] By thus simplifying taxation, officials eliminated many abuses by which the wealthy and powerful had avoided their responsibilities. Through the levy of one payment in silver to cover the many miscellaneous labor services—such as the courier service and the militia—the government could hire people efficiently and fairly to perform these tasks. Hai Jui,[38] Lü K'un, and Yang Tung-ming all grappled with the shift to the Single-Whip method of taxation.[39]

---

control). For a fascinating account of the commercialization of rural society in Fukien province during the sixteenth century, see Evelyn Sakakida Rawski, *Agricultural Change and the Peasant Economy of South China*, in particular pp. 1–100. Much can also be gleaned from Mark Elvin, *The Pattern of the Chinese Past*, pp. 268–84. See also Fu I-ling, *Ming-Ch'ing shih-tai shang-jen chi shang-yeh tzu-pen*, in particular pp. 18, 20–23. For a review of the books by Perkins, Elvin, and Rawski, see Tsing Yuan, "Continuities and Discontinuities in Chinese Agriculture, 1550–1700."

36. William S. Atwell, "Notes on Silver, Foreign Trade, and the Late Ming Economy."

37. For a discussion of the Single-Whip system, see Liang Fang-chung, *The Single-Whip Method of Taxation in China*. Much can also be gleaned from Ray Huang, *Taxation and Government Finance in 16th Century Ming China*. Huang notes that the Single-Whip system was introduced in the south long before the north (p. 120) and that it met with much resistance in the north (p. 299).

38. Chiang Hsing-yü, *Hai Jui*, pp. 74–82.

39. Lü K'un reports that the Single-Whip system was put into effect in

The increased production of cotton also stimulated the economic change. In part, the trend derived from the policies of the early Ming emperors who ordered the imperial government to make payments in cotton rather than in grain. By the sixteenth century, according to one estimate, the imperial government needed not less than five or six million bolts of cotton just for the annual salaries for the military.[40] In fact cotton became so popular during the Wan-li period that a hundred new stores specializing in cotton socks opened up in one area alone.[41] Realizing how lucrative the new textile industry had become, local officials occasionally encouraged the common people to take up the weaving of cotton. Lü K'un, for example, drew up an elaborate plan for teaching the men and women of Shansi to weave cotton. He recruited ten carpenters to teach other carpenters how to construct looms and spinning wheels; he used official funds to provide each household with one catty of ginned cotton; and he recruited weavers to instruct the people in the skill. This plan, he hoped, would enrich the whole province.[42]

Peasants who found opportunities to weave for middlemen or to sell surplus crops to the towns, often yielded to the temptation to specialize[43] and consequently became entangled in and dependent on large interregional economic networks. To facilitate the exchange of resources between the major urban areas and the rural villages, periodic markets and small towns proliferated.[44]

If some rural areas consequently prospered, ominous

---

his area in 1585. Everyone initially welcomed the reform. After a few years, however, difficulties arose regarding additional payment for labor services (*CWCWC*, 5:54a–55a).

40. Yen Chung-p'ing, *Chung-kuo mien-fang chih shih kao*, p. 15. Also see Mi Chü Wiens, "Cotton Textile Production and Rural Social Transformation in Early Modern China."

41. Cited in Fu I-ling, *Ming-Ch'ing shih-tai*, p. 11.

42. *SCL*, 2:9b–10a. This passage has been partially translated in Mi Chü Wiens, "Cotton Textile Production," p. 517, and Joanna F. Handlin, "Lü K'un's New Audience: The Influence of Women's Literacy on Sixteenth-Century Thought," p. 26.

43. Fu I-ling, *Ming-tai Chiang-nan shih-min ching-chi shih-t'an*, pp. 48–49.

44. On the proliferation of markets during the Ming, see Elvin, *Pattern of the Chinese Past*, pp. 269–71; and Fu I-ling, *Ming-tai Chiang-nan*, pp. 103–4.

signs that the commercialization might lead to severe social discord also surfaced. The introduction of money, many scholars feared, had tainted the traditional ideals. Lü observed that financial disagreements turned brothers into enemies.[45] One rural lecturer noted that children's filial allegiance toward their parents ceased as soon as they got their hands on money.[46] Others moaned that everyone had grown competitive, greedy, and selfish.

Economic prosperity blurred social distinctions. Sumptuary regulations withered away as wealthy townspeople sported the caps formerly worn only by "budding scholars" (*hsiu-ts'ai*)[47] and men dressed effeminately.[48] The prosperity caused Lü K'un to worry that peasants were extravagantly indulging in meat or wine, gambling in the market towns, or, worst of all, contributing their savings to potentially rebellious millenarian groups.[49] Indeed, according to a report of 1565, the White Lotus sect could afford to construct forty-five temples and attract ten thousand followers in the province of Hopei alone.[50]

The economic changes necessitated social adjustments, not all of which were successful. As towns grew more attractive, landowners turned absentee, and the paternalistic ties between them and their tenants gave way to impersonal businesslike relationships. So, at least, observed Lü K'un, who looked back wistfully to the Liang and Sung dynasties when, he believed, landlords took good care of the hired laborers on whom they depended for protection and work.

45. Lü K'un, *Tsung-yüeh ko,* in *Lü tzu i-shu,* 1b.

46. Cited from *Hsiang-ch'eng hsien chih* (Wan-li ed.) in Wang Lan-yin, "Ming-tai chih hsiang-yüeh yü min-chung chiao-yü." *Shih-ta yüeh-k'an* 21:115–116 (1935).

47. Fu I-ling, *Ming-tai Chiang-nan,* p. 102.

48. Ibid., p. 107.

49. *SCL,* 2:18b; 2:16a–b.

50. Cited in Li Shou-k'ung, "Ming-tai pai-lien k'ao-lüeh," p. 44. For Lü K'un's warnings against joining pernicious heterodox sects, see Lü K'un, *Tsung-yüeh ko,* 21b. In his famous memorial of 1597, "Yu-wei shu," Lü mentions as one of four categories of potential rebels the White Lotus who meet at night and whose leaders could command enormous followings (*CWCWC,* 1:6b). For a thoughtful discussion of the White Lotus, see Daniel L. Overmyer, *Folk Buddhist Religion: Dissenting Sects in Late Traditional China.* For a partial translation of Lü's memorial, see ibid., p. 28.

"Now," observed Lü, "when the tenants ask for help, the landlords ask for high interest."[51] Lü also noted that market towns were cheating the villages, using inaccurate scales, bullying the ignorant in transactions, and levying excess taxes.[52]

The use of silver stimulated the economy and made beneficial tax reforms possible, but the fluctuating supply created much anxiety. One official who noted that silver had become the main medium of exchange also commented on the difficulties caused by the popular preference for silver over copper. As people abandoned the use of copper, the price of silver became highly inflated and the conversion of produce into silver for the payment of taxes consequently became increasingly complex.[53] Peasants and craftsmen, vulnerable to fluctuations in both the supply of silver and the market demand for specialized products, gave vent to their frustrations throughout the late Ming. Bandits roamed the countryside, weavers rioted, and members of the White Lotus sect rose up with the hope of hastening a messianic salvation.[54]

In a second noteworthy change, the prosperity of the period stimulated the democratization of education. The founding emperor of the Ming, T'ai-tsu—who had risen to power from peasant origins and who consequently envied and distrusted the urbane scholars in his bureaucracy—

51. *SCL*, 2:7b.

52. *SCL*, 3:42b–43a. In Fukien, commercialization had an altogether different effect on landlord-tenant relations. Absentee landlords, unable to control and supervise their tenants, settled for fixed, low-risk incomes (Rawski, *Agricultural Change*, pp. 28–29). On contractual relations, see Fu I-ling, *Ming-tai Chiang-nan*, p. 27.

53. From the biography of Chin Hsüeh-yen in *Ming shih*, 214:5669–70; cited and translated in Peterson, *Bitter Gourd*, p. 69.

54. On the role of overseas trade in the silver supply in China, see Atwell, "Notes on Silver, Foreign Trade, and the Late Ming Economy." When interruptions in the flow of silver from the Americas to China were particularly marked during the 1630s and 1640s both urban riots and tenant uprisings gained intensity (ibid., p. 16). For a concise survey of Ming riots and a suggestive comparison of Ming and Ch'ing responses to unrest, see Tsing Yuan, "Urban Riots and Disturbances," in particular pp. 285–296 and 311–312. For an uprising of weavers in Su-chou, see Charles O. Hucker, "Su-chou and the Agents of Wei Chung-hsien, 1626," in *Two Studies on Ming History*, pp. 41–83. See also, Fu I-ling, *Ming-tai Chiang-nan*, pp. 88–9 and 94–5. See also James Bunyan Parsons, *Peasant Rebellions of the Late Ming*.

wished education to be available to all and monopolized by none. He therefore instructed that community schools be established in every hsien.[55] Although his program met with only limited success, officials in charge of local administration, like Lü K'un, and also gentry, like Yang Tung-ming, did from time to time try to set up community schools.[56]

The community schools provided students with functional literacy. In one year, boys could master roughly two thousand characters, and in two to three years, they could learn to read and write simple materials.[57] A Korean monk visiting

55. Maintaining control over the community schools once they were set up was a problem for the early rulers that resulted in several policy changes. In 1375, T'ai-tsu instructed officials to establish community schools. In 1383, he instructed the common people to set up the community schools and forbade the officials to interfere. In 1436, both local education and provincial officials were instructed to oversee the community schools. In 1465, it was made clear that attending the community schools should be voluntary for those who were impoverished (*Ta Ming hui-tien*, 78:22b–23a). For a fine survey and analysis of reports in local gazetteers and other materials on community schools, see Wang Lan-yin, "Ming-tai chih hsiang-yüeh yü min-chung chiao-yü," and "Ming-tai chih she-hsüeh." Much information on the community schools can also be gleaned from: Tadao Sakai, *Chūgoku zensho no kenkyū*, and Evelyn Sakakida Rawski, *Education and Popular Literacy in Ch'ing China*, chapter 2. I agree with Rawski that there is no clear and consistent distinction between the two terms for "community school," *she-hsüeh* and *i-hsüeh* (p. 35).

56. Lü offered the following plan for staffing the community schools: "Today in selecting teachers for the communities (*she*), one should try to select twenty or more who are over forty, who are still pure in heart, and are as determined as an upright scholar, regardless of whether they have been to school or not. The magistrates should assemble them at the Confucian Temple and give them rations for their daily food. First teach them by expounding on [Chu Hsi's] *Hsiao-hsüeh* and the *Hsiao ching* and [have them] learn the characters and *fan-ch'ieh* spellings. After a year, if . . . their pronunciation, . . . their understanding of the literary principles, and their lecturing and explanations are roughly correct—the magistrates will visit the school to examine them and select those who are fit to teach others. Then distribute them among the community schools" (*SCL*, 3:7b). See also Yang Tung-ming, "I-hsüeh chi" with Colophon of 1601 by Chou Tzu-hsün in *SCKK*, 3:1a–10a; and Chou Ju-teng, "Chien she-hsüeh wen-i" in *Tung-yüeh cheng-hsüeh lu*, 13:27a–33a.

57. For a fascinating and concise evaluation of numerous aspects of popular education—literacy rates, printing, and sponsorship and financing of schools—see Rawski, *Education and Popular Literacy*, especially pp. 4 and 53. Although Rawski's book is ostensibly about the Ch'ing, it contains much information on or germane to the late Ming. For a detailed survey of primers used in elementary education and of pedagogy, see Chang Chih-kung, *Ch'uan-t'ung yü-wen chiao-yü ch'u-t'an*. Chang frequently touched on

China in the 1480s reported that in one prosperous area "even village children, ferrymen and sailors could read,"[58] and recent estimates for the Ch'ing dynasty suggest that 30 to 45 per cent of the male population and 2 to 10 per cent of the female population enjoyed functional literacy.[59]

To attract such semi-literate readers, publishers and authors lavishly illustrated their books, wrote in the informal vernacular style, and often added explanations and keys to the pronunciations of difficult characters. Thus alongside the classics and other serious works there now competed for the reader's attention numerous unscholarly genres—easy, practical, or entertaining—that suited the impatient and poorly educated. Abridged, simplified versions of the classics helped lazy students to prepare for the civil service examinations. Practical household handbooks informed the common people on such everyday matters as how to care for their cats, how to blend fragrances for soaps, and how to schedule chores throughout the year.[60] Vernacular fiction also flourished during the sixteenth century. Subjects ranging from religious salvation and supernatural fantasies to tales of crime and passion satisfied diverse popular interests. Restless youths vicariously enjoyed the heroic adventures of the Robin Hood types portrayed in *Shui-hu chuan* [The Water Margin]—an episodic novel against which Feng Ts'ung-wu warned his students.[61] And idle, housebound women found escape in the titillating erotic love stories, just barely disguised as didactic literature.[62]

Lü K'un (ibid., pp. 25, 51, 86, 92, and 122). Rawski draws heavily from Chang's work.

58. John Meskill, tr., *Ch'oe Pu's Diary: A Record of Drifting Across the Sea*, p. 155. Ch'oe Pu, who traveled to China during the late fifteenth century was referring to the Chiang-nan region of central China, where, he noted, literacy was much higher than in the north.

59. Rawski, *Education and Popular Literacy*, p. 23.

60. For "A Classic on buying a cat" (*Na mao ching*) by Yü Tsung-pen of the Yüan dynasty, see *Chü-chia pi-pei*, 7th *ts'e*, 1a–b. On fragrances for washing clothes and hair, see ibid., 9th *ts'e*, 9b–10a. For a month by month list of household chores, see ibid., 9th *ts'e*.

61. *FSHC*, 6:8a. For an abridged translation of this novel, see J. H. Jackson, *Water Margin*.

62. See, for example, *Chin P'ing Mei*, tr. as *The Golden Lotus* by Clement

As literacy spread, the assumption that achieving the goal of sagehood or moral perfection was difficult gave way to the belief that learning should be widespread, pleasurable, and easy. Literacy, one gazetteer declared, was as essential to life as breathing.[63] Sages, who in former times had appeared only once every few centuries, now filled the streets; and students who were loath to make sacrifices for their education were reassured that "wine, women, wealth, and passion do not block the road to enlightenment."[64]

Most influential in paving the way for new definitions of education was the famous philosopher and statesman, Wang Shou-jen (1472–1529), more familiarly called Wang Yang-ming. In reaction to an earlier view of the philosopher Chu Hsi (1130–1200) that principle (*li*) inhered in all things and could be perceived through the investigation of the external world (*ko-wu*), Wang maintained that principle could be found within one's own mind through introspection. As a student, Wang had despaired of understanding Chu Hsi's outmoded commentaries to the Classics, had tossed his books aside, and had tried to understand the concept of *ko-wu* by contemplating bamboo instead. He was unsuccessful and after seven days fell ill from the mental strain. Only years later when serving in a very difficult post among Miao aborigines in the backward region of Kweichow did he achieve enlightenment. Suddenly in the middle of the night, he excitedly realized that for understanding the Way of the sages "one's own nature is self-sufficient and it is wrong to seek for principle outside of it."[65] On the basis of this insight, Wang elaborated on the concept of "innate knowledge"

Egerton. For a description of the pornography of the period, see Robert Hans van Gulik, *Sexual Life in Ancient China*, pp. 263–335.

63. *Shao-wu fu chih* (1543), 7:1a.

64. Liang Ch'i-ch'ao, *Intellectual Trends*, p. 28.

65. For information on Wang Shou-jen, see: Wei-ming Tu, *Neo-Confucian Thought in Action: Wang Yang-ming's Youth (1472–1509)*; and Fung Yu-lan, *A History of Chinese Philosophy*, 2:596–623. For a trans. of some of Wang's works, see Wang Yang-ming, *Instructions for Practical Living and Other Neo-Confucian Writings*. For a discussion of Wang's influence on late Ming thought, see Wm. Theodore de Bary, "Individualism and Humanitarianism in Late Ming Thought," pp. 12–14; 145–245.

(*liang-chih*).[66] Wang believed that through the extension of innate knowledge (*chih liang-chih*) each person could achieve moral perfection.[67]

Wang's teaching that the authority for moral principles rested within the mind, and should be understood, therefore, through personal experience rather than by conforming to external standards, paved the way for the moral relativism and individualism of the sixteenth century. In his famous discussion with two disciples at T'ien-ch'üan Bridge,[68] Wang concurred that one could achieve enlightenment either spontaneously and intuitively, as advocated by one disciple, Wang Chi (1378–1460), or through earnest effort, as advocated by another disciple, Ch'ien Te-hung (1497–1574).[69] The method should be chosen, Wang Yang-ming explained, not according to external standards, but according to the student's native ability. In teaching others, Wang further believed, one of four axioms should be stressed to suit the level of the student's intelligence. One of these axioms—"In the original substance of the mind there is no distinction of good and evil"—was interpreted by members of the next generation to give license to moral relativism. Thus Wang's tolerance of different approaches to knowledge sowed, much against Wang's own intentions, the seeds for the philosophical disputes that later divided the scholar-officials.

Through the proselytizing of his diverse followers, Wang Yang-ming's teachings spread like wildfire and touched men like Wang Ken (1483–1540), the son of an uneducated salt merchant.[70] Wang Ken attended for only five years one of those village schools the emperor T'ai-tsu had promoted, and never attempted to take the civil service examinations. Nonetheless, he harbored grand ambitions to save the world. He dreamed that when a crowd of thousands was screaming in terror because the sky was falling, he alone shouldered

66. *Mencius* VIIA, in Legge *Chinese Classics*, 2:456. Wang Yang-ming, *Instructions for Practical Living*, pp. 145–46; 116–17.

67. Fung Yu-lan, *History of Chinese Philosophy*, 2:605–10.

68. Wang Yang-ming, *Instructions for Practical Living*, p. 244.

69. Biography of Wang Chi by Julia Ching in *DMB*, pp. 1349–55. Biography of Ch'ien Te-hung by Julia Ching in *DMB*, pp. 241–44.

70. Biography of Wang Ken by Julia Ching in *DMB*, pp. 1382–85. For a

the sky and won the praise and gratitude of all. He had perceived, his dream intimated, that in real life the commoners were so eager for instruction that even he, albeit poorly educated, could gain prominence without an official position. Fired by a sense of mission, Wang Ken wandered throughout the countryside to teach artisans and peasants. As in his dream, so in real life he attracted enormous audiences; and on his death he left behind devoted disciples who energetically carried on his work.

Ho Hsin-yin (1517–79) also followed in the wake of Wang Yang-ming. Ho was initially somewhat more conventional than Wang Ken and took the district examinations in 1546. But when persuaded by one of Wang Ken's followers that an official career was fruitless, Ho desisted from taking further examinations and found other ways to serve his society. He organized his lineage to work as a cooperative and to follow egalitarian principles. He established a boarding school with the aim of removing children from parental influence and instructing them in his new principles. He even went so far as to unite his lineage against excessive taxation by the local bureaucracy. For this last act, he barely escaped punishment. During the rest of his life he wandered about lecturing, sometimes forming alliances with dubious fringe social groups. He was consequently arrested on the charge of banditry and died in prison.[71]

While some like Wang Ken rushed to the countryside to teach artisans and peasants, others attracted large followings to their academies in the bustling urban centers.[72] Each disciple, each academy founder, inspired by Wang Yang-ming's view that principle rested within the mind, developed his own philosophy and hence fostered an atmosphere of intellectual and moral relativism. In tune with that mood, one late Ming novel (*Hsi-yu chi*) satirized the view that the three

---

discussion of Wang's thought, see Jung Chao-tsu, *Ming-tai ssu-hsiang shih*, pp. 150–59. See also de Bary, "Individualism" pp. 157–71.

71. For information on Ho Hsin-yin, see the biography by Wu Pei-yi and Julia Ching in *DMB*, pp. 513–15; de Bary, "Individualism," pp. 178–88; and Ronald G. Dimberg, *The Sage and Society: The Life and Thought of Ho Hsin-yin*. For Ho's essays, see Jung Chao-tsu, ed., *Ho Hsin-yin chi*.

72. Ping-ti Ho, *Ladder of Success*, p. 199.

hundred sixty conflicting schools of wisdom alike lead to the one goal, self-attainment.[73]

The spread of literacy and the prosperity of the late Ming must be understood in conjunction with a third major trend—the growing alienation of scholar-officials from the autocratic and irresponsible late Ming emperors. The Ming rulers could afford to oppress, demean, and dismiss their officials because the spread of education had expanded the available pool of scholars. Hai Jui and Feng Ts'ung-wu barely escaped death for their forthright criticisms of the Chia-ching and Wan-li emperors. Lü K'un was painfully aware that speaking carelessly in court frequently led to disaster.

Playing an important role in strengthening the state from 1567 to 1582 was the powerful minister Chang Chü-cheng (1525–82). Chang called for lessening discussion, enforcing the law, improving the livelihood of the people, and strengthening military preparedness.[74] His pragmatic policies, designed to strengthen the state and benefit the peasantry, would not tolerate the interference of young students in the affairs of local government, or the wrangling among scholar-officials in the private academies. For this, Chang won the enmity of many. At the same time, Chang did much to check the extravagant and irresponsible tendencies of his emperors.[75] He prevailed on the Wan-li emperor, for example, to desist from repairing the palaces and lavishing gifts on his favorites.

Chang Chü-cheng died in 1582, whereupon order at court rapidly disintegrated. In 1589 the Wan-li emperor, Shen-tsung, stopped holding audiences and then refused, for almost thirty years, to respond to petitions. Because the emperor neglected government affairs, new appointments could not be made, and the bureaucracy became severely understaffed. With the authoritative guidance of the emperor lost, factionalism divided the officials at court, and numerous controversies arose—over the location of the imperial tomb

73. Wu Ch'eng-en, *Monkey*, p. 21.

74. Biography of Chang by Robert B. Crawford and L. Carrington Goodrich in *DMB*, pp. 53–61. See also Robert B. Crawford, "Chang Chü-cheng's Legalism," pp. 367–414.

75. *DMB*, p. 59.

(1585); over the appointment of the heir apparent (1586–1601); over the merit evaluations (1593 and 1604); and over the role of eunuchs in collecting special mining and market taxes—to name only a few.[76]

The suspension for a year of censorate officials, and the erratic demotions and dismissals of others, further confounded and demoralized officialdom. Toward the end of Shen-tsung's reign officials felt a deep sense of crisis, which fastened on three cases: in 1615, "the case of the attack with a club," when someone broke into the palace and threatened the heir apparent's life; in 1620, "the case of the red pills," when the emperor, already severely ill, was believed to have been murdered by red pills administered as a last resort by one of his officials; and, also in 1620, "the case of the removal from the palace," when various people at court maneuvered for control over the boy heir apparent.[77]

Shaken by the moral relativism and the heightened sense of crisis, a number of upright scholars—including many who had been dismissed from government service—banded together, first in 1604 and then more determinedly in the 1620s, at the Tung-lin Academy to clarify their moral standards and to root out the evil influences at court. Yet, even as they criticized the inner court, in particular the eunuch Wei Chung-hsien, the Tung-lin members also blamed the laxity of their own peers for the moral confusion. Specifically they singled out the numerous heterodox thinkers who had drifted away from Wang Yang-ming's original teachings to iconoclastic, selfish, and individualistic views.[78]

76. See the informative biography of the Wan-li emperor, Chu I-chün, by Charles O. Hucker in *DMB*, pp. 324–37.

77. For information on the three cases, see the biography of Kao P'an-lung by Charles O. Hucker in *DMB*, pp. 705–6.

78. Charles O. Hucker, "The Tung-lin Movement of the Late Ming Period," pp. 144–45. Heinrich Busch, "The Tung-lin Shu-yüan and Its Political and Philosophical Significance." Seventeenth-century materials are replete with diatribes against the followers of Wang Shou-jen. See for example the writings of Chang Lü-hsiang, *Yang-yüan hsien-sheng ch'üan-chi*, 27:11b–12a; 31:23b. See also Lu Lung-ch'i, *San-yü t'ang wen-chi*, 2.2a–8b, where he criticized the pernicious influence of Zen Buddhism on late-Ming thought; blamed the fall of the Ming dynasty on the failure of its scholars; and maintained that even the upright leaders of the Tung-lin movement, Ku Hsien-ch'eng and Kao P'an-lung, shared many of Wang

The Tung-lin group's outraged cries against Wang's followers have led many historians to conclude that the ground swell of experimental ideas inspired by Wang was thoroughly eliminated. The policy of the Ch'ing, who conquered China in 1644 and who proved to be masterful architects of orthodoxy, appeared to corroborate this view. The late Ming rulers, the Ch'ing claimed, had lost the Mandate of Heaven by neglecting their responsibilities; but worse, the Ch'ing warned all scholars, the heterodox followers of Wang Yang-ming had hastened the decline of the Ming. By playing on the scholars' feelings of guilt in this manner, the Ch'ing rulers promoted an atmosphere of caution and self-watchfulness.

Although Ch'ing policy did to some extent shape intellectual activity, the heroism of the Tung-lin party and the attitudes of the Ch'ing rulers have in fact obscured important Ming currents that continued uninterrupted after 1644, among them the concern for simplicity and utility, intense self-watchfulness, and even the penchant for crises. The reorientation that stirred up those currents is the subject of this book.

Shou-jen's faults. In particular Lu criticized Wang Ken, Wang Chi, Lo Ju-fang, and Chou Ju-teng.

2

Sages

What defines the dimensions of man? Scholars, often inspired by the models of past sages and heroes or fired by a sense of mission, boldly and confidently took on formidable opponents and fought for noble causes. Their determination, their commitment, and the grand scope of their visions enlarged them and commanded the respect of their followers. Wang Yang-ming's convictions gave him the courage to educate and improve the living conditions of aborigines in the Kweichow wilderness even while he suffered the disgrace of exile and the pains of social isolation. Lo Ju-fang resolutely defended the importance both of lecturing and of the student's loyalty to his teacher. Hai Jui, in his lifelong fight for justice, risked death in criticizing his emperor, and disrepute in opposing the well-connected landlords of the Kiangnan area. These are but a few examples of those who achieved larger-than-life stature.

Every period produces men who in their commitment to noble causes test the boundaries of acceptable political and social behavior. But as these boundaries shift from era to era—as the institutions from which men draw strength for their actions and the channels through which they communicate change—so do the talents and actions through which men rise above their times. Thus the precise ingredients of greatness change even while the general concept remains the same.

During the decades following Wang Yang-ming, scholars enjoyed considerable latitude to develop individualistic, even eccentric ideas. Among the institutions that enabled them to do so were the private academies. These had prospered during the Sung dynasty, fallen into disrepair during the Yuan, and enjoyed an energetic revival during the Ming. Ming officials and scholars hastened to reconstruct academy buildings that had deteriorated, to convert ancestral halls into schools, and to add libraries, dormitories, and refectories to existing institutions. Between the Yuan and Ming dynasties, the number of private academies rose, according to one count, in Honan from six to eighty, in Chekiang from four to fifty-four, in Kiangsi from eleven to fifty-six, and in Fukien from eight to eighty-three.[1] Although these figures were based on the incomplete surveys of gazetteers, the sudden expansion is clear. By 1525, Wang Yang-ming had cause to remark that to supplement the officially sponsored schools, which had become inadequate, "private academies had been constructed in all the famous and beautiful places."[2]

Men joined the private academies for several reasons. There, merchants found opportunities to make advantageous contacts with officials. Indeed, commercial interests often merged with and bolstered scholarly concerns, as when salt merchants invited Chan Jo-shui (1466–1560) to lecture.[3] At the private academies, those preparing for the examinations sought instruction, moral support, and perhaps most important—as numerous academy regulations against pandering to visiting officials might indicate—useful social connections. In addition, through the academies officials extended their patronage, built up their reputations and hence formed valuable political connections. Thus the rise of the academies owed much to the alliance between students who wished to avoid the burdensome corvée labor and officials who wished to establish reputations through the academies.[4] Most notably, Hsü Chieh (1494–1579) took on students as a young official and strongly supported scholarly associations. When he became grand secretary in 1552, those with political ambitions found it advantageous to establish academies that could offer hospitality to officials on tour.[5] The academy craze

1. Okubo Hideko, *Min Shin jidai shoin no kenkyū*, pp. 78–84.
2. Wang Shou-jen, *Wang Yang-ming ch'üan-shu*, 7:18b–20a.
3. Biography of Chan Jo-shui by Chaoying Fang in *DMB*, p. 28.
4. Hsü Hsüeh-chü, *Kuo-ch'ao tien-hui*, 130:5b. Cited in Tilemann Grimm, "Ming Education Intendants," p. 139.
5. See John Meskill, "Academies and Politics in the Ming Dynasty,"

that was sweeping through China during Lo Ju-fang's lifetime contributed much to his rise to fame.

Another opportunity for individual initiative occurred at the level of local administration following the breakdown of the *li-chia*. According to the *li-chia* system devised by Ming T'ai-tsu, rural society was organized into "administrative neighborhoods," or *li*, which consisted of 110 households—ten wealthy families responsible for the leadership and ten units, or *chia*, of ten households each. Each unit was responsible for collecting taxes and organizing the corvée labor. However, with the increase in population and the concomitant decrease in the per capita holdings of land, the quotas—which were not adjusted to changing conditions—became increasingly difficult to meet. As landowners devised means to evade their tax responsibilities, the organizational structure of rural society broke down and left unprecedentedly large room for the initiative of the local gentry (which this study defines as former officials), provincial officials, and degree-holders.[6] Thus Ho Hsin-yin, who had passed only the district examination and had failed to win an official appointment, could apply his energies and talents on his own initiative to organizing his lineage. And Hai Jui, following the disintegration of the *li-chia*, could expand the duties of the magistrate.[7]

Also offering new opportunities for leadership was the floating population of the semi-educated, who had, for example, given real form to Wang Ken's dream of saving mankind from a falling sky. With the spread of printing, and specifically with the application of printing to everyday matters, the possibility of communicating directly with the common people became real. As the sections on Lü K'un and the military general Ch'i Chi-kuang (1528–88) will show,[8] the spread of printing gave prominence to new types of social relations

---

p. 162. See also *MJHA*, 27:1b. On Hsü Chieh, see the biography by Chaoying and Lienche Tu Fang in *DMB*, pp. 570–76.

6. John R. Watt, *The District Magistrate*, pp. 105–6; 111–138. See also Y. Yamada, "Min Shin jidai no sonraku jichi ni tsuite (1)," 214–30.

7. Watt, *District Magistrate*, pp. 137–38, citing *Hai Jui chi* (hereafter *HJC*), pp. 145–46.

8. See chapter 7 below.

and made it possible to harness the energies of large groups for cooperative endeavors.

The wide variety of opportunities allowed mid-sixteenth-century men ample room to express their talents fully and in vivid ways that refuse to fade even with the passage of time. Available were the means, the channels of communication, and the institutions, to have an impact, albeit fleetingly, on society.

Lo and Hai carried out principles that in themselves had great vitality. The courageous of the next generation—such as the participants of the Tung-lin movement—acted according to principles that were verified by an identification with real crises. Both Lo and Hai had undauntingly and unselfconsciously lived by their principles and risen above their critics. Men of the next generation, cramped by a consciousness of the boundaries to their permissible behavior, were more easily engaged by their critics. Where Lo and Hai had acted individually, the Tung-lin acted as a group. The adjustments to the sense of restrictions, in particular the identification of values with crises and the incorporation of individual behavior into group action are evident in the writings of Lü K'un.[9]

In 1553, the Grand Secretary Hsü Chieh lectured for two months in the Ling-chi Temple in Peking. Excitement filled the air as several thousands crowded in to participate in the "learned discussions."[10] It was the year when students who had already passed the *chü-jen* degree in the provincial examinations poured into the capital to compete for the *chin-shih* degree. Among the aspirants that year were Lo Ju-fang of Nan-ch'eng, Kiangsi, and Hai Jui of Ch'iung-shan, Hainan Island. Only about three hundred would pass the difficult metropolitan and palace examinations necessary to earn the *chin-shih* degree. The stakes were high: direct entrance into the middle ranks of officialdom on the one hand; either an assignment to a low post or a sheepish return to one's expectant family on the other.

9. See chapter 7 below.

10. Lo Ju-fang, *Hsü-t'an chih-ch'üan* (hereafter *HTCC*), 2:40a. *HTCC* was originally printed in Soochow, according to the editors of *Lo Chin-hsi wen-chi*, preliminary *chüan*, p. 13b.

Lo had already attended several such meetings on his way up the examination ladder. Preparing for the examinations had filled him with horrifying anxieties, and he found comfort in huddling together with students of "like resolve" (*t'ung-chih*). As a young man in 1531, Lo had set his mind on becoming a sage and had started a diary to keep track of his faults.[11] In 1532, he cloistered himself in a monastery and tried to quiet his thoughts by contemplating the purity of water reflected in a mirror. These early efforts ended in a nervous collapse, an illness that, according to Lo's father, resulted from internal rather than external problems.[12] In 1536, a visit to the Confucian temple renewed Lo's determination to take the provincial examination, which he then failed in 1540. In his disappointment, Lo responded to a sign that read "Emergency aid for sickness of the heart" only to find, not a doctor, but the lecturer Yen Chün.[13] Yen, a disciple of Wang Ken, was, like Wang, one of many semi-educated men of that time who could find gratifying ways to use their rough education without submitting to the rigorous classical training necessary for entering the civil service. From Yen, Lo learned how to maintain a sense of equilibrium.[14]

In 1543, Lo passed the *chü-jen* degree and then proceeded in 1544 to the capital to try his luck at the *chin-shih* examination. He attended a large meeting at the Ling-chi Temple. Among his companions were Hsü Yüeh and T'an Lun (1520–

11. Biography of Lo by Julia Ching in *DMB*, pp. 975–78; *MJHA*, 34:1a–3a; and *Ming shih*, 283:3186. Biographies by Lo's admirers, T'an Hsi-ssu, Liu Yüan-ch'ing, Wang Shih-huai, and Chou Ju-teng; and epitaphs, rich in biographical information, by Yang Ch'i-yüan, Chao Chih-kao, and Tsou Yüan-piao, can be found in *Fu-chi*, 2 *chüan*, in *Chin-hsi tzu chi*. The various accounts sometimes contradict one another on small details. The most complete biography can be found in *HTCC*, 2:36a–69a. See also Li Chih, *Hsü Tsang-shu*, 22:444–46. Small bits of information, mostly inconsequential, can also be found in *Tung-ch'ang fu chih* (1808), 15:17a; 20:40b; *T'ai-hu hsien chih* (1872), 15:10a; 16:2a; *Ning-kuo fu chih*, (1919), 3:15a; 5:26b–27a. For an analysis of Lo's thought, in particular the evolution of his ideas from those of Wang Chi and Wang Ken, see Araki Kengo, *Mindai shisō kenkyū*, chap. 5. The ideas presented below are based on Joanna F. Handlin, "Hai Jui and Lo Ju-fang: Alternative Routes to Fame in the Sixteenth Century."

12. *HTCC*, 2:37a.

13. *HTCC*, 2:37a. See also *MJHA*, 34:1b–2b.

14. *HTCC*, 2:37b.

77).[15] Hsü Yüeh was from Lo's province, Kiangsi, and had been one of Yen Chün's teachers. He had already earned the *chin-shih* degree in 1532, and was now in a position to guide Yen's protégé, Lo, through the examination procedures. T'an Lun, also of Kiangsi, was to pass the *chin-shih* examination that year. He would then start his active military career training troops, fighting the pirates along the Chekiang coast, cooperating with the famous general, Ch'i Chi-kuang, and exchanging views with none other than Hai Jui.[16] Lo in the end did not take the final palace examination, according to some accounts because his aging father had fallen ill.[17]

In 1545, detained at home by his father's illness, Lo built a library where scholars from everywhere congregated to discuss such idealist Neo-Confucian philosophers as Ch'eng Hao (1032–85), Lu Hsiang-shan (1139–93), Wang Yang-ming, and Wang Ken.[18] By 1553, Lo had built up the moral support of a vast network of friends and had enjoyed the opportunity for almost an additional decade of study. Thus fortified, he appeared at the Ling-chi Temple to listen to Hsü Chieh and was soon after to pass the final palace examination.[19]

Hai Jui's path to the metropolitan examination in 1553 also started with an early determination to become a sage.[20] As was the case with Lo Ju-fang, his progress was slow and difficult. He did not earn the *chü-jen* degree until 1549. He failed

15. *HTCC*, 2:38a. For Hsü Yüeh, see *MJHA*, 32:14b–15a; *Ming shih*, 283:3186.

16. Biography of T'an Lun by Chaoying Fang in *DMB*, pp. 1243–46; *Ming shih*, 222:2559–60.

17. *HTCC*. 2:38a–b. 18. *HTCC*, 2:38b.

19. *HTCC*, 2:4a. It was at this time, in 1553, that Lo formed a pact with Chiang Pao, who like Lo earned the *chin-shih* degree that year, and Hu Lu-shan, Tsou Shan, Keng Ting-hsiang, and Liu Ying-feng, who were to earn it in 1556. See T'an Hsi-ssu, "Huang Ming li-hsüeh ming-ch'en chuan" in *Chin-hsi-tzu fu-chi*, 1:1b.

20. In 1526 at fourteen *sui*. See the chronological biography (*nien-p'u*), compiled by Wang Kuo-hsien in *HJC*, p. 578. Biography of Hai by Chaoying Fang in *DMB*, pp. 474–79; and *Ming shih*, 226:2602–4. For a translation of Hai's biography in *Ming shih*, see Ernst Wolff, "A Preliminary Study of Hai Jui: His Biography in the Ming-shih," pp. 147–61. For a critical biography of Hai, see Chiang Hsing-yü, *Hai Jui*. Several biographies in addition to the *nien-p'u* have also been reprinted in *HJC*, pp. 525–603. For a partial translation of one of Hai's works on local government, "Hsing-ko

the metropolitan examination in 1550 and was again to fail in 1553. The two contemporaries coped with the obstacles to office in sharply different ways. Lo had undergone frequent spiritual crises; Hai Jui displayed from his fourteenth year a steadfast commitment to being "pure of mind" (*chen-hsin*) and strictly adhered to proper social rituals.[21] Lo cultivated peer support; Hai, according to available information, formed no important and lasting contacts. Whether Hai even attended the lectures at the Ling-chi Temple, where his competitors scrambled for patronage, is not known. Later in life, Hai Jui scorned those who tried to build up social influence; and, an activist by nature, he was impatient with "learned discussions." Even as young men taking the metropolitan examinations in 1553, Lo and Hai were making very different judgments about what deserved note in their writings.

After Lo and Hai took the *chin-shih* examination, their paths diverged markedly, because of differences not so much in their official duties as in how they interpreted their opportunities. In 1554, Lo was assigned district magistrate of T'ai-hu, Anhwei, but he displayed his greatest talents as a lecturer rather than as an administrator. In 1554, Hai Jui received a minor post as instructor in Nan-p'ing, Fukien, but he gained fame as a forceful administrator rather than as a teacher.

Lo Ju-fang and Hai Jui were almost exact contemporaries and therefore to some extent shared the same milieu. Both were familiar with Wang Yang-ming's thought. Lo drew much inspiration from two of Wang's followers and often specifically discoursed on Wang's views.[22] Hai Jui sometimes cited Wang as an authority[23] and sometimes criticized him.[24] In addition, the social networks to which Lo and Hai belonged frequently overlapped. Keng Ting-hsiang, one of Lo's

---

t'iao-li," see Michel Cartier, *Une Réforme Locale en Chine au XVIe Siècle: Hai Rui à Chun'an 1558–1562.*

21. See the discussion of Hai Jui further on in this chapter.

22. See, for example, Lo Ju-fang, *Hsü-chiang Lo Chin-hsi hsien-sheng ch'üan chi,* 6:38a. The two followers were Wang Ken and Wang Chi. For a discussion of their influence on Lo and on Lo's philosophical views in general, see Araki Kengo, *Mindai shisō kenkyū,* chap. 5.

23. *HJC,* pp. 97 and 185. 24. *HJC,* p. 211.

closest friends, in 1566 defended Hai Jui, who had been imprisoned for criticizing the emperor.[25] Li Chih (1527–1602), who had participated in "learned discussions" with Lo, wrote an admiring biography of Hai.[26] Hai corresponded frequently with T'an Lun, who had been one of Lo's companions at the Ling-chi Temple in 1544.[27] Hai Jui also corresponded with Chou Ssu-chiu, who in 1586 traveled about with Lo Ju-fang.[28] Chou hailed from Keng Ting-hsiang's hometown, Ma-ch'eng, knew Li Chih well,[29] and had served in Hai Jui's hometown, Ch'iung-shan.[30]

The lives of Lo and Hai suggest some of the difficulties the next generation would face; for both men were aware that they were carefully watched by the powerful Grand Secretary, Chang Chü-cheng, whose pragmatic policies aimed at strengthening the state. In 1573, shortly after becoming Grand Secretary, Chang challenged Lo Ju-fang's philosophical views[31] and sent an official to check up on Hai Jui.[32] Finally, both Lo and Hai commanded the attention of such prominent writers as Tsou Yüan-piao.[33] In short, Hai and Lo alike were not only sensitive to the popularizing philosophical influences of Wang Yang-ming but also themselves became significant reference points for the next generation.

Precisely because the initial social and career opportuni-

25. Keng Ting-hsiang, *Keng T'ien-t'ai hsien-sheng wen-chi*, 2:21a–22b. Keng also wrote a biography of Hai (ibid., 16:1a–4b).

26. Li Chih, *Hsü Ts'ang shu*, 23:471–73. Also reprinted in *HJC*, pp. 545–47.

27. *HJC*, pp. 416–17; 422; 435–36; and 426.

28. *HJC*, p. 466; *HTCC*, 2:61b.

29. In a letter to Chou Ssu-chiu, Yang Ch'i-yüan commented that he had recently read Li Chih's *Fen shu* and felt that Chou was fortunate to be with Li Chih night and day [*Ch'ung-k'o*] *Yang Fu-so hsien-sheng chia ts'ang wen-chi*, 6:12a). Yang also wrote an epitaph on Chou (*Ma-ch'eng hsien chih* [1882], 33:64a–66b). Chou and Keng both passed the *chü-jen* degree in 1552 (*Ma-ch'eng hsien chih*, 14:20a) and the *chin-shih* degree in 1553 and 1556 respectively (ibid., 14:20b).

30. *Ch'iung-shan hsien chih* (1857), 7:42b–43a.

31. *HTCC*, 2:47a–b. For information on the proscriptions of the private academies, see Sheng Lang-hsi, *Chung-kuo shu-yüan chih-tu*, pp. 85–87; John Meskill, "Academies and Politics."

32. Wolff, "A Preliminary Study," p. 159.

33. Tsou, "Hai Chung-chieh kung wen-chi hsü," reprinted in *HJC*, pp. 606–7. Tsou, *Yüan-hsüeh chi*, 6A:49a–53b. Also in *Chin-hsi-tzu fu-chi*, 2:17b–22b.

ties open to Lo and Hai were so similar, the sharp divergence in their final destinations—what they wrote about and how they perceived the world—is significant. That Lo and Hai created such different patterns out of similar material and potentially similar careers makes it possible to sort out the personal traits and the assumptions about society associated with a devotion to education on the one hand and administration on the other.

Lo Ju-fang, Educator

Lo Ju-fang won praise for his service both in organizing local volunteer efforts and in fulfilling his responsibilities as an official. Upon returning to his hometown in 1551, even before earning the *chin-shih* degree, he commissioned several buildings—a charitable granary, a charitable study-hall (*i-kuan*), and an ancestral temple—and put aside a trust of sacrificial lands. In addition, he repaired the ancestral tombs and lectured at the local shrine in order to edify the country people.[34] When Lo became magistrate of Ning-kuo, Anhwei, he again enterprisingly devoted himself to the welfare of the people and built a hall for a private academy in 1562.[35] So industriously did he serve Ning-kuo that the inhabitants were loath to see him leave and wrote "A Record of Grasping the Cart Wheels" to commemorate his outstanding service.[36] During his official career, Lo energetically promoted education, reformed prisoners, and—as vice commissioner of the military farms in Yunnan—solved irrigation problems and even devised ingenious strategies against some Burmese rebels. Lo performed his duties effectively and, according to all accounts, deeply touched the hearts of the people wherever he served.[37]

Overshadowing Lo's accomplishments as a local official was his success as one of the most influential and widely re-

34. *HTCC*, 2:39b–40a. 35. *HTCC*, 2:44a. 36. *HTCC*, 2:45a.

37. The people of T'ai-hu—where Lo served as magistrate in 1553—erected a shrine to commemorate Lo along with four other gentlemen (*T'ai-hu hsien chih* [1872], 15:10a).

vered lecturers of his day. Indeed, Lo's administrative policies never crystallized to leave their mark on others, and only a lean record of his accomplishments as an administrator remains. Lo's few works on the problems officials faced—two brief pieces on the history of monetary exchange and a pamphlet on water control—are no longer extant.[38] Lo's recorded dialogues, in contrast, were reprinted in edition after edition by his followers. It was in the role of educator that he flourished.

Of Lo's skillful lecturing, the seventeenth-century historian Huang Tsung-hsi noted: "In light conversations or serious speeches, wherever Lo's words fell, it was like the [sudden] spread of spring or the peal of thunder. [Mr. Lo] could instantaneously enlighten the moral natures even of those people who had never known learning."[39] Often as many as four to five hundred listeners attended Lo's meetings for "learned discussions."[40] On one occasion between forty and fifty thousand people flocked to a lecture he gave at a rural meeting. Lending veracity to these seemingly exaggerated figures, the account of the rural meeting explained that the vastness of the audience necessitated special arrangements: scattered throughout the audience were platforms from which eight or nine "hollerers" amplified the lecture. The account further noted that the hubbub of the enormous audience at first made hearing difficult; but singing gradually brought the crowds under control, and once Lo appeared, a hushed silence reigned.[41] Whatever their literal accuracy,

38. An extensive bibliography of over ninety works by Lo and dialogues recorded by his disciples, with brief remarks on dates of compilation, on whether they were published, and on whether they were still extant when the bibliography was compiled, can be found in *Lo Ming-te wen-chi*, preliminary *chüan*, pp. 12b–15b. The two works on monetary exchange, *Ming t'ung-pao i*, 1 *chüan*, and *Kuang t'ung-pao i*, 1 *chüan*, are mentioned in *Ssu-k'u ch'üan-shu tsung-mu, ch'in-ting*, 84:10a–b. Only the first of these is listed in the bibliography in *Lo Ming-te wen-chi*, preliminary *chüan*, p. 14a. The pamphlet on water control, *T'ien-nan shui-li ts'e*, was listed in the bibliography as no longer extant (ibid., p. 14a). Almost all the other works in the bibliography relate to philosophical rather than practical matters.

39. *MJHA*, 34:2a–b.

40. *HTCC*, 1:69a.

41. Lo Ju-fang, *Hsiang-yüeh ch'üan-shu* in Lo, *Hsü-chiang Lo Chin-hsi hsien-sheng ch'üan-chi*, 13:16b. *Chüan* number is not marked in the text. For another comment on Lo's large audience, see *HTCC*, 1:7a.

these figures, along with the testimonies of Lo's numerous talented admirers, point to both the widespread demand for lecturers and to Lo's undeniable influence as a teacher.

Initially, deep anxiety of spirit over preparing for the civil service had driven Lo to meet with men of like resolve. In time, however, his lecturing became so successful as to gain him a life independent of the examinations.

In 1565, long after Lo had finally earned the highest degree in 1553, he persuaded Hsü Chieh to sponsor lectures at the Ling-chi Temple on the grounds that "talented men were necessary."[42] In 1566, "scholars from all directions" flocked to Lo's library. Lo's anxiety as student had given way to a mission as teacher. In 1571, after the death of his mother two years earlier and before his return to office in 1572, Lo wandered about, visiting his comrades and holding large meetings in many provinces including Shantung, Kiangsi, Kwangtung, and Hunan.[43] Records of the discussions (*hui-yü*) in each place were kept. In 1573, on his return north to office, Lo stopped at Kiangsi to hold a big meeting for ten days. He then followed the Yangtze River east, passing through such places as Jao-chou (Kiangsi), An-ch'ing (Anhwei), Ning-kuo (Anhwei), Nanking, and Yangchow. Those of like resolve frequently invited Lo to lecture. Ts'ao Yin-ju, Chiao Hung, and Chai Ch'iu-t'an accompanied Lo on the boat from Nanking to Yangchow for about ten days. Not one day passed without gentry and scholars—including Li Chih—hastening to meet with Lo.[44]

At this time, Lo met with Chang Chü-cheng. The conversation was tense and guarded, because Chang was suspicious of the "learned discussions" organized by Lo and his friends. When asked where his good friend, Hu Chih (1517–85), was stationed, Lo responded that Hu was about to return from Kwangsi. The account of this exchange commented that Chang must have sensed that Lo shared Hu Chih's hostility towards Chang. Chang therefore assigned Lo to Tung-ch'ang, Shantung.[45]

In Tung-ch'ang, Lo promptly sponsored the restoration of

42. *HTCC*, 2:44a. 43. *HTCC*, 2:46b.
44. *HTCC*, 2:31b–32a; 2:46b–47a. 45. *HTCC*, 2:47b.

the Confucian temple and the temple of the city god. After a brief and successful term, he was transferred to the remote western province of Yunnan. En route, in 1574, he returned home, where for his sixtieth birthday several hundred disciples and friends assembled at a monastery for a large ten-day meeting.[46] By then, according to one report, Lo's teaching had become more refined and powerful, and his followers increased daily.[47] Lo tried in vain to send a memorial requesting retirement and was advised in reply that he must hasten south before the deadline.[48] Meanwhile Lo heard that several who had attended the meeting at the monastery planned to climb Hua Mountain in northwestern Kiangsu. Lo had long wished to make that trip and agreed to accompany the others on the way to another large meeting to be held in Lo-an (Shantung). At the mountain top, several of Lo's companions remarked that the extraordinary view strengthened their belief in the marvels of the Way of the Sages.[49] Thus within the framework of official duties and between assignments, Lo pressed for opportunities to lecture to the people and hold "learned discussions" with his friends. Even in governing Ning-kuo and Tung-ch'ang, he applied himself most energetically to projects that would improve education—the construction of a private academy and the repair of temples that could serve as lecture halls.

After serving industriously in Yunnan, Lo went in 1577 to the capital to present a congratulatory memorial to the throne. In 1578, he returned home. During the next decade, Lo alternately traveled about and received guests at home. After a trip south to Kwangtung and Fukien with his two sons, Lo repaired his library in 1583 and took up residence there. In 1584, disciples from near and far convened for a month-long meeting to celebrate their master's seventieth birthday.[50] He traveled about to visit such friends and mentors as Tsou Shan, Yen Chün, and Hu Chih. Even in the last two years of his life he held one large meeting after another for "learned discussions."[51]

46. *HTCC*, 2:48a.
47. Lo, *Hsü-chiang Lo Chin-hsi hsien-sheng ch'üan-chi*, p. 8a.
48. *HTCC*, 2:48a. 49. *HTCC*, 2:48b. 50. *HTCC*, 2:61a.
51. *HTCC*, 2:60b–61a.

Towards the end of Lo's life and after his death, friends and followers hastened to honor their mentor by publishing collections of his essays and lectures, by writing up his biography, and by composing testimonials of gratitude. No less than forty-seven admirers, representing a wide range of interests, appended their names to one publication of Lo's writings. The list placed Lo's admirers in three categories: (1) three friends, including Keng Ting-hsiang, a socially well-connected scholar-official who followed the views of Wang Yang-ming, and Hu Chih, an advocate of Ch'an Buddhism; (2) eighteen disciples, including T'ang Hsien-tsu (1550–1616), the famous dramatist, and Yüan Huang (1533–1606), best known for his belief in man's control over his own destiny and in the unity of the three religions; and (3) twenty-six "later students" of Lo's thought. This last category included Chiao Hung, a student of Keng Ting-hsiang; Chang Yüan-pien, a student of Wang Chi and a protégé of Lo's antagonist, Chang Chü-cheng; Chou Ju-teng (1547–1629 [?]), known for his synthesis of Buddhism and Confucianism; and Tsou Yüan-piao, official and philosopher, who in 1622 founded the controversial Shou-shan Academy. The list, in short, represented a diversity of interests, geographical origins, philosophical affiliations, and talents.[52] In addition to those listed were many other prominent thinkers—including Ho Hsin-yin, Li Chih, and Hsü Fu-yüan (1535–1604)[53]—who had exchanged ideas with or been touched by Lo.

Just why Lo's lectures were so alluring is hard to discern from the surviving records of his dialogues. As some observed, Lo "spoke better than he wrote."[54] Nonetheless, the recorded dialogues do indicate his deep sensitivity to his audience, for he responded quickly to any silences and puzzle-

52. The list is drawn from Lo, *Hsü-chiang Lo Chin-hsi hsien-sheng ch'üan-chi*, preface, pp. 1a–3b. See the biography of T'ang Hsien-tsu by Chao-ying Fang in *ECCP*, pp. 708–9. See also C. T. Hsia, "Time and the Human Condition in the Plays of T'ang Hsien-tsu."

53. On the acquaintance between Lo and Ho, who were both students of Yen Chün, see *MJHA*, 32:2a. On Li Chih and Lo, see *HTCC*, 2:31a–b. For letters from Lo to Hsü Fu-yüan, see *Lo Ming-te wen-chi*, 5:6b–10b.

54. Stated by T'ao Wang-ling in his preface to Lo, *Hsü-chiang Lo hsien-sheng ch'üan-chi*, p. 1a. Cited without reference to T'ao by Huang Tsung-hsi in *MJHA*, 34:2a.

ment that swept across the faces of his listeners.[55] Above all, Lo's dialogues convey an expansive mood and sparkle with a reassuring optimism. Lo unwaveringly expressed confidence in the concepts of humaneness (*jen*), filiality, the oneness of all things, innate knowledge (*liang-chih*) and the "perpetual renewal of life" (*sheng-sheng*). His deep faith in these concepts moved students to grasp their meaning. A charismatic figure who filled a social need, he was a mediator through whom others could communicate and establish a sense of community. Thus his thought, although unsystematic in its written form, remained a common point of reference for his juniors. Even after Lo Ju-fang died, his followers continued to use his works as a focus for periodic study sessions.[56]

In part, Lo drew strength from the camaraderie of scholar-official friends such as Keng Ting-hsiang and Hu Chih. In part, he also drew strength from the demand for lecturers—whether for entertainment or for religious improvement—that was spreading rapidly among the common people. Throughout Lo's recorded dialogues are numerous phrases that reveal his awareness of an expanded audience. He talked of "daily utility for the common people" (*pai-hsing jih-yung*) and of "ignorant men and women" (*yü-fu yü-fu*). He believed that "the explication of texts would transform scholars and the people;"[57] that even prisoners should be educated;[58] and that "learning should be simple and moving."[59] To this extent the trend to popularize education had touched Lo.

Lo's own philosophical views had been partly shaped by Yen Chün, who had been only superficially familiar with the classics but had nonetheless found an audience. Yen Chün in turn had been a disciple of Wang Ken, who, although poorly educated, had zealously instructed artisans and peasants. Lo was clearly aware that the interest in learning was rapidly spreading. Without explicitly mentioning a particular social group, one of Lo's followers imagined that each of his nine companions would instruct ten men who would in turn each instruct ten more "until myriads and then the whole world would be reached."[60] And had Lo already learned from Keng

55. *HTCC*, 1:69a. 56. *HTCC*, 1:21b. 57. *HTCC*, 2:40b.
58. *MJHA*, 34:3a. 59. *HTCC*, 2:21b. 60. *HTCC*, 2:21b.

Ting-hsiang of the rapidly growing reputation of his contemporary, the religious proselytizer Lin Chao-en (1517–98)? Lo's acquaintance with Keng Ting-hsiang suggests that this was the case. In 1564, Keng invited Lo and his disciple, Ts'ao Yin-ju, to the Ming-tao Academy in Nanking.[61] In a memorial to the throne requesting that access to office be widened to accommodate new talent, Keng specifically mentioned Lo's disciple, Ts'ao Yin-ju, Kuan Chih-tao (1536–1608)—whom Lo met at the Ming-tao Academy in 1564—and Lin Chao-en.[62] Also it was just around then, from 1562 to 1564, that Ho Hsin-yin, who had already established a friendship with Keng in 1560, visited and praised Lin. Lin had passed the district examination, but a religious experience had directed him away from the civil service. About the time that Lo was crowding into the Ling-chi Temple to hear Hsü Chieh in Peking in 1553, Lin was embarking on a career as religious teacher.[63] In the 1570s, Lo traveled throughout the southern provinces of Fukien and Kwangtung where Lin was by then widely known.[64]

Lo's awareness of a mass audience contributed to his buoyant optimism but can only partly account for his unusual ability to command a large following. Contributing above all to his strength was his confidence in his authority to teach. This confidence is apparent in the aloofness from the common people in his instructions for the rural lectures (*hsiang-yüeh*), which one of his many followers pulled together in 1597, ten years after Lo's death.

The institution of the *hsiang-yüeh* dates back to *Lü-shih hsiang-yüeh* [The *hsiang-yüeh* of Mr. Lü] of the eleventh century.[65] As there envisioned, the *hsiang-yüeh* was a voluntary

61. *HTCC*, 2:17b. Together with Kuan Chih-tao and Chiao Hung, they took an oath (*HTCC*, 2:18a).

62. Keng, *Keng T'ien-t'ai hsien-sheng wen-chi*, 2:17b.

63. Judith A. Berling, *The Syncretic Religion of Lin Chao-en*, pp. 81–84.

64. *HTCC*, 2:59b.

65. One version of *Lü-shih hsiang-yüeh* is available in Ch'en Hung-mou, ed., *Hsün-su i-kuei*, 1:5a–7b. Information on *hsiang-yüeh* was drawn from: Tadao Sakai, *Chūgoku zensho no kenkyū*, pp. 40–73; and Wang Lan-yin, "Ming-tai chih hsiang-yüeh yü min-chung chiao-yü." Wang's article provides some fascinating examples of lectures written in the vernacular language during the late Ming, pp. 116–20. For a discussion of *hsiang-yüeh* during the Ch'ing period, see Hsiao, *Rural China*, pp. 184–205.

agreement, probably of the well-to-do, to join in association to correct one another's faults for moral self-cultivation and to help the poor in times of difficulty so that they would not turn to evil. Those who failed to be cooperative would be evicted from the group.[66]

During the Ming, the bureaucratic elite appropriated the *hsiang-yüeh* as a lecture program for the moral education of the common people. In 1518, Wang Yang-ming used the *hsiang-yüeh* to pacify the socially unstable area of southern Kan-chou, Kiangsi.[67] By 1554 or so, the *hsiang-yüeh* had reemerged in a distinctly new form. It was no longer a voluntary association but one that the planners expected all the common people of the community to join. The sanctions had also changed. To encourage cooperation among members of a voluntary association, the threat of exclusion had been sufficient. To encourage compliance by members of a mandatory organization, a combination of instruction and coercion was necessary. For this reason the *hsiang-yüeh* at this time merged with the institution of mutual surveillance, the *pao-chia*.[68]

The *pao-chia* also dates back to the Sung dynasty, to the statesman Wang An-shih (1021–86), who around 1070 planned to organize ten households into a *pao*; fifty *pao* into a large *pao*; and ten large *pao* into a general (*tu*) *pao*. The members of each *pao* were to share the responsibility both for military conscription and for any robberies or murders committed within that unit. Not moral suasion but a system of punishments and rewards insured cooperation.[69]

Wang Yang-ming had instituted a variation of the *pao-chia* system several times. For the purpose of mutual surveillance, he organized ten households into one *p'ai*; ten *p'ai* into a *chia*; and ten *chia* into a *pao*. Wang undoubtedly hoped that

66. *Lü-shih hsiang-yüeh* in Ch'en Hung-mou, ed., *Hsün-su i-kuei*, 1:6b.

67. Wang, *Instructions for Practical Living*, pp. 298–306.

68. On the merging of *pao-chia* and *hsiang-yüeh* methods, see Sakai, *Chūgoku zensho*, pp. 40–44.

69. Information on *pao-chia* has been drawn from the following sources: Wen Chün-t'ien, *Chung-kuo pao-chia chih-tu k'ao*; Philip A. Kuhn, *Rebellion and Its Enemies in Late Imperial China*, pp. 24–28; and H. R. Williamson, *Wang An-shih*, 1:177–212. For a discussion of *pao-chia* during the Ch'ing, see Hsiao, *Rural China*, pp. 43–83.

the lecture efforts of *hsiang-yüeh* would supplement and soften the coercive control of *pao-chia*. However, he did not acually combine the *pao-chia* with the *hsiang-yüeh*, not in writing at any rate.[70] It was not until the next generation that the two institutions were truly synthesized, first loosely and unreflectively by Lo Ju-fang, and then more fully and deliberately by Lü K'un.[71] Just how Lü K'un interpreted these institutions will be discussed later. What is important here is what Lo's writings on *hsiang-yüeh* reveal about his attitudes toward the common people.

In these writings Lo made concessions to an unscholarly non-elite audience. To entertain an audience whose patience for moral lectures must have been short, Lo urged everyone to bring his own utensils for enjoyable rounds of tea[72] and to sing songs between the speeches.[73] To enliven the terse messages of the philosophers, Lo used a few colorful examples. When elucidating Chang Tsai's *Hsi-ming* [Western Inscription], for example, Lo stated, "If someone tramples on a chicken or breaks a flower, he is upset," and then rhetorically asked, "How much more so if one harms one's own kind?!"[74] On one occasion, Lo even slipped into vernacular language.[75]

Despite Lo's concessions to the common people by incorporating colloquial phrases into his lectures, the popular audience did not affect his thought deeply.[76] Rather he consistently remained above and distinct from the non-elite[77] and

70. See, for example, Wang, *Instructions for Practical Living*, pp. 293–95.

71. Lo Ju-fang, *Hsiang-yüeh ch'üan-shu*. For Lü K'un's guidelines for *hsiang-yüeh*, see *SCL*, 3:1a–7a; *chüan* 5. For an interesting version of the amalgamation of *pao-chia* and *hsiang-yüeh*, see Hsü Fu-yüan, *Ching-ho t'ang chi*, 7:5a–8a. Taking inspiration from Wang Shou-jen (ibid., 7:6a), Hsü argues that *pao-chia* must be combined with *hsiang-yüeh*, community granaries, and community schools in order to succeed (ibid., 7:5a). He explains that originally *pao-chia* took precedence over *hsiang-yüeh* but that the old system must be abandoned because good leaders to whom *pao-chia* can be entrusted are scarce (ibid., 7:7a).

72. Lo, *Hsiang-yüeh ch'üan-shu*, 13:4b. 73. Ibid., 13:16b.

74. Ibid., 13:7b. 75. Ibid., 13:12a; Sakai, *Chūgoku zensho*, p. 49.

76. I agree with Tadao Sakai's view that although Lo used the vernacular, his writings show little evidence of popular belief (*Chūgoku zensho*, p. 56). This view contrasts with the evaluation of Lo by Araki Kengo, *Mindai shisō kenkyū*, p. 128.

77. Lo lectured separately to scholars and common people on the one hand and gentry on the other (*Hsiang-yüeh ch'üan-shu*, 13:43b).

confident that he had the authority to instruct the people. Lo in part drew authority from the worthies of the past—the Sung dynasty essay on *hsiang-yüeh* by the revered Lü and the words of Mencius and Chang Tsai. But above all, he cited as an authority the Six Injunctions of Ming T'ai-tsu and focused some of the *hsiang-yüeh* lectures on them.[78] These may be roughly summarized as: Be filial and obey your parents; respect your elders; live harmoniously; instruct your children and grandchildren; work peacefully; and do not commit evil. By instructing that the injunctions be read six times a month, Lo reminded both his underlings and the people that he represented imperial authority.[79] Relying on the injunctions of T'ai-tsu and the teachings of the past, Lo could confidently assume the role of educator and ceremonial leader.

Exposure to the unruly masses did not significantly open Lo's eyes to social problems or mar his faith in the basic goodness of man. Only on rare occasions did Lo give a place, and then always a small one, to evil. He recognized, for example, that the purpose of the Six Injunctions was to lead people to "do good and be warned against doing evil";[80] he urged the members of the *hsiang-yüeh* to correct one another's faults;[81] and he reminded them that the purpose of the meetings was moral reform.[82] On the whole, however, Lo remained steadfastly optimistic that humaneness would prevail and rarely acknowledged the flawed nature of man. Once he conceded that someone who beat his father and cursed his mother was, to be sure, evil. But even then Lo quickly added that the wrongdoer undoubtedly understood his behavior to be bad and could therefore be said to have a conscience—hence, the capacity for goodness.[83] Basically Lo believed that "good and evil originally were inseparable principles; if one wants to do good and is fully diligent and

78. For Lo's lectures on the Six Injunctions, see *Hsiang-yüeh ch'üan-shu*, 13:5a–9b. For a discussion of the Six Injunctions, see Watt, *The District Magistrate*, p. 114, and Sakai, *Chūgoku zensho*, pp. 39–57. For a translation of Chang Tsai's "Western Inscription," see Wing-tsit Chan, *A Source Book in Chinese Philosophy*, pp. 497–98.

79. Lo, *Hsiang-yüeh ch'üan-shu*, 13:2a; 10b.

80. Ibid., 13:10b. 81. Ibid., 13:13a. 82. Ibid.

83. *HTCC*, 1:38b–39a. The word translated as "conscience" is *liang-chih*.

serious, then one naturally will be unwilling to do anything bad."[84]

On one occasion, Lo recognized that people are sometimes self-centered: "Being good without any regard for others only benefits one's own self-cultivation and is therefore deficient."[85] However, he responded to social tensions and selfishness by persistently reaffirming the values of filiality and humaneness, and by exhorting the members of the *hsiang-yüeh* "mutually to encourage everyone in one's lineage, village, and clubs to be filial."[86] Lo firmly continued to model all behavior on filiality and brotherly love and to base his conception of community on the value of humaneness. His attitude, later pages will show, contrasts sharply with the cynical realism of writers like Hai Jui and Lü K'un.

Lo felt buoyed by the large audiences that seemed to confirm the validity of his views, and he often adjusted his style to the level of the common people. But shaping his response to the common people was above all his unwavering confidence in the power of his ideals and in his position as moral leader. This must be understood in terms of his attitude towards authority in general.

Authority figures had loomed large in Lo's youth. He periodically submitted to and sought the aid and comfort of teachers. When the young Lo had a nervous breakdown in 1531, he found a cure in the guidance of his father and the texts of Wang Yang-ming. When Lo experienced a second spiritual crisis he sought help from the famous lecturer Yen Chün. Lo had yielded to the guidance of his seniors, gradually converted to their values, and, once initiated, easily assumed the role of teacher. Only after he had the opportunity to demonstrate his devotion to Yen Chün did Lo's career as a lecturer really take off. In 1568 Yen Chün was imprisoned in Nanking. Lo promptly borrowed two hundred taels, bought a boat, and rushed with his two sons and several disciples to ransom Yen. Someone asked Lo: "Yen Chün is inferior to you; why do you treat him like a teacher?" Lo shrugged the

84. Lo, *Hsiang-yüeh ch'üan-shu*, 13:10b.
85. Ibid., 13:12a–b. 86. Ibid.

challenge off with the reply that not even one hundred Lo Ju-fangs could equal a Yen Chün. Lo then took Yen Chün into his own home. In a record of Lo's relationship with Yen, Tsou Yüan-piao observed that Yen was poor and regarded Lo's house as his private treasury, giving money away according to his whims. Lo was already quite old, Tsou continued, but whenever Yen got angry, Lo knelt down to let Yen slap his cheeks. Only after Yen's anger had dissipated would Lo rise. Yen was, according to Tsou, extremely difficult and added nothing whatsoever to Lo's learning. Nonetheless, Lo served Yen unfailingly; and Yen got from Lo more than a grandfather could expect from filial sons and loving grandsons.[87] Even as a highly popular lecturer, Lo refused to take "the teacher's seat" at meetings.[88] Lo's symbolic acquiescence to a superior authority effectively persuaded his followers of the validity of the teacher's authority. And Lo's loyal sacrifice of his own wealth to free and support Yen verified Lo's ideals. Lo's trust in personal relations had shaped his capacity to expect trust in others. He assumed most naturally the role of teacher he had so highly valued and displayed his greatest strength, not as an official, but as a lecturer.

In 1579, Hsü Chieh died. Promptly, Chang Chü-cheng, long his rival, proscribed the academies. Chang Chü-cheng had fiercely criticized learned discussions throughout his tenure of office. In an essay against learned discussions, Chang once wrote:

> The *Shu ching* [Book of History] says, "Make the five human relationships widely known." What is meant by "widely" is to educate patiently men of different innate abilities—the dull and the bright, the strong and the weak—and to induce the worthy to bow and comply and the unworthy to look up and try. That is all. Today, people do not understand the meaning of "widely" and are overindulgent and lax, buying fame from the people, to such an extent that

87. *HTCC*, 2:45b–46a. 88. *HTCC*, 2:45b.

> scholars act proud and boastful; and their ways deteriorate daily.

And then, chastising those presumptuous scholars who had assumed the task of setting morals straight, he continued: "Occasionally there are one or two who try to correct [the situation]. But they too emphasize show and speak empty words, opening their own heterodox paths. This is called using meat to drive away snakes and wood to put out fires."[89]

Chang's surveillance failed to shake Lo. Indeed Lo was so confident in his views that he lightheartedly shrugged off all criticism. Some, noting his eagerness to embrace all with a spirit of oneness, accused Lo of promulgating "universal love" (*chien-ai*), a concept which scholar-officials believed threatened the concept of filiality on which the Confucian order rested.[90] When someone asked Lo how his view that "everything was of the same essence" (*hun-jan t'ung-t'i*) differed from "universal love," Lo answered so briefly as to sound somewhat evasive. Explaining that the word for "essence" (*t'i*) also meant "body," and that the body is composed of differentiated limbs and organs, Lo asked, "How can love not be differentiated?"[91]

The next generation could not so uninhibitedly derive a sense of exhilaration from addressing large audiences. Those who commanded mass followings were condemned as demagogues, self-indulgently and frivolously trying to build reputations on their large followings. Nor could lecturers of the next generation so freely claim the authority to carry out their missions. Instead, as the contrasting example of Feng Ts'ung-wu will fully demonstrate, they became increasingly conscious of their accountability to their critics and to the government they served. Thus Lo enjoyed a position that

89. Cited in Chang Hsüan, *Hsi-yüan wen-chien lu*, 45:13a. See also, John Meskill, "Academies and Politics in the Ming Dynasty," and Tilemann Grimm, "Some Remarks on the Suppression of Shu-yüan in Ming China."

90. The concept of "undifferentiated love," often translated as "universal love," dates back to Mo Tzu. See Fung Yu-lan, *A History of Chinese Philosophy*, 1:76–105.

91. *HTCC*, 1:30b.

was just barely showing signs of weakness during his lifetime and ceased to be tenable during the next generation.

Hai Jui, Administrator

Lo Ju-fang started his career as a magistrate, but he built most vigorously on the opportunities of the popular lecturer. Hai Jui started his career as a school instructor, but assumed heroic stature in the arenas of court politics and local government. He devoted only a very small portion of his writings to the subjects of teaching and philosophy. However important he might have thought these areas to be in theory, in practice he focused his writings on the problems of local administration. His fame was based not on his thought, but on his deeds as an official and his detailed regulations for tax collection, mutual surveillance, and construction projects. Lo's strength was based on his appeal to students. Hai drew strength not from a heady confidence in "humaneness," or a charismatic presence, but from a firm adherence to principles of fairness and to impersonal laws and regulations.

Hai Jui's rise from a humble instructor to an influential censor-in-chief in Nanking was marked by a series of confrontations in which he both alienated many of his peers and grew more confident in and committed to the authority of legal forms. As a school instructor, Hai Jui justified his refusal to kneel before visiting superior officials by citing the regulation that standing should suffice. The school, he claimed, should not be humbled. As magistrate of Ch'un-an, Chekiang, Hai Jui fearlessly confiscated silver from the ostentatiously extravagant and officious son of a powerful governor. The young man could not truly be the governor's son, Hai skillfully argued, because the governor was known to place a high value on moderation and had instructed that touring officials should receive only simple hospitality.[92] Similarly, Hai Jui offended a visiting censor-in-chief in Chekiang by treating him frugally. Hai stubbornly maintained that the

92. *DMB*, p. 473; Wolff, "A Preliminary Study," p. 150.

district was too poor to accommodate the censor's large cavalcade of carriages. By relying on legal sanctions and campaigning for justice in this manner, Hai Jui, even as a mere magistrate, repeatedly freed himself from the net of personal relations.

As Hai Jui won higher positions, and as he gained confidence in the legal ground on which he stood, he intrepidly took on more powerful opponents. In 1565, after becoming Secretary of the Ministry of Revenue, Hai Jui wrote a daring, outspoken memorial criticizing the emperor Shih-tsung—who reigned from 1521 to 1567—for extravagantly seeking Taoist immortality, for misusing state revenues to build superfluous mansions, and for failing to hold court. Most scathingly of all, Hai concluded that conditions under Shih-tsung were even worse than those under an infamous emperor of the Han dynasty. The enraged Shih-tsung wished to have Hai Jui seized immediately, but a eunuch advised the emperor that Hai, who had already bought a coffin in anticipation of the punishment he would receive, would not escape. A few months later, Hai was imprisoned. However, according to the official history of the Ming dynasty, the emperor's timely death brought amnesty to Hai Jui.[93] Undoubtedly the narrow escape, no less than the victories in previous battles, armed Hai Jui with a fearless confidence in his principles, for he then proceeded to challenge the powerful families of the Sung-chiang area. There Hai used the Single-Whip method of taxation to eradicate the corrupt practices by which the powerful had shifted tax burdens onto the small landholders, thus driving them into debt and appropriating their land. Hai Jui had already successfully redistributed the responsibilities for taxes and corvée labor in Ch'un-an, where he had served from 1558 to 1562. Many there had abandoned their land because they could not pay the high taxes. Hai induced them to resume tilling their fields by promising them three tax-free years.[94] But in Sung-chiang,

93. For a translation of the memorial, see Wolff, "A Preliminary Study," pp. 151–56.

94. Chiang Hsing-yü, *Hai Jui*, pp. 20–22. For some insights into the plight of the small landholders during the late Ming, see Elvin, *Pattern of the Chinese Past*, pp. 235–67.

where he had to fight against politically powerful men like Hsü Chieh, Hai was unsuccessful and was forced to retire in 1570.

That Lo Ju-fang and Hai Jui made such different uses of careers that had started out so similarly stems in part from differences in their personalities, particularly in the way each reacted to authority. In contrast to Lo Ju-fang, Hai Jui dissociated values from any personalized authority. His father had died when Hai was in his fourth year, and no teacher figured prominently in Hai's development. Hai defined his values independently of friends and teachers,[95] as is apparent in his elaboration on the famous essay on teachers by Han Yü (786–824).[96] Accepting that teachers were essential to the transmission of the Way, Han Yü had argued that possession of knowledge, not seniority or high station, qualified one to be a teacher. The teacher, according to Han, was not necessarily superior to the disciple, and men of high status should therefore not feel ashamed to study with teachers. "It is simply that the teacher has learned the Way before others, and has specialized in the art of instruction."[97] Hai Jui expressed praise for Han Yü's essay, but also some doubts. He feared that "if there are no teachers or friends outside of the self, then acting in accord with the Way might be difficult." Hai Jui therefore sought moral instruction, not from a teacher, but by summoning a spirit before him. Upon hearing the spirit speak, Hai trembled as though "a stern teacher had instructed him and straightforward friends had cautioned him."[98] In other words, Hai Jui's foremost "teachers and friends" consisted of internalized values divorced from actual social relations. No wonder, then, that he respected all sorts of depersonalized types of authority, in particular, laws and institutional structures.

The divergence in the careers of Lo and Hai also reflected

95. In his biography of Hai, Chiang Hsing-yü states that Chao Chen-chi (1508–76) was Hai's "teacher and companion," but gives no source for this view (*Hai Jui*, p. 116). I have been unable to find any material throwing light on Hai's relationship other than Hai's brief letter to Chao, *HJC*, p. 422. For Chao's biography, see *MJHA*, 33:1a–3a.

96. *HJC*, pp. 1–2. For a translation of Han Yü's famous "Shih-shuo" (Discourse on teachers), see de Bary, ed., *Sources of Chinese Tradition*, pp. 429–30.

97. Han Yü, "Discourse on teachers," p. 430.

98. *HJC*, pp. 1–2.

differences in their perceptions of the world. The harmonious social relations envisioned by Lo Ju-fang are nowhere evident in Hai Jui's writings. While Lo occasionally noted *en passant* that some people committed evil, his faith in human goodness overwhelmed his perception of reality. Overlooking whatever dark stories might have accounted for the prisoners of Ning-kuo hsien and failing to probe into the social reasons for their crimes, Lo instructed the criminals to attend his lectures—so strong was his confidence in the efficacy of moral suasion. One skeptic asked whether he could indeed govern Ning-kuo simply by lecturing on the Six Imperial Injunctions, but such questions made no impression on him.[99]

From their writings alone one could hardly believe that Hai and Lo shared the same world. In contrast to the steadfastly optimistic Lo, Hai Jui despaired that "no one trusted anyone from top to bottom in the social hierarchy"[100] and that social discord was apparent everywhere. Hai Jui believed that people were greedy and "hastened to wherever there was profit";[101] and that self-interest so dominated society that men would deceive and cheat even their own nephews.[102] Distrustful and cynical, Hai Jui observed that the sense of community had everywhere disintegrated to give way to economic disequilibrium and tensions between "you and me."[103] The superiors in the hsien bureaucracy, "like hired laborers," interpreted their service in terms of salary while neglecting the original meaning of officialdom.[104] The elders, to whom Hai would have liked to entrust the tasks of local government, were unreliable;[105] moved by "the money spirits," they only wished to fatten their private sacks. The village headmen (*hsiang-kuan*) gradually grew rich while the people produced less. The gentry for twenty years, according to Hai, had resembled tigers who seize the meat of the people;[106] and officials had rapaciously squeezed profit from the governed.[107]

99. *HTCC*, 2:42b.
100. *HJC*, p. 74. Translated by Cartier, *Une Réforme*, see p. 128.
101. *HJC*, p. 145. For similar complaints, see *HJC*, p. 5, and *HJC*, p. 28.
102. *HJC*, p. 157. For other comments on "profit," see *HJC*, pp. 40, 95, 96, and 98.
103. *HJC*, p. 157.
104. *HJC*, p. 48; Cartier, *Une Réforme*, p. 100.
105. *HJC*, p. 150.
106. *HJC*, p. 238.
107. *HJC*, p. 353.

Hai Jui also blamed social discord on the very *sheng-yüan*, or "budding scholars" (*hsiu-ts'ai*), who filled the ranks of Lo Ju-fang's vast audiences. The number of *sheng-yüan*, who were recipients of the first degree in the civil service examinations, had expanded greatly by the sixteenth century. From 1438 to the last decades of the dynasty, the number dramatically rose from one hundred to four hundred per cent, varying with the geographical location.[108] The degree-holder was exempted from the corvée labor and received monthly stipends. At the same time, he was required to enroll in the prefectural or county schools and subjected to the discipline of the school officials.[109] Thus the dynasty, fearful that scholars barred from any hope of entering the civil service would turn rebellious, had co-opted them by liberally granting the first degree.

At the same time, the dynasty carefully restricted the quotas for the higher degrees, usually necessary to qualify for office. Consequently the *sheng-yüan*, frustrated by the lack of opportunity to rise, became notorious troublemakers as they channeled their energies and talents into other pursuits. Numerous references to those arrested began to pop up in sixteenth-century accounts as *sheng-yüan* stirred up land disputes or led protests against excess taxation.[110] Worse, the expansion of their ranks had, as Hai Jui perceived, become a costly burden on the people.[111] Not only were the *sheng-yüan* exempt from the corvée labor,[112] but those selected as "tribute students" (*kung-sheng*) to prepare for the metropolitan examinations received allowances. Hai Jui argued that a reduction of quotas would save expenses, would facilitate the selection of the best, and would prevent indulgent favoritism toward the unqualified children of official families.[113]

Hai Jui rarely missed a chance to rage against the *sheng-yüan*. He disparaged the young *sheng-yüan* for lacking man-

108. Ho, *Ladder of Success*, pp. 174, 177. 109. Ibid., p. 172.

110. See, for example, Feng Ch'i, *Pei-hai chi*, 33:21a. See also *SCL*, 1:20a–b.

111. *HJC*, p. 92.

112. For a discussion of the social status of *sheng-yüan*, see Ho, *Ladder of Success*, pp. 35–41.

113. *HJC*, p. 93. For a discussion of *kung-sheng*, see Ho, *Ladder of Success*, pp. 27–32.

ners and treating their elders contemptuously.[114] He complained that the custom of serving wine to educational and district officials only encouraged the *sheng-yüan* to compete for profit.[115] Citing Mencius's dictum that "Men must be decided on what they will NOT do and then they are able to act with vigour in *what they ought to do,*" Hai despaired, "Today most 'budding scholars' resemble loose women rather than virgins."[116]

Hai Jui complained that true scholars rarely litigated but that *sheng-yüan* often did;[117] that many *sheng-yüan* were liberally treated but rarely returned the favor to the emperor; and that superiors encouraged students to think in terms of reputation and influence.[118] Hai further found distressing the fact that the "budding scholars" and other insignificant students who had no authority could flatter and talk their way around the school officials.[119]

Lo Ju-fang euphorically embraced a sense of oneness. Hai felt divided even from those who had passed the first degree. Lo never expressed the slightest distrust in human nature, even when drawing up plans for *hsiang-yüeh* for the rural uneducated. Hai Jui, in contrast, was by nature suspicious. As instructor of the district school in Nan-p'ing, he commanded that records be kept of the residences and social connections of the students. Specifically he wished to know the names of their teachers and with which *sheng-yüan* the students consorted.[120]

Problems that failed to find their way into Lo's writings intruded mercilessly into Hai's consciousness. Hai was acutely aware that pirates along the coast were causing the people misery;[121] that excessive corvée had provoked rebellions such as that of the water-carriers;[122] that people were joining the

114. *HJC*, p. 90.

115. Ibid., p. 96. See also p. 94 (Cartier, *Une Réforme*, p. 134); and p. 53 (Cartier, pp. 113–4). See also Hai's instructions that *sheng-yüan* desist from receiving and sending off officials (*HJC*, p. 24).

116. *HJC*, p. 54 (Cartier, *Une Réforme*, p. 114). For the passage by Mencius, see Legge, *The Chinese Classics*, 2:321. Emphases are Legge's.

117. *HJC*, p. 114. 118. *HJC*, p. 53.

119. *HJC*, p. 353.

120. *HJC*, p. 18. 121. *HJC*, pp. 439–40.

122. *HJC*, p. 26. See also p. 31.

heterodox White Lotus Society;[123] and that in 1560, squabbles over mining rights had led to riots which resulted in pillage, the burning of official residences, and deaths.[124]

To bring social harmony to his chaotic and contentious world, Hai Jui relied heavily on laws and regulations. He frequently cited the *Ta Ming hui-tien* [Collected Statutes of the Ming Dynasty]; he wrote numerous regulations to standardize practices; and he appreciated that laws could be used to establish routines.[125] Hai Jui was confident that he was a man of principle, capable of using laws properly; but he distrusted law in the hands of others and observed that litigation was tearing apart the social fabric. He noted that the selfish, competitive, and profit-seeking people of Ch'un-an "believe that committing fraud for gain is heroic . . . that instigating lawsuits to win victories is a sign of bravery. They fail to consider the misery that follows the litigation."[126] Hai Jui incessantly railed against litigation. He complained that lawsuits daily were growing more complicated, and no one could stop them;[127] that perverse litigation was increasing;[128] and that overindulgent provincial officials had let it get out of hand in the Kiangnan area.[129]

Hai Jui's conviction that he was principled while others were not resulted in some arbitrary policies. Fearing, for example, that prolonged litigation would expand opportunities for corruption and dissension, Hai advocated that whenever legal cases were doubtful, one should make clear-cut judgments simply to end the dispute. He opposed those wishy-washy compromisers (*ho-shih lao-jen*) who spread uncertainty through such judgments as "the plaintiff is sixty per cent at fault and the defendant forty per cent responsible." Such

123. *HJC*, p. 277. For a discussion of the White Lotus, see T'ao Hsi-sheng, "Ming-tai mi-lo pai-lien chiao chi ch'i-t'a yao-tsei;" Li Shou-k'ung, "Ming-tai pai-lien k'ao lüeh," pp. 17–47; and Daniel L. Overmyer, *Folk Buddhist Religion*.

124. *HJC*, p. 144 (Cartier, *Une Réforme*, p. 149).

125. For examples of Hai citing the *Ta Ming hui-tien*, see *HJC*, pp. 74 and 247. See also Liang Yün-lung, "Hai Chung-chieh kung hsing-chuang," *HJC*, p. 536.

126. *HJC*, p. 114. Cartier has omitted this and other illuminating passages concerning the litigiousness of the people of Ch'un-an from his translation.

127. *HJC*, pp. 114 and 157. 128. *HJC*, p. 251. 129. *HJC*, p. 275.

compromises, according to Hai Jui, only postponed the resolution of conflicts, and paved the way for time-consuming court appeals.[130] Furthermore, Hai Jui noted, the reversal of law cases confused the clerks in their record-keeping and befuddled the "small people," who in any case did not care whether the decisions were principled, but only whether they had saved face.[131]

To maintain order and to fight against the disruptive forces of greed, Hai Jui advocated a "fixed view." He believed that scholars, like gold and jade with a fixed value in the marketplace, should never let themselves be influenced by praise and slander. Even when right and wrong were turned upside down, Hai confidently asserted, the correct view would eventually emerge.[132]

Adamantly opposing compromise, Hai Jui declared: "Great men and gentlemen have a fixed view. . . . If what is preserved is not fixed and one suddenly says, 'change with the times' (*pien-t'ung sui-shih*) and abandons the rules of propriety for vulgarities, following this today and that tomorrow . . . to what low depths will one sink! Now if one today abandons the rules of propriety in order to flatter others, tomorrow one will certainly be incapable of maintaining the Way to set the world right." In conclusion, Hai asked how anyone under such conditions could be suitable to serve his country, and then warned that one therefore must "consistently and vigilantly put into effect the rules of propriety and the regulations of the founding emperor."[133]

Inflexible in his opinions, Hai Jui also frequently derided the "self-righteous hypocrites" (*hsiang-yüan*), those obsequious and weak officials who easily bent moral principles. Hai steadfastly maintained that "there is a proper principle in regard to what is straight and crooked in the world."[134] Any-

130. *HJC*, p. 117. 131. *HJC*, p. 116.
132. *HJC*, p. 106. 133. *HJC*, p. 24.
134. *HJC*, p. 117. Confucius had said of the *hsiang-yüan*, "Your good careful people of the villages are the thieves of virtue" (Legge, *Chinese Classics*, 1:324). Also cited in *Mencius* VIIB, in Legge, *Chinese Classics*, 2:499. For other examples of Hai's attack against the *hsiang-yüan*, see *HJC*, pp. 248 and 317–18. In his preface to Hai Jui's writings, Chang Po-hsing draws special attention to Hai's criticisms of the compromising *hsiang-yüan*. See "Hai Kang-feng hsien-sheng wen-chi hsü," *HJC*, pp. 617–18.

one who tried to compromise between "righteousness and profit"—or between caring for the people and entertaining visiting officials—had, according to Hai, destroyed the integrity of the mind and would never become a sage.[135]

Hai Jui's obdurate devotion to justice and his valiant effort to impose order on society through the application of laws and regulations won him fame and heroic stature in the popular imagination. Shortly after he died, numerous stories and plays celebrated Hai Jui's fair and perspicacious judgments as magistrate.[136] One collection consists of seventy-one cases presumably settled by Hai Jui when serving as magistrate of Ch'un-an. Although the preface states that the stories were based on notes taken by someone who had witnessed Hai Jui in action, all the stories appear to be apocryphal, and the biographical information on Hai Jui is erroneous. Nonetheless the stories demonstrate that Hai Jui's values of public-mindedness and legal justice found fertile soil in the popular imagination.[137] Hai Jui understood that small landowners, suffering from the effects of commercialization, clamored for protection. Perceiving that the "voice of the people was small" and that there was a "public opinion (*kung-i*) that could not of its own accord reach the top,"[138] Hai knew that an arena where he could carry out his commitment to justice awaited him. That the times were ripe for displacing personal with legal influence had strengthened Hai Jui in his battles against oppressive landlords.

Hai Jui died impoverished, owning a mere eight taels, a light gown, and a few old clothes; one man praised him for "not fearing death, not loving money, and not establishing political parties."[139] In the eyes of his fellow-officials, however, Hai Jui appeared harshly uncompromising, overly re-

135. *HJC*, p. 106.

136. For a discussion of literature celebrating Hai Jui as judge, see Chiang Hsing-yü, *Hai Jui*, pp. 127–28. For a brief discussion of the recent controversy about Hai, see Wolff, "A Preliminary Study," pp. 147–48.

137. For Hai Jui's arbitrations on various murder cases and on a dispute over grain, see the records of his investigations (*ts'an yü*), *HJC*, pp. 169–78. For the collection of seventy-one apocryphal cases, see Li Ch'un-fang, ed., *Hai Kang-feng chü-kuan kung-an chuan*.

138. *HJC*, p. 106.

139. Chou Hui, *Chin-ling so-shih*, cited in *HJC*, p. 638.

liant on external forms, and generally out of tune with his peers. Unlike Lo Ju-fang, Hai Jui attracted few unquestioningly loyal admirers; although his policies may have been "on behalf of the state and the people,"[140] they alienated his colleagues. "The whole court could not stand Hai Jui's pure and self-sacrificing deeds," one writer noted before adding the twist, "nor could they match him."[141] Even those who acknowledged Hai Jui's strengths judiciously weighed his virtues against his pigheaded brashness. Thus, Ho Liang-chün (1506–73) praised Hai for his fearlessness, his lack of greed, and his strong will. "Truly an exceptional fellow!" Ho exclaimed, and then added, "It's just that he was somewhat crazy and rarely penetrating; he repeatedly chased after ridiculous dreams, and he thoroughly lacked the air of a scholar-official (*shih-ta-fu*)."[142] Ho observed that Hai's policies created havoc in economic relations and that, by loving the people, Hai had "in reality killed them. How can this be called good government?!"[143]

Ho Liang-chün, who was a wealthy landlord from Sung-chiang, clearly found Hai Jui's plans for land redistribution threatening. Many of Hai's critics, like Ho, undoubtedly had vested interests in land. Even so, their attacks show that Hai Jui's policies failed to take into account the political realities of a landholding bureaucracy. In refusing to make concessions to the landed bureaucrats, Hai occupied a position that was politically untenable.

Hai Jui himself had denounced those who were litigious; at the same time, he used laws against some of his most powerful peers. Thus he set himself apart from others and seemed excessively self-righteous. More important, the manner in which Hai used laws must have offended even the most moral among the bureaucratic elite. As the contrasting example of Lü K'un will show, Hai Jui's inflexible adherence to regulations denied even upright and selfless officials the lati-

140. Yüan Shang-pin, Preface to *Hai Chung-chieh kung wen-chi*, cited in *HJC*, p. 605.

141. Chou Hui, *Chin-ling so-shih*, cited in *HJC*, p. 639.

142. Ho Liang-chün, *Ssu-yu-chai ts'ung-shuo*, cited in *HJC*, p. 633. See the biography of Ho by Chaoying Fang in *DMB*, pp. 515–18.

143. Ho Liang-chün, *Ssu-yu-chai ts'ung-shuo*, cited in *HJC*, p. 634.

tude to exercise independent moral judgment and threatened to subordinate them, like functionaries, to a rigid routine. Hai's ultimate goal—a clearly defined harmonious and just social order—was moral and humane, but the means by which he tried single-handedly to achieve it appeared arbitrary. How Lü K'un infused laws and regulations with a humanistic spirit will be the subject of a subsequent chapter.

3

Yang Tung-ming: In His Hometown

Yang Tung-ming's climb up the civil service ladder started auspiciously. He won the *chü-jen* degree in 1576, and the *chin-shih* in 1580. After serving as a drafter in the Central Drafting Office, he earned an appointment as supervising secretary in 1589. In office, Yang displayed rectitude and courage. In 1595, he served as an examiner in the metropolitan examinations and selected twenty of the candidates, including some who were to become well-known, but to maintain his integrity he refused to take advantage of those social connections.[1]

Yang's promising rise coincided with the decade of turmoil that followed the death of the powerful Grand Secretary Chang Chü-cheng in 1582. Many hastened to settle grievances that had piled up under his stern rule, and a disconcertingly rapid and unpredictable turnover of the metropolitan personnel took place. In particular, those who had been dismissed for criticizing Chang Chü-cheng's failure to observe mourning for his father saw an opportunity, with the evaluation of metropolitan officials in 1593, to restore "good elements" to court. To the atmosphere of factional strife was added mounting anxiety over the selection of an heir apparent and the Japanese invasion of Korea in 1592. The

1. For biographical information on Yang, see the biography by Huang P'ei and Julia Ching in *DMB*, pp. 1546–7; *Ming shih*, 241:2749; *MJHA*, 29:8b–9a; *Yü-ch'eng hsien chih* (1895), 3:10b, 12b; 5:2b, 5a, 24a, 26a; 6:11a–14b; T'ang Pin, *Lo-hsüeh pien*, 4:79b–80b; Sun Ch'i-feng, *Li-hsüeh tsung-chuan*, 23:55a–57b; and Sun Ch'i-feng, *Chung-chou jen-wu k'ao*, 2:41a. For a list of Yang's twenty successful examination candidates, see *SCKK*, 4:20a. Among them was Liu I-ching (1567–1637), whose biography can be found in *Ming shih*, 240:2737. On Yang's refusal to cultivate these connections for private ends, see *Yü-ch'eng hsien chih*, 6:12b.

battle of the "pure critics" against the Grand Secretariat resulted in mass dismissals and the resignation of many "good elements."[2]

Yang Tung-ming frequently addressed memorials to the throne, intrepidly "speaking out when others dared not," in the words of an admirer. In one memorial, Yang requested that the good elements, including Chao Nan-hsing (1550–1628), Shih Meng-lin (*chin-shih*, 1583), and Wang Ju-hsün (1551–1610) be recalled.[3] In another, Yang hastened to the defense of Li Ts'ai (*chin-shih*, 1562) who had been imprisoned in 1588.[4] But Yang lacked both the shrewdness and the voice to deal effectively with the precarious metropolitan politics. Of his memorials only one, submitted in 1594 on the famine in his own province of Honan, elicited a response. For taking sides in a factional struggle in 1595 Yang was demoted to a minor appointment as commissary of the Records Office in Shensi. Soon after he was forced to retire to his hometown, Yü-ch'eng. Before Yang was reappointed to office in 1620 and promoted to Junior Vice Minister of Justice in 1621, he had spent over twenty-five of his mature years at home, painfully aware of the obstacles to accomplishing anything at court and frustrated in his political ambitions.

Demoted and disappointed, Yang faced on his return to Yü-ch'eng the perplexing question: "Are gentlemen really on the same level as commoners just because they live in the country?"[5] How Yang distinguished himself, what image he chose to etch for himself under those trying circumstances, is the subject of this chapter.

Immediately on his return home in 1595, Yang commissioned a Pavilion of Broken Willow Branches—a metaphor for

2. For a brief outline of the battle between the good and bad elements, see the biography of Ku Hsien-ch'eng by Heinrich Busch in *DMB*, pp. 736–39.

3. For praise of Yang's moral courage, see the preface to *Ch'ing-so chin yen* by Ch'iao Yin, p. 2b. For Yang's defense of the "good elements," see *Ch'ing-so chin yen*, 1:19b–21a. See biography of Chao Nan-hsing by Chaoying Fang and Lee Hwa-chou in *DMB*, pp. 128–132. For Shih Meng-lin, see *Ming shih*, 231:2653 and *MJHA*, 60:4a. For Wang Ju-hsün, see *Ming shih*, 235:2685.

4. *Ch'ing-so chin yen*, 2:10a–12a. Biography of Li Ts'ai by Julia Ching in *DMB*, pp. 874–877.

5. *SCKK*, 1:12b.

parting friends—to be built as a guest house where scholars from distant places could stay and discuss textual problems in the Classics. Over a hundred scholars passed through, including several who had been listed among Lo Ju-fang's admirers—Keng Ting-hsiang and Yang Ch'i-yüan—and such other famous officials of the period as Tsou Yüan-piao, Feng Ts'ung-wu, Lü K'un and Wei Yün-chen.[6] When Yang was not receiving guests, he traveled about to lecture. On passing through Hsin-an, Honan, in 1596, Yang lectured for Meng Hua-li to over seventy students.[7] We also learn from the gazetteer of Yü-ch'eng of a Wang Meng-feng who in his youth accompanied Yang on his lecture tours.[8] By welcoming guests to his Pavilion of Broken Willow Branches and by accepting invitations to speak away from home, Yang maintained connections, even while in retirement, with prominent scholars—many of whom had been dismissed from office in the 1590s. Promptly on his return to office in 1621, Yang cooperated with two of these, Feng Ts'ung-wu and Tsou Yüan-piao—both of whom had similarly surfaced from long retirements—in founding the Shou-shan Academy.[9]

Yang had found his way into central social circles and had engaged in learned discussions. However, it was not in the contemplative life of the academy but in the active organization of local volunteer efforts that Yang Tung-ming took pride, and it was for his activities rather than his thought that Yang won most praise. Indeed, Yang maintained that gentlemen living in the country could justifiably close their doors only when nothing was happening; during times of

6. *Yü-ch'eng hsien chih*, 6:11a–12b. Also mentioned among Yang's friends were Chang Yüan-pien and Meng Ch'iu, who died in 1588 and 1589 respectively. The gazetteer is incorrect, therefore, in listing them among those who visited the lodge Yang had built in 1595. According to another entry in the gazetteer, Yang's younger brother, Tung-kuang, cooperated in having the hall built for lecturing (ibid., 6:15a). For Wei Yün-chen, see *Ming shih*, 232:2658–2659.

7. "Hsing-hsüeh hui-yüeh hsü" by Meng Hua-li, *SCKK*, 4:1a. Meng had, like Yang, been a victim of factional strife and had been dismissed. See *Ming shih*, 283:3191, and *MJHA*, 29:8a.

8. For a brief biography of Wang Meng-feng, see *Yü-ch'eng hsien chih*, 6:17a.

9. See the biography of Yang by Sun Ch'i-feng, *Chung-chou jen-wu k'ao*, 1:41a.

crises such as natural disasters or military uprisings, they had a responsibility to act.[10] Accordingly, in organizing his miscellaneous writings Yang gave primary place not to his recorded dialogues, letters, or philosophical essays, as was conventional, but to the records of his local volunteer activities in his hometown. These activities Yang Tung-ming first undertook on a brief sojourn in his hometown in 1590 and then during his retirement from 1595 to 1620.

The record of activities Yang sponsored is impressive and includes setting up regulations for the granary of the neighboring Ts'ao hsien,[11] honoring the local elders with a drinking ceremony and a record of their biographies,[12] establishing and hiring teachers for a community school to which students from everywhere flocked,[13] sponsoring the repair of dikes in 1601, setting up soup kitchens during the severe snow storms of 1602,[14] running a grain equalization program,[15] and sponsoring the reconstruction of a school in 1606.[16] In assuming so much responsibility for local affairs, Yang conformed to a pattern that had for centuries been common for retired officials. In writing so extensively about his activities and in giving those writings a central place—rather than letting them slip unobtrusively into genealogies or gazetteers—Yang made a statement about himself that also tells us something about his times.

Yang's commemorations of local activities—whether the foundation of a local granary or the start of a new society—are straightforward, unadorned, and pragmatic. In these Yang listed, sometimes tediously, the donors for a grain equalization plan[17] and the elders who deserved community respect;[18] or Yang outlined regulations for feeding the poor or running a school.[19] In publishing these pieces, Yang did

10. *SCKK*, 1:13b–14a.

11. *SCKK*, 1:1a–4b. Ts'ao hsien was in Shantung, just over the border from Honan, about 110 *li* from Yang's home town.

12. "Ching lao lu," *SCKK*, *chüan* 2. For guidelines for the drinking ceremony, see *Ta Ming hui-tien*, 79:1a–7b. For a general description of the ceremony as practiced during the Ch'ing dynasty, see Hsiao, *Rural China*, pp. 208–20.

13. *SCKK*, 3:1a–b. 14. *SCKK*, 1:15b. 15. *SCKK*, 1:14a–b.

16. *SCKK*, 1:22b–25a. 17. *SCKK*, 1:15a. 18. *SCKK*, 2:3b–9a.

19. *SCKK*, 3:1a–b.

not seek to show off his scholarship, but his leadership. Close identification with his hometown, personal experiences, and even concern for the operation of status and wealth were the ingredients Yang used to advertise himself to his peers.

Both Yang's connections with many renowned scholars and his status as a retired official enhanced his authority at home. According to his accounts, the local people frequently turned to him for leadership—as when three district students asked him to compile a "meeting agreement."[20] Yang also won the cooperation of officials in neighboring hsien and a visiting magistrate, Wang Na-yen.[21]

Further contributing to Yang's authority at home was his great financial power, derived from precisely what sources is not known. Yang used his wealth liberally to set the pace for charity and to challenge the well-to-do of his district to sponsor welfare activities. Yang was wealthy enough, for example, to maintain at least four wives. He could also support the energetic charitable activities of his second wife, *née* Ch'iu, who one year directed that one hundred rolls of cloth be woven and made into clothes for the destitute.[22] Yang could also afford to sponsor the repair of the Temple of the City God and the construction of at least four temples and shrines.[23]

Other expenses that Yang incurred included bimonthly dues of two bits of silver to The Society for Sharing Goodness (*T'ung-shan hui*);[24] and monthly contributions to The Society for Spreading Humaneness (*Kuang-jen hui*).[25] Although Yang did not specify the amount of individual contributions, forty-two members, including Yang and his two brothers, contributed about 6 taels a month. To the grain equalization program, Yang Tung-ming contributed 34 taels and his two brothers 33 taels each. The Yang brothers thus contributed 100, or over one-half of the 170 taels collected. The contribu-

20. *SCKK*, 4:4a.

21. *Yü-ch'eng hsien chih*, 2:9b; 3:4a. *SCKK*, 1:11b.

22. *Yü-ch'eng hsien chih*, 7:3a–b; 7:21a; 8:2b.

23. Ibid., 3:10b; 3:12b–13a. Yang and his younger brother also jointly built a hall for scholars (ibid., 6:15b).

24. *SCKK*, 1:8a.

25. *SCKK*, 1:11b.

tions of the Yang family far outshone the contributions—10 taels each—of the three Fan brothers of another leading local family.[26]

Through philanthropic activities, Yang Tung-ming touched many areas of local society. For the charitable school, Yang used funds from his own pocket to hire three teachers.[27] Because the official allowance for distributing gruel to wanderers was insufficient, Yang and his brothers, Tung-kuang and Tung-shu, decided to supplement it in 1602.[28] Tung-kuang, who was familiar with the art of medicine, also distributed drugs throughout the area.[29]

Charitable work was necessitated by the harsh and disruptive environment of the area. Yü-ch'eng was vulnerable to the shifting course of the nearby Yellow River. When the river flooded and changed course in 1530, for example, the people of Yü-ch'eng had to change the location of their town.[30] During the Wan-li period, Yü-ch'eng further suffered a sequence of harmful frosts, famine, floods, and plague, which called for the charity of the wealthy.[31]

In Yang's district at least a few widows could avoid falling back on their parents or committing suicide by weaving to support their children.[32] Such reports of self-reliant women corroborate the findings of economic historians that during the late sixteenth century the market economy had penetrated the rural areas of northern China.[33]

But economic relations were fragile, and during periods of

26. *SCKK*, 1:15a. The Fan clan, which claimed descent from the famous Fan Chung-yen, is heavily represented in *Yü-ch'eng hsien chih*. See in particular, the biography of Fan Chih-mou (6:16a–b). There are some indications that the Fan clan had hit on hard times. Fan Chih-mou had seven brothers and two sisters. In order to meet the family's responsibilities for the *corvée* labor, Fan's mother organized women to embroider materials they could exchange for food (7:20b).

27. *SCKK*, 3:1b. 28. *SCKK*, 1:15b.

29. *Yü-ch'eng hsien chih*, 5:15b. For a biography of Yang Tung-kuang, see ibid., 6:15b–16a.

30. Ibid., 1:8a. 31. Ibid., 10:10b–11a.

32. See, for example, the biographies of Yang's wives, *née* Wang and *née* Tai (ibid., 7:4a–b).

33. For the spread of the cotton textile industry to the north during the late sixteenth century, see Yen Chung-p'ing, *Chung-kuo mien-fang-chih shih-kao*, especially pp. 19–20. For Lü K'un's efforts to train people to weave cotton, see *SCL*, 2:9b–10a.

stress the area paid a high price for the benefits of commercialization. Those who made their living by weaving, or who had otherwise profited from commercial opportunities, depended on a complex system of exchange and were consequently vulnerable whenever poor harvests upset the economic equilibrium of the area. Thus the famines of the mid-1590s had alarmed Yang. He realized that one must make a special effort to win the hearts of the village lads so that they would not turn into desperadoes.[34] He also feared that vagrants from other areas might disrupt life at Yü-ch'eng. In particular, because the land around Yü-ch'eng was marshy,[35] the walls of the town had a special utility in providing protection from floods to inhabitants of the surrounding areas.[36] Those who enjoyed living within the walls had to promote harmonious social relations with the less fortunate who lived outside if riots were to be avoided during crises. Therefore Yang instructed that the soup kitchen should "not distinguish the natives from the wanderers . . . and should give to whomever comes." By stipulating that all recipients must register the day before appearing at the soup kitchen, Yang hoped to bring them under the control of his community.[37]

The social and economic pressures of Yü-ch'eng may have determined the ultimate shape of his voluntary associations, but Yang's impulse to organize activities went far beyond relief for immediate crises. One of the first societies Yang organized, in 1590 on a brief return home before his retirement, was entirely unpragmatic—a society of elders who initially met for the unabashed enjoyment of drinking and storytelling in the romantic (*feng-liu*) tradition. Yang soon found the meetings of The Society for Sharing Pleasure (*T'ung yüeh hui*) dull and meaningless. He therefore decided to redirect the group toward more worthy goals. He altered the program to accomplish good deeds and changed the name to The Society for Sharing Goodness. Using monthly dues and the fines from those who missed meetings, the group sponsored road and bridge repair, as well as financial assistance

34. *SCKK*, 3:1a.
35. *Yü-ch'eng hsien chih*, 9:6a.
36. Ibid., 9:8a.
37. *SCKK*, 1:17a.

with marriages and funerals. Only to some extent was the original function of the group preserved. The members were allowed to drink without limit at the monthly meetings but were warned "not to become intoxicated and dissipated" and not to eat too extravagantly.[38]

Yang gradually extended his influence beyond The Society for Sharing Goodness. In 1591, because so many scholars of the area had admired that society, Yang organized an additional thirty-one men, or as he put it, virtually "all the wealthy and powerful" of the town, into a Society for Spreading Humaneness. The regulations for the second group were patterned on those for the first; but the membership differed. All twelve members of the first group had a degree or had held minor official posts. The members of the second group were younger and of lower status. They included ten members of the Fan clan—all of whom were students of the Imperial Academy (*chien-sheng*)—Yang Tung-ming's younger brothers, several clerks (*li-tien*), scholars who had passed the first degree (*sheng-yüan*), "local guests" (*hsiang-pin*), and several "local people" (*hsiang-min*). This group attracted the patronage, to the tune of seven taels, of three officials who were natives of the neighboring district of Shang-ch'iu.[39]

In 1593, Yang joined the members of The Society for Sharing Goodness to sponsor the repair of a pavilion where they then held a drinking ceremony for the senior men of the area.[40] Such ceremonies were traditionally held from time to time to encourage the people to respect the aged and virtuous. After the event, Yang's comrades made further financial contributions to publish a volume of accounts of the men to set for posterity the example of respecting one's elders.[41]

38. *SCKK*, 1:6b–9a.

39. Yang stated that the regulations for the *Kuang-jen hui* were roughly the same as those of the *T'ung-shan hui* and therefore did not need to be repeated (*SCKK*, 1:11a). For the list of participants, see *SCKK*, 1:11a–b. *Chien-sheng*, or students of the Imperial Academy, were holders of the first degree with special privileges that included eligibility for office and access to library and tutorial facilities. For a summary of changes in the status of *chien-sheng* during the Ming, see Ping-ti Ho, *The Ladder of Success in Imperial China*, pp. 32–33.

40. *SCKK*, 2:1a.

41. *SCKK*, 2:2a–b.

In 1596, Yang organized The Society for Promoting Learning (*Hsing-hsüeh hui*).[42] The list for that society consisted of eighty-six members including two instructors, four assistant instructors, and numerous scholars of the area: two *chin-shih*, four *chü-jen*, nine tribute students, thirty-five *sheng-yüan*. In addition, numerous disciples from surrounding hsien had joined. Yang also listed the twenty scholars from other provinces whom he had selected in the *chin-shih* examination of 1595. In short, the membership of The Society for Promoting Learning was extensive in both size and geographic representation.[43]

In 1601, Yang organized yet another group, this time in response to a natural disaster. Heavy rains had ruined the crops, and sounds of wailing could, according to Yang's account, be heard from ninety per cent of the village homes. Because vagrants had drifted into Yü-ch'eng, the price of grain suddenly rose. Some feared the famine would be even more severe than that of 1594 and that people would be driven to eating human flesh. Consequently Yang and over a dozen others, including a few minor bureaucrats, several *sheng-yüan*, two "local people" and a local farmer (*i-nung min*) contributed 170 taels for over 300 bushels of grain, which they planned to distribute among the poor to keep the market prices down in the spring.[44]

The membership lists for the various groups formed by Yang overlapped only in a few instances. Because the groups were almost mutually exclusive, it is clear that Yang was a pivotal figure, a key organizer who through these associations extended his influence to different sectors of local society—to officials in neighboring districts as well as to rising "budding scholars" and prosperous commoners.

Yang expressed his interest in learned discussions by establishing the guest house for scholar-officials, and by sponsoring both The Society for Promoting Learning and, upon return to office, the Shou-shan Academy. He also believed

42. *SCKK*, 4:2b–4b.

43. For lists of the comrades, the men Yang had selected when serving as an examiner in Peking, and the disciples of The Society for Promoting Learning, see *SCKK*, 4:18b–22a.

44. *SCKK*, 1:14a–15a.

that his learned discussions with The Society for Promoting Learning were important enough to be recorded.[45] Yang was, as Lü K'un noted, outgoing and gregarious.[46] In the end, however, it was Yang's activist side, the side committed to "statecraft and practical learning" (*ching-chi shih-hsüeh*)—learning which according to Lü K'un had been "obtained outside [the realm] of words"—that flourished.[47]

Yang's bent toward writing about practical matters becomes most apparent in the light of his close contact with members of the T'ai-chou branch of the Wang Yang-ming school of thought, a branch noted for the popularization of sagehood through lecturing. According to Lü K'un, Yang Tung-ming derived some of his ideas from Yang Ch'i-yüan, who was in turn a follower of none other than the lecturer Lo Ju-fang.[48] In the spirit of Lo Ju-fang, Yang maintained that "intuitive knowledge" (*liang-chih*) predisposed men toward goodness, that "the hearts of rich and poor, worthy and ignorant were basically the same,"[49] that moral education would effectively increase the number of good people,[50] and—with a trace of hesitancy—that everyone could become a sage.[51]

Like Lo, Yang also believed in the efficacy of moral suasion. Even to solve such practical problems as banditry, Yang promoted education. By founding a community school, by providing free instruction for the poor, Yang hoped to deter the young from evil even during times of famine.[52] Education was also the key to social harmony in Yang's policy for the charitable soup kitchen. After eating, the destitute were required to listen to short didactic songs that conveyed such simple moral messages as "Those who are good will earn clothes and food."[53]

As persistent as Yang was in his educational efforts, he ultimately lacked the heady optimism of his predecessor Lo Ju-fang. Unlike the followers of Wang Yang-ming, who believed that everyone could become a sage, Yang noted de-

45. *SCKK, chüan* 5. 46. *CWCWC*, 3:17b.
47. *CWCWC*, 3:17b–18b. 48. *CWCWC*, 3:17b. 49. *SCKK*. 1:21a.
50. In a letter to Lü K'un, *SCKK*, 7:47b. 51. *SCKK*, 4:3a–b.
52. *SCKK*, 3:1a. 53. *SCKK*, 1:17a–b.

spairingly that only four sages had appeared in over two hundred years.[54] He sensed that learned discussions had become suspect. Someone had challenged Yang, "What is lecturing for?"[55] And Lü K'un in a letter had frankly warned Yang against "lecturing and empty talk" and favored instead "statecraft and practicality."[56]

In response, Yang defended lecturing in terms acceptable to his well-meaning critics. To one he retorted, "How is lecturing unrelated to practical use?" and then explained that lecture meetings gave people the opportunity to test their ideas in order to settle their doubts, to help one another in self-cultivation, and to correct one another's faults. He concluded that "nine out of ten of those who embody the Way and stress human relationships have benefitted from lecturing."[57]

Yang's defense, however, was weak. He conceded that some indeed lectured simply in order to establish a following to spread their fame.[58] He had observed: "Although there are many study societies, few [members] in each group become enlightened and many remain benighted."[59] Yang had also perceived that scholarship in his time was getting out of hand, that Li Chih, for example, had published, along with some fine insights, numerous seditious thoughts in his *Hsü Fen shu* [Sequel to a Book to Be Burned].[60]

Doubts even about the effectiveness of words, shared by many late Ming thinkers, crept into Yang's writings.[61] Yang noted in a letter to Lü K'un that the illiterate monk Hui-neng (638–713) had after all become a famous Buddhist priest without reading books. When someone asked Yang whether one therefore need not consult the laws perfected by the

54. *SCKK*, 4:3a. 55. *SCKK*, 6:10a.

56. Yang acknowledged Lü's letter in a letter to Lü (*SCKK*, 7:46b). This particular letter from Lü to Yang is not preserved in *CWCWC*.

57. *SCKK*, 6:11a–12b. 58. *SCKK*, 6:11b.

59. *SCKK*, 6:31a. 60. *SCKK*, 7:7b.

61. Questions about the value of words date at least as far back as Chuang Tzu but gained unprecedented centrality during the Ming. See David S. Nivison, "The Problem of 'Knowledge' and 'Action' in Chinese Thought since Wang Yang-ming." In particular, see Nivison's comments on "an attitude of suspicion toward abstract statement" and on "a general suspicion of 'words'" (ibid., pp. 119–121).

sages and whether Confucius, then, was also in error, Yang protested: "Of course not. From ancient times, when did the great sages ever dispense with learning? One must look at *how* one studies. If one takes the self as the basis, then the self will use the past; if one takes the past as the basis, then the self will be mired in the past." Yang explained that the ancients formulated laws only after devoting much thought to their basic virtuous nature and that people later relied on the ready-made laws for their convenience.[62] The ancients were simply the first to understand what was common to all human minds. "It is not that the ancients were capable and later people were not," Yang stated, and then he concluded that the Six Classics are all commentaries on the self and that there are aspects of the self which the Six Classics cannot exhaust. In this manner Yang maintained respect for the wisdom of the sages—in other words, for bookish knowledge or received opinion—while making room for personal, or experiential knowledge.[63]

Thus if Yang defended lecturing, he had departed far from Lo Ju-fang, with whom he was, through Yang Ch'i-yüan, tenuously affiliated—at least according to Lü K'un. When someone asked why Yang Tung-ming had rejected a friend's advice not to hold lecture meetings, Yang, lacking Lo's self-confidence, replied: "I am an average man (*chung-jen*). Meeting with friends lifts my spirits; in isolation I become lax. If I abandon learned discussions I am afraid I will become endlessly dissipated and gradually confused."[64]

Lo Ju-fang had felt buoyed by the message he had to convey; Yang felt subdued and tentative. Lo Ju-fang had destroyed a record he kept of his faults; the self-doubtful men of Yang's generation found comfort in sharing their experiences and even their failings. Lo Ju-fang had boldly defended the role of teacher; lecturers of Yang's generation defended themselves against accusations of trying to establish networks through their disciples. Accordingly, Yang played down the role of leadership in learned discussions and stressed instead the importance of learning from "bene-

62. *SCKK*, 7:45a–b. Emphasis mine. Hui-neng (638–713), a Zen master, advocated sudden enlightenment.

63. *SCKK*, 7:46a. 64. *SCKK*, 6:25b.

ficial friends" (*i-yu*).[65] In defining the goal of lecturing as the improvement of self as much as the education of others, Yang paid the price of self-abnegation for his learned discussions. Lo Ju-fang had boldly interpreted Confucianism and relied on the Six Imperial Injunctions as a sanction for his own mission. He suffered no doubts that he had the authority to spread his teachings. Yang yielded passively to the mounting opposition to learned discussions that Chang Chü-cheng's disapproval of Lo Ju-fang had foreshadowed.

After spending a decade in Yü-ch'eng, Yang was painfully conscious that an era was ending. In an essay written shortly after 1606, just as he approached old age, Yang maintained that without a faith in worthies, the country would be desolate. True, Yang added, the number of worthies was limited and from ancient times it had always been impossible to find many of them. Nonetheless, he noted that before 1587 there had been quite a few worthies with the result that the empire had been peaceful. But later, the court became faction-ridden, many officials were dismissed, slanderous rumors circulated, and confusion arose. After bemoaning that "Heaven has failed to bless the state and the worthies have by now all died," Yang listed those who had recently died, including: Chang Yüan-pien (d. 1588), Meng Ch'iu (d. 1589), Keng Ting-hsiang (d. 1596), Meng Hua-li (d. 1597), Teng I-tsan (d. 1599), Yang Ch'i-yüan (d. 1599), Feng Ying-ching (d. 1606), and Wei Yün-chen (d. 1606).[66] Yang observed that everyone must die, but he added that the death of sages left the world feeling empty and helpless in emergencies. Thinking about it, Yang concluded, was chilling.[67]

In writing about local affairs Yang took his hometown as the center from which he extended his influence. Yang's relations with active officials lent him authority at home; but broad political issues faded from view and gave way, in the surviving written record at least, to local concerns.

65. See Yang's defense of "seeking beneficial friends" in *SCKK*, 7:47a. For Yang's statement that friendship had been inaccurately rated as the last of the five human relationships, see *SCKK*, 4:11a–12a.

66. *SCKK*, 6:64b. For Feng Ying-ching, see *Ming shih*, 237:2708–2709, and *MJHA*, 24:17b. For Teng I-tsan, see *Ming shih*, 283:3191, and *MJHA*, 21:1a–b.

67. *SCKK*, 6:64b–65a.

In his commemorative pieces (*chi* and *hsü*), Yang Tung-ming invariably stepped boldly into the center of the stage and dominated the scene, sometimes immodestly. In commemorating a project to control river floods, for example, Yang stressed that he had personally inspected the work, and complimented himself for having astutely improved the methods for repairing a breach in the dikes.[68] Again somewhat self-congratulatorily, Yang reported that on retirement he had joined forces with other gentlemen to establish the community granary of Ts'ao hsien because he had found bookish solitude unsatisfying.[69]

Yang's commemorative pieces are personal, localized, and specific. Only rarely do they open with a description of an exemplary historical figure or an outline of some commendable precedent. Yang acknowledged inspiration from the past when he cited in his "Record of Charitable Fields" the example of Fan Chung-yen (982–1052), and when he recalled the grain equalization method of the ancients as a solution to the famine of 1601.[70] Yang also alluded to the great Neo-Confucian philosophers, undoubtedly to display his erudition, when he addressed the young scholars of The Society for Promoting Learning.[71] More often, however, rather than move from some formal example to the specific case, Yang opened with an intimate autobiographical account of how he became involved in the task. Yang took his own experience as the point of departure. Thus in one essay, he casually opened with the autobiographical statement, "When I passed through Chi hsien."[72] And in another essay, Yang summarized his reactions to and reasons for giving new direction to The Society for Sharing Pleasure.[73]

Details of local affairs loomed large in Yang's writings and often crowded out grander concerns. Yang dwelled, for example, on a poor widower from the mountains, Chang Ch'ang-an, whom The Society for Spreading Humaneness had agreed to sponsor. Because Chang knew something about medicine, the Society decided to pay for Chang's sec-

68. *SCKK*, 1:18a. 69. *SCKK*, 1:1a.

70. For Yang's allusion to Fan Chung-yen, see *SCKK*, 9:5a. For Yang's allusion to Neo-Confucian thinkers, see *SCKK*, 1:14a.

71. *SCKK*, 4:2b. 72. *SCKK*, 1:4b. 73. *SCKK*, 1:6b–8a.

ond marriage to free him to practice his skill. Mr. Fan, a member of the Society who was well-versed in medicine, selected prescriptions to insure that Chang would deliver efficacious care. Several hundred people a day asked for medical attention, and everyone, according to Yang, was thankful.[74]

Similarly preoccupied with local details, Yang made room for the idiosyncracies and strong points of each old man in the volume of biographies published to commemorate the elders. In one biography, rather than simply transmit, as had Lo Ju-fang, moral instructions from the founding emperor or the great sages to the common people, Yang elicited a moral point from an uneducated elder. Reported Yang:

> When Li Ch'ou came to my feast, he sat stiffly all day like a clay statue. I said, "You are so senile, you can't utter a word." The old man said: "Not so. People survive by relying on the material force (*ch'i*) in their hearts. If one speaks too much, eventually the material force will be destroyed, dissipated and wasted, and the body will consequently die." Startled, I said, . . . "Now I know that those who talk excessively not only invite criticism but are very far from the proper way to longevity."[75]

Even if one purpose of such drinking ceremonies was to elicit comments from the elders, Yang's willingness to record the event in print, to give importance to rather than patronizingly dismiss the information gathered from his inferiors, suggests that his social orientation was very different from Lo Ju-fang's.

In another way Yang moved from the specific to the general. He evoked sympathy for a cause not by affirming the dictates of some authority but by displaying his own emotional response to a subject. In many of his accounts, whether of dike repair, marriage-aid societies, or commemorating the aged, Yang Tung-ming opened by striking an emotional chord. In "A Record of Grain Distribution," Yang recounted how in 1608 he had grieved to hear the death cries

74. *SCKK,* 1:9b–10a. 75. *SCKK,* 2:4b–5a.

of those starving in Yü-ch'eng.[76] In "A Record of Sponsoring Marriages," Yang expressed pity for those poor young men and women who remained single beyond the marriageable age.[77]

Even in his formal "Chi-min t'u-shuo shu" ["Illustrated Memorial on the Starving"] of 1594, Yang's close, emotional identification with his hometown is forcefully clear. The plight of the people of Honan moved Yang "to weep so profusely that he could barely put his brush to paper."[78] He backed his appeal to the emperor not with reasoned arguments based on the exhortations of the classics, but with unsparingly vivid descriptions. He reported that "the starving, who had formerly sold their children, were now chopping up their corpses; those who had formerly simply abandoned the bodies of their relatives, were now devouring their flesh."[79] He further stated that he could not bear to describe the scenes he had witnessed—people "cutting grasses on which they could survive and scraping bark off trees to fill their stomachs; everyone looked ghost-like, their faces withered and yellow."[80]

Yang Tung-ming concluded the memorial on famine on a note of frustration; he explained that because he lacked the talent to articulate the plight of the starving, he had supplemented the text with illustrations.[81] To be sure, the famine was so severe that another official submitted bird droppings along with his memorial to show the emperor what the famine had driven the starving to eat.[82] But the point remains that Yang, whose talent in composing memorials was mediocre, expressed himself most forcefully when he identified closely with his community. It is perhaps not accidental that

76. *SCKK*, 1:19b. 77. *SCKK*, 1:21a.

78. *Yü-ch'eng hsien chih*, 8:7a. T'an Ch'ien, *Kuo-ch'üeh*, 5:4722. For a discussion of this and other famines in Honan, see Shui-yuen Yim, "Famine Relief Statistics as a Guide to the Population of Sixteenth-Century China: A Case Study of Honan Province," pp. 1–30.

79. "Chi-min t'u-shuo shu" in *Yü-ch'eng hsien chih*, 8:8a.

80. Ibid., 8:7b–8a. 81. Ibid., 8:11a.

82. T'an Ch'ien, *Kuo-ch'üeh*, 5:4723. In response to such pleas, Cheng Kuei-fei contributed 5000 taels to the central states. See the biography of Cheng Kuei-fei by Chaoying Fang in *DMB*, pp. 209–11, in particular, p. 210.

of all his memorials only the one on the famine in Honan won attention.

Yang's emotionalism, avoidance of formal solutions, and inclusion of numerous specific details lent veracity to his writings. A friend of many years, Lü K'un, admired Yang's work for its direct unpretentious style. Lü had been Yang's examiner, was impressed by Yang's virtuous demeanor, and consequently gave his son, Chih-wei, in marriage to Yang's daughter. Lü K'un perceptively praised Yang Tung-ming for writing "without one redundancy, without one cliché." Every word that flowed from Yang's heart was, according to Lü, "trenchant and real."[83]

If Yang's writings on local affairs were "trenchant and real," they expressed a narrow self-centered world, and consequently his writings were of limited significance. According to the gazetteer of Yü-ch'eng, Yang edited several philosophical texts and wrote four works each on metaphysical and practical matters.[84] But of his large corpus, only one or two copies of a few titles remain. These include *Shan-chü kung-k'o* [Accomplishments during Retirement], *Lun-hsing i-yen* [Personal Opinions on the Nature of Man], *Ch'ing-so chin-yen*, a collection of Yang's memorials, and his memorial requesting famine relief, "An Illustrated Memorial on the Starving."[85] One might blame historical accident for the loss: in 1635, shortly after Yang's death, bandits swept through and destroyed much of Yü-ch'eng.[86] But this argument, resting on localized destruction, assumes that his writings never circulated widely. Indeed, only the memorial on the starving and a few excerpts from Yang's other works were ever reprinted.[87] Yang's surviving writings are neither complex nor

83. "Preface to *Yang Chin-an wen-chi*," in *CWCWC*, 3:17b–18b.

84. *DMB* attributes ten titles to Yang (p. 1547). More accurately, Yang edited several and wrote eight (*Yü-ch'eng hsien chih*, 6:13b).

85. Copies of *Shan-chü kung-k'o* are available in the Naikaku Bunko Library, Tokyo, and the Gest Library, Princeton University. One copy of *Ch'ing-so chin yen* and one of *Lun hsing i yen* are both available in the Gest Library. "Chi-min t'u-shuo shu" was reprinted in *Yü-ch'eng hsien chih*, 8:6b–11b.

86. *Yü-ch'eng hsien chih*, 1:8b.

87. Several essays from *SCKK* have been reprinted in *Yü-ch'eng hsien*

intriguing. Colorless and unexceptional, they lack the erudition of Wang Yang-ming, the organizational skills of Hai Jui, the biting sarcasm of Li Chih, and the metaphorical language of Lü K'un.

A tomb inscription Yang wrote to commemorate his friend, Meng Ch'iu, reveals the limitations of the experiential approach. Yang opened with a summary of the circumstances that led him to write it: his friends Meng Hua-li and Tsou Yüan-piao had already written a biography and epitaph of Meng Ch'iu, respectively; Meng Hua-li then asked Yang to write the inscription; Yang modestly refused; Meng Hua-li argued with him; Yang finally changed his mind. Only after drifting through the circumstances that led up to writing the inscription did Yang finally proceed to elaborate on Meng Ch'iu's accomplishments. The inscription thus smacks of self-advertisement. Yang's personal account clutters up the opening and draws attention to the act of writing the inscription, which appears trivial in light of the main purpose—to honor the deceased Meng Ch'iu.[88]

Yang's inclination to stress his personal experiences found more suitable material in the affairs of his hometown. There, as the organizer of activities, Yang was in fact in the center of, or identified with, events that were, in their own small context, important. In retreat, managing hometown affairs, Yang could feel central and strong. There his personal outlook and ineloquent voice forcefully matched what he had to say. As late Ming scholars came to criticize "empty talk" and as practical learning gained respect, those who like Yang lacked the talent to formulate great philosophical syntheses or to work within the elaborate guidelines of formal literary compositions, could nonetheless find opportunities to leave a slight mark.

However, Yang lacked the talent to rise above his times. Since he took his personal responses to specific hometown affairs as a guide, Yang failed to generalize policies in terms that could apply elsewhere. His activities were so localized that his influence was never far-reaching. In Yü-ch'eng, Yang

---

chih, chüan 8. Sections of *Lun hsing i yen* are included in Sun Ch'i-feng, *Li-hsüeh tsung chuan*, 23:57b–62a.

88. *SCKK*, 9:17b–19b.

acquiesced to the inevitable realities of local politics and made room for considerations of status and wealth. Yang took pride in the fact that "all the wealthy and powerful" had joined the Society for Spreading Humaneness.[89] He enhanced the membership list of the Society for Promoting Learning by including the names of the twenty *chin-shih* he had passed as an examiner.[90] And he paid meticulous attention to status and wealth in compiling membership lists, specifying for example, that where he had contributed thirty-four ounces of silver to one cause, his two younger brothers each contributed only thirty-three.[91] Boxed into local affairs by political pressures and enervated in the area of learned discussions, Yang lacked the ingenuity to find either a language or a conceptual framework through which particularistic local interests and personal experiences could be synthesized with the broad values of the bureaucratic elite. In contrast to his mentor Lü K'un, Yang could not break out of the boundaries that had closed in on scholar-officials.

89. *SCKK*, 1:9b. 90. *SCKK*, 4:20a. 91. *SCKK*, 1:15a.

4

Feng Ts'ung-wu: In the Academy

Yang Tung-ming admired his friend Feng Ts'ung-wu (1566–1627[?]) for being "a hero . . . not an average person."[1] Like Yang, Feng was a victim of the unstable political intrigues of the 1590s and spent twenty-five years, from 1596 to 1621, in retirement. But Feng used his time differently. While Yang gravitated toward an active life, establishing local volunteer organizations, Feng spent his time contemplatively, studying and lecturing. Thus the two men, who shared the same social milieu, who experienced similar political difficulties, and who in their final years even co-sponsored the Shou-shan Academy, manifest distinct facets of the very same world.[2] Each represents alternatives available to the other, and each therefore illuminates the implications of the choices made by the other.

Feng hailed from a well-to-do family of Ch'ang-an, Shensi. His father, Feng Yu (1507–65), known for his fondness of philosophy, had been a provincial graduate in 1534, held a minor position as vice prefect of Pao-ting, Pei Chih-li, and was sufficiently wealthy to set aside some lands in trust for his lineage.[3]

1. In a letter to Lü K'un, *SCKK*, 7:48b–49a.

2. For the Shou-shan Academy, see the biography of Tsou Yüan-piao by Charles O. Hucker in *DMB*, p. 1313.

3. Biography of Feng by Charles O. Hucker in *DMB*, pp. 458–59; *MJHA*, 41:1a–2a; *Ming shih*, 243:2769; *Ch'ang-an hsien chih* (1668), 7:13b; and Sun Ch'i-feng, *Li-hsüeh tsung-chuan*, 23:19a–b. For a discussion of Feng's thought in the context of other Ming philosophers—his attitudes toward Buddhism, and how both Feng and his teacher, Hsü Fu-yüan, modified or clarified Wang Yang-ming's view of intuitive knowledge so as

Feng Ts'ung-wu passed the metropolitan examinations in 1589, served as a Hanlin Academy bachelor, and was then appointed an investigating censor in 1591. In 1592, he intrepidly wrote a memorial criticizing the emperor for "enjoying long nights drinking" and neglecting his duties. The enraged emperor ordered Feng flogged in court. Fortunately an official used the birthday of the emperor's mother as a pretext to win amnesty for Feng.[4] Feng took sick leave in 1592, and resumed office in 1596, but not for long. The emperor, eager for an excuse to get rid of the critical Feng, had accused him along with other censors for failing to bring to light the misdeeds of a disgraced eunuch. Within a year, Feng lost his position and was scratched entirely from the civil service roster.

With each vicissitude in his political life, Feng's commitment to lecturing steadily deepened. Sickly from birth, he had even as a child disliked active play and leaned toward a contemplative life. With the exception of a few critical pieces on the well-field system, the policies of Wang An-shih, and corruption in the administration of salt transportation, Feng did not comment upon specific administrative matters.[5] His writings left no room for topics that plagued many of his contemporaries—the organization of *pao-chia*, *hsiang-yüeh*, and granaries at the local level; or defense of the borders at the national level. Even Feng's memorials gave vent to moral exhortations rather than to recommendations for more efficient administration. Thus his writings concentrate on philosophical issues and include an analysis of the idealist school of Neo-Confucianism (*hsin-hsüeh*) with particular criticisms of Wang Yang-ming's tendencies towards Ch'an Buddhism (*Pien-hsüeh lu*); a critical survey of thinkers of the Yuan dynasty (*Yüan-ju k'ao lüeh*); a survey of the thinkers of his home province of Shensi (*Kuan-hsüeh pien*); his "Shan li t'u-

---

to avoid the late sixteenth-century trend toward moral relativism—see Okada Takehiko, *Ō Yōmei to Minmatsu no Jugako* (Tokyo, 1970), pp. 304–14.

4. Feng Ts'ung-wu, [*Feng*] *Shao-hsü chi* (hereafter *FSHC*), 18:4a–9b.

5. For comments on Feng's childhood sickliness, see preface to "Pien-hsüeh lu" by Yang Hao in *FSHC*, 1:7b. For essays on the well-field system, see *FSHC*, 3:35b–36b, 41a–b. For salt administration, see *FSHC*, 18:17a–20b.

shuo" ["Explanation of the Chart of Goodness and Profit"]; and his comments on the Classics, *I-ssu lu* ["Records of Thoughts on Doubtful Points"].[6]

During his two terms of leave, Feng slipped into the role of scholar rather than administrator. In 1592, Feng initially isolated himself. Some evenings, two or three comrades visited him to distract him from his illness by discussing the meaning of classical texts, playing lute songs, and chanting poetry until daybreak.[7] In 1595, Feng accepted invitations to address students in various districts of Shantung province.[8] In 1596, he resumed office briefly, only to be expelled from the civil service that very same year. In 1596 he lectured at the Pao-ch'ing Temple in Ch'ang-an, but after falling sick in 1598, secluded himself for nine years.[9]

In late 1606 Feng resumed lecturing.[10] As had been the case with Lo Ju-fang, the popularization of education created a demand for Feng's instruction. Feng welcomed "all farmers, artisans and merchants who have determination" to attend his lectures.[11] One associate observed of his followers, "There are many who are poor and do not have the opportunity to study,"[12] and Feng took great pride in the benefits that "learned discussions" brought to a poor scholar named Chu.[13] By 1609, Feng's audiences had outgrown the capacity of the Pao-ch'ing Temple. Consequently some officials put aside a trust of public fields and sponsored the construction of the Kuan-chung Academy to the east of the temple. There, audiences of several thousands listened to Feng lecture.[14] Thus Feng was a talented lecturer who could attract a large, socially diverse following and win the support and confidence of officials.

With his inner circle of comrades, Feng traveled about. In

6. "Pien-hsüeh lu," *FSHC, chüan* 1. For a critique of *Yüan-ju k'ao-lüeh*, see *Ssu-k'u ch'üan-shu ts'ung-mu, ch'in-ting*, 58:11b–12b. *Kuan hsüeh pien*, *FSHC, chüan* 19–20; "Shan li t'u-shuo," *FSHC, chüan* 8; *I-ssu lu*, *FSHC, chüan* 2–3.

7. *FSHC*, 2:8a. 8. *FSHC*, 4:22a.

9. Preface to "Pien hsüeh lu," by Yang Hao in *FSHC*, 1:8a.

10. *FSHC*, 15:38a–b. 11. *FSHC*, 6:9b.

12. *FSHC*, 11:14a. 13. *FSHC*, 17:4a–6a.

14. *Hsien-ning hsien chih* (1819), 3:15a. See also Feng's account of the Kuan-chung Academy (*FSHC*, 15:1a–5b; and 15:38a).

the spring of 1608, taking advantage of the fine weather, he guided several dozen disciples on a brief outing.[15] Again in the spring of 1611, Feng and several dozen companions visited a shrine in Hopei.[16] Wherever he traveled, he was much in demand. After visiting the Hung-tao Academy and a shrine dedicated to three famous men, he held a discussion with his companions.[17] On returning to Ch'ang-an after visiting that shrine, he met with one hundred disciples at a temple.[18] In addition to these excursions, only briefly noted in Feng's collected writings, he undoubtedly took many others. We know, for example, that Feng visited the guest house Yang had built in Yü-ch'eng.[19]

To commemorate his discussions, Feng left behind extensive records, or "recorded dialogues" (*yü-lu*), which provided answers to questions on textual problems and moral issues raised by his followers. Feng took the compilation of these dialogues very seriously. He reported, for example, that when illness prevented him from writing up a report of the 1608 spring outing, he took care to incorporate the notes a few years later into an account of a ten-day meeting with over a hundred men at the T'ai-hua Academy.[20]

In light of Feng's comradely enjoyment of outings and the large appreciative audiences, ranging in size from several dozen to thousands, Feng's "recorded dialogues" sound surprisingly defensive. They express no signs that the responsive following flattered or exhilarated him, and they lack the expansive optimism that had characterized Lo Ju-fang.

Feng was defensive against the legacy of Chang Chü-cheng's proscription of the academies and criticisms of Lo Ju-fang. Chang had moreover menacingly warned Meng Ch'iu, who moved in the same circles as Feng, that Meng was a good official but should desist from lecturing.[21] Looking back on that period, Feng's friend, Tsou Yüan-piao, observed in

15. *FSHC*, 9:2a–2b.
16. *FSHC*, 11:1a–b. The text specifies "Hopei." The official name during the Ming was Pei Chih-li.
17. *FSHC*, 11:13a.
18. *FSHC*, 11:16a.
19. *Yü-ch'eng hsien chih*, 6:12b.
20. *FSHC*, 9:3a.
21. Cited in Meng Ch'iu, *Meng Wo-ch'iang hsien-sheng chi*, 7:16a. For Meng's defense against criticism that learned discussion, or lecturing, is "empty," see ibid., 2:21a–b.

1602: "Holding learned discussions was easy under Hsü Chieh and difficult under Chang Chü-cheng."[22] Feng also felt vulnerable to the criticisms against Lo Ju-fang for encouraging universal love. Someone asked Feng whether wanting "everyone to be a gentleman or a good person would not degenerate into universal love." Feng replied that when asked a similar question Lo had responded, "What I fear is that people will remain cruel-hearted and have no love that could degenerate." Feng endorsed Lo's "well-chosen words" and worried only that people feared "universal love" more than selfishness.[23]

Unlike Lo Ju-fang, who had steadfastly concentrated his attention on the message he wished to convey, Feng became mired in dialogues with his antagonists. Indeed, criticisms against the academies continued to engage his attention long after Chang Chü-cheng had died. Feng conceded that with the proliferation of the academies the quality of Confucian scholarship had deteriorated. He noted that in perusing local gazetteers he had found that even remote places harbored anywhere from ten to several dozen temples. "As for the private academies," he added, "they are even more numerous than the stars." Some are located in ancient scenic sites; others in public buildings or dilapidated temples. "Alas," Feng sighed, "No wonder heterodoxy is increasing, and Confucian scholars are on the decline."[24]

Feng was aware that the academy associates often deviated far from the spirit of Confucianism. When someone asked Feng why one should bother establishing the academies, the members of which were not all "true Confucians," Feng made the rather lame response: although those in the temples were not all "true Buddhists," no one ever hesitated about establishing temples.[25] Feng understood, for example, that those who lectured were suspected of trying to establish reputations for themselves. Someone who had stopped lecturing after having been so reproached explained to Feng, "Just after lecturing, others follow up with their own words;

22. Tsou's preface, written in 1602, is included in Chang Yüan-pien, *Chang Yang-ho wen-hsüan*, pp. 3–4.
23. *FSHC*, 8:12b–14b. For the passage by Lo, see *HTCC*, 1:30b.
24. *FSHC*, 13:46b. 25. Ibid.

what is the use?" In response Feng asked, "When you lectured in the past—was it in fact for others or for yourself? If for others, then you should feel sympathetic with what they say as though it was for yourself . . . and if you stop [lecturing] because of slanderous remarks . . . then it is because you are lecturing to establish a reputation."[26]

Unlike Lo Ju-fang, whom no criticisms shook, Feng was on guard to defend a territory for scholars. He argued: "The educational officials are limited in number, but the academies are not. The academies truly supplement what the educational officials have failed to accomplish."[27] While out of office, Feng relied on those in office and responded to their pressures. Officials, after all, sponsored the Kuan-chung Academy where Feng lectured. Thus, as strongly opposed as Feng was to the corrupt elements in the government, he did not turn countercultural or heterodox. Rather he accommodated those in power by avoiding sensitive political topics. To defend the academies, Feng capitulated to his critics and accepted restrictions on the activities of the academies.

Fearful of criticism that he was seeking fame, Feng, like Yang Tung-ming, retreated from assertions of his superior authority as a teacher. Rather, to brush aside accusations that he was seeking fame, Feng humbly denied his strengths: "Confucius worried about 'the failure to discuss what is learned;' how much more [worrisome] for scholars. Therefore we nowadays hold learned discussions not only to teach others but to improve ourselves. Why? [Because] the human heart is easily dissipated, and learning is difficult to exhaust."[28]

Lo Ju-fang had trusted that his listeners would readily respond to appeals to humaneness, and that education would bring all men into the community of sages. Feng believed in man's capacity for sagehood, but focused his attention on human failings. "People are not sages," he stated, and then asked, "Who can be without faults?"[29] Lo Ju-fang was so confident that humaneness would prevail that he did not write rules of conduct for his study groups; even in address-

26. *FSHC*, 14:4a–b. 27. *FSHC*, 13:47b.
28. *FSHC*, 6:3a. Legge, *Chinese Classics*, 1:195.
29. *FSHC*, 6:4b; see also 6:5a.

ing the rural uneducated, he favored using moral suasion over spelling out admonitions. By contrast, Feng carefully outlined proscriptions; he assumed that men would veer toward evil if boundaries to behavior were not carefully delineated.

Lo Ju-fang took for granted a spontaneous group spirit. Feng assumed that people were by nature contentious, and he consequently expressed deep distrust for the academy associates. Rarely do members of a study group argue, Feng protested, but then promptly instructed the associates how "everyone should try to restore order" should arguments arise.[30] "In discussions," Feng elsewhere advised the associates, "one should strive for equanimity, free oneself of all biases and yield to other persons. . . . Even if still believing oneself correct, one should by no means again bring up the topic for discussion."[31] Perceiving the study groups to be divided and contentious, Feng further warned members: "When in a crowd, do not shout and speak high-flown words as though no one was present."[32]

Lo took for granted a universal commitment to humaneness. For him, the bonds that held society together required no conscious exposition. Feng was painfully aware that the members of his community were self-centered and that some objective framework—in the form of rules, constraints, or even verbal contracts—was therefore necessary to define and maintain a sense of community. Feng commented in a letter to Tsou Yüan-piao that the neglect of the rules for proper behavior had greatly harmed the Way.[33] And to Kao P'an-lung, Feng wrote: "In learned discussions today, one must preserve a sense of fear within and abide by regulations without."[34]

Several sets of stern regulations that Feng outlined for the academies convey his distrust of human nature. In a "meeting agreement" of 1596 for those convening at the Pao-ch'ing Temple, Feng noted that the participants—who usually joined the study societies not to pursue learning but to scramble for useful social connections—disrupted the meet-

30. *FSHC*, 5:4a. 31. *FSHC*, 6:2a–b.
32. *FSHC*, 6:7b. 33. *FSHC*, 15:43a. 34. *FSHC*, 15:58a.

ings.[35] Consequently Feng warned, "Those who are relatives or old friends should not use the study meetings to socialize as they please"[36] and should not curry favor for advancement by generously sending off visiting officials.[37] Doubting whether the academy associates would exercise good judgment, Feng further admonished, "Do not consort with diviners, masters of [the black] arts, planchette-manipulators, exorcists and other such unreliable men;" and "Do not read *The Water Margin* . . . and other such harmful books."[38] Doubting, moreover, whether the members were even capable of humaneness, Feng exhorted: "Do not ridicule and insult the poor or covet and slander the rich."[39]

A preface one member of Feng's study group wrote in 1598 to a "meeting agreement" implied that verbal contracts were necessary when social relations were poor. The preface stated, "Sometimes scholars sharing the same lodging will have nothing to do with one another, and sometimes [scholars] a thousand *li* apart are [so close that they seem to be] shoulder to shoulder; it is a matter of whether their minds are united or not. If they are truly united, then even without meetings there is a meeting of minds. A meeting agreement without a contract is the ideal agreement. Therefore a meeting of minds is better than meeting face to face, and a spiritual agreement is better than a verbal contract."[40]

Even the sense of community within families and lineages, Feng unwittingly acknowledged, could no longer be taken for granted. Thus he warned young students: "Do not be so presumptuous about [your knowledge of] literature as to find fault with the teachings of your father or older brothers;" and "Do not have such a high regard for yourself as to insult your relatives, friends, lineages, and clubs."[41]

Signs of distrust run through many of Feng's essays. Rather than urge the academy associates to be generous leaders in the spirit of the oneness of all things, Feng, accent-

35. *FSHC*, 6:7b; 6:2a. 36. *FSHC*, 6:2a. 37. *FSHC*, 6:7b.
38. Ibid., 6:8b. For English versions of *Shui-hu-chuan*, see Pearl Buck, *All Men are Brothers* or J. H. Jackson, *Water Margin*. For a discussion of the favorable criticisms of *Shui-hu-chuan* during the late Ming, see Richard G. Irwin, *The Evolution of a Chinese Novel: Shui-hu-chuan*.
39. *FSHC*, 6:8a. 40. *FSHC*, 5:1b. 41. *FSHC*, 6:7b.

ing his negative expectations of human behavior, warned: "Do not forget to return the books you borrow; and do not damage or soil them."[42]

Associated with Feng's sense of distrust was his awareness that everyone occupied not only a realm that was public, or open (*kung*), but one that was private, or self-centered (*ssu*). Accordingly, Feng admonished the associates, "Do not go into other people's libraries to snoop in their private books and records;" and "Do not . . . discuss other people's private affairs."[43] Conscious of the private realm, Feng modified—or elaborated on—Wang Yang-ming's definition of "intuitive knowledge," which Feng believed was Wang's noteworthy contribution to the study of sagehood. On "intuitive knowledge," Feng commented: "We do not know whether everyone can apprehend the specks of true and false in each person's heart."[44] A later chapter will discuss the method of self-cultivation associated with the view that each person possessed an interior world of "specks of true and false," a world that was beyond the reach of others, and that therefore necessitated the deliberate and conscious sharing of experiences. For the moment, suffice it to say that Feng's keen awareness of each person's interior world underscored his sense of distrust and prompted him to rely on regulations.

Feng further acknowledged that the political and legal activities of the participants in the academies often proved treacherous and disruptive. He warned the members: "Do not compose verses, plays, popular songs, and couplets to satirize and criticize current events and bring about the downfall of your comrades;" and "Do not compose anonymous placards, written accusations, or letters for the private assignations of other people."[45] These two rules, Feng noted, were often disobeyed. Finally, so that they would remain above suspicion of being heterodox or seditious, Feng prohibited members from discussing such political topics as court and border affairs, or the evaluation of officials.[46] Rather they should concentrate on the Four Books, the Five Classics, and such Neo-Confucian texts as *Chin-ssu lu* [Re-

42. *FSHC*, 6:8a. 43. *FSHC*, 6:8a–b. 44. *FSHC*, 6:3b–4a.
45. *FSHC*, 6:8a–b. 46. *FSHC*, 6:1b.

flections on Things at Hand] compiled by Chu Hsi and Lü Tsu-ch'ien.[47]

At the same time, Feng responded to the demands of his time that learning be useful. He thus urged those who met at the Pao-ch'ing Temple to refrain from "empty discussions and to respect practical action."[48] The avoidance of politics precisely when practical action was so strongly stressed must have intensified a feeling of uselessness among Feng's academy associates.[49]

Between the demands that learning be useful and that learning remain apolitical, there remained little ground on which Feng could justify lecturing. Thus, if Feng was defensive against the critics of lecturing, he grew downright evasive when asked how philosophical debates related to practical action. Someone challenged Feng: "Recently 'lecturers' all discuss the abstruse and do not realize that 'carrying out what one professes' (*kung-hsing*) is enough; what need is there for lecturing?" Feng replied: "The cure for the disease of abstruseness lies in 'carrying out what one professes' . . . but why say there is no need for lecturing?"[50] Similarly, when someone citing the precept, "Scholars should not speak but act," asked, "Why lecture?" Feng again failed to explain just why lecturing was valuable. Prevaricating, he replied instead, "The word 'speak' here does not refer to lecturing," and then explained that "speak" referred to such behavior as talking gratuitously about other people's faults while neglecting to examine one's own.[51]

The proliferation of philosophical differences among lecturers further drained learned discussions of their moral force. Though some lecturers gained a sense of identity by

47. *FSHC*, 6:2b. For a translation of Chu Hsi's work, *Reflections on Things at Hand*.

48. *FSHC*, 6:2a.

49. For an illuminating interpretation of this problem, see Frederic Wakeman, Jr., "The Price of Autonomy: Intellectuals in Ming and Ch'ing Politics." See also Charles O. Hucker, "The Tung-lin Movement of the Late Ming Period."

50. *FSHC*, 7:29a. The phrase *kung-hsing* is drawn from "carrying out in his conduct what he professes" (Confucius, *Analects*, in Legge, *Chinese Classics*, 1:205).

51. *FSHC*, 6:6a–b.

associating with the academies, the academies maintained their sense of purpose through philosophical debates that splintered the larger community of scholars and officials. Conflicting interpretations of the classics, each upheld by an institution of large membership, proliferated and diminished the significance of any one philosophical view. Furthermore, the feuds, although waged most energetically, often had no purpose other than maintaining the identity of the academies and thus fizzled into petty squabbles without any real function.[52] Moreover, because friendships frequently crossed philosophical schools, it became apparent that opinions reflected neither social networks nor political positions. For example, Feng, who vehemently opposed Buddhism,[53] had long befriended and in 1621 even jointly started the Shou-shan Academy with Tsou Yüan-piao, who condoned the synthesis of Buddhism and Confucianism. Under such circumstances, "learned discussions" began to appear "empty" and superficial.

Having divorced lecturing from political concerns, Feng instead defended its utility on purely moral grounds as "a method of cultivating virtue . . . without which one cannot distinguish between right and wrong."[54] But Feng's moral defense of lecturing was shaky. In a piece, "Ch'in-chien shuo" ["On Diligence and Frugality"], Feng defends "learned discussions" on the grounds that they bring material rewards. Feng tells of two scholars (*shih-fu*). One participated in learned discussions; the other did not "believe in study." Both were from wealthy families and taught their sons to be "diligent and frugal." As young men, the two sons were extravagant and lazy, but they later reformed their ways and turned responsible and obedient. The son of the man who favored learned discussions read books, sought friends of fine character, and treated most generously his lineage and village. His family grew prosperous and well-known, and he became a famous scholar. The son who was not brought up to study

52. For example, comments by Chang Yüan-pien that everyone in a crowd "has his strong point and his opinion" (*Chang Yang-ho wen-hsüan*, p. 1). He also stated that everyone at court has an opinion and belongs to a party (ibid., p. 21).

53. See, for example, *FSHC*, *chüan* 1.

54. *FSHC*, 6:3a.

was also frugal, but stingy, with the result that the relatives grew resentful, lawsuits arose, and the family fortune declined. In the end, the village would not even accommodate him. The two sons, Feng concluded, were the same in frugality, diligence, and filiality, but the fates of their families greatly differed. Why? Because of the extent of their learning.[55]

In arguing that learned discussions were necessary to "make real" one's diligence and frugality, Feng drew special attention to those qualities associated with the gentlemanly pursuit of learning—such as the style of life and the broad network of friends—which only distantly concern morality. Moreover, in acknowledging that the son who did not believe in learning was diligent and filial, Feng unwittingly dissociated morality from learning and justified learning as a key to worldly success.[56]

That "learned discussions" were losing significance became apparent in several other ways. First, Feng defined many of his own views by attacking other intellectual positions. He attacked Mo Tzu for advocating universal love and Yang Chu for promoting self-centeredness. He attacked legalistic thinkers for favoring considerations of state power and wealth, and he attacked Buddhist adherents for their amoral denial of the existence of good and evil.[57] Such offensiveness would not have been necessary had he been confident of the intrinsic merits of his own position.

Second, the appropriateness of lecturing had become a much debated issue, a topic that often competed with and even overshadowed the discussion of actual philosophical problems. That Feng was so deeply entangled in these debates suggests an inability to base his position on an authority separate from or stronger than that of his critics. Further indicating the weakness of his intellectual stand was his inability to rise above a concern for fame. An antagonist asked:

55. *FSHC*, 14:8a–b.

56. In fact, Feng could not rise entirely above considerations of reputation and morality. Elsewhere he slips inadvertently into using good fortune and disaster as sanctions for moral behavior: "Of those who speak with care and watch their actions, who is not respected, who is not prosperous? Of those who speak carelessly and act recklessly, who does not lose respect, who does not invite disaster?" (*FSHC*, 7:20b).

57. *FSHC*, 1:18b.

"The ancient sages just lectured and left it at that. Why is it necessary to establish a reputation for lecturing?" Feng replied: "Had the ancients just lectured without establishing a reputation . . . then later generations would not know there was such a thing as lecturing. . . . How could that have been their intention?"[58] Just as worldly success rather than morality had verified the value of learning in the essay, "On Diligence and Frugality," so fame rather than the message communicated verified the value of lecturing. Lo Ju-fang had been able to deflect criticisms that he was trying to establish a reputation because he believed he served ideals whose importance and validity existed independently of his efforts. Feng could not disentangle the validity and survival of "learned discussions" from the reputation of the teacher.

Third, as lecturing came under attack, the relationship of scholarship to morality demanded reevaluation. The dissociation of learning from morality, apparent in the piece "On Diligence and Frugality" discussed above, is evident in another essay Feng wrote. There Feng argued that brilliance and literary effort would enhance the efforts of those who were already on the way to sagehood, but would only exacerbate the errors of those who had gone astray.[59] How learning and morality were related had become an issue.

Fourth, Feng often viewed philosophical differences dispassionately as objects for scholarly inquiry. In compiling two surveys of great thinkers (*Kuan-hsüeh pien* and *Yüan-ju k'ao-lüeh*), Feng felt no compulsion to synthesize past scholarship, to iron out the differences among the scholars, or even to pass judgments on their strengths and weaknesses. In the preface to *Kuan-hsüeh pien*, he simply stated that although the scholars varied in many respects, they were alike in being true to the spirit of Confucius. His outlook thus left room for the display of a wide variety of opinions.[60]

It is not accidental that such compendia first appeared in the late Ming when scholars felt some distance from, or had perspective on, thought as an object of study.[61] Following

58. *FSHC*, 6:5b. 59. *FSHC*, 8:7b–8a. 60. *FSHC*, p. 2a.

61. For a brief summary of both the rise of evidential studies and sources on the subject, see chapter 1 above.

this trend during the next dynasty, Huang Tsung-hsi organized his *Record of Ming Philosophers* by taking into consideration social affiliations and geographical contexts—in other words, criteria other than the degree of philosophical correctness—to impose order upon the confusing array of ideas.[62]

Further indicating Feng's objective view of knowledge was his consciousness that learning was something in which one believed or had faith (*hsin*). The father of the unfortunate son in Feng's essay, "On Diligence and Frugality," did not "believe in learning."[63] Elsewhere Feng more fully declared: "In learned discussions, it is most important to open up the way for belief. Now, consider someone who does not believe in learning; will speaking to him about [such matters as] the mind and body, character and fate, have an effect? Therefore, only after opening up the way for belief will one be able to speak [effectively]."[64] Ideas take hold as much because a place awaits them as because of their intrinsic merit. Thus in the continuation to this passage, Feng uneasily acknowledged that non-Confucian ideas could also slip in as the objects of faith: "After opening up the way for trust, one must guard against superstitious beliefs. . . . If Buddhism and Taoism get mixed in, then I am afraid that the greater [the capacity for] belief, the further away will one be [from Confucianism]."[65] Feng's definition of learning in terms of the place it filled—as object of belief—not only suggests a lack of confidence in the inherent truth of any one doctrine, but also throws light on his willingness to treat numerous interpretations of Confucianism interchangeably in his compendia.

So shaky was the foundation for Feng's moral values that he felt threatened by the values of wealth and power associated with the practical goals of the state. Consequently Feng frequently criticized the ancient legalistic thinkers Han Fei Tzu and Kuan Chung,[66] and the Sung dynasty statesman,

62. Other such biographical compendia include: Chou Ju-teng, *Sheng-hsüeh tsung-chuan* (*DMB*, p. 273); Wei I-ao, *Pei-hsüeh pien* (published, 1646), (*ECCP*, p. 672); T'ang Pin, *Lo hsüeh pien* (*ECCP*, p. 710); and Sun Ch'i-feng, *Chung-chou jen-wu k'ao* (*ECCP*, p. 672).

63. *FSHC*, 14:8a–9a.

64. *FSHC*, 13:25a.

65. *FSHC*, 13:25a–b.

66. *FSHC*, 7:2a.

Wang An-shih, who he believed resembled the legalistic minister Li Ssu (d. 208 B.C.).[67] Feng allowed that Wang had had the welfare of the state at heart, but Feng argued that Wang's neglect of the values of "filiality, brotherly love, humaneness, and righteousness" had ultimately led to disaster.[68] Then, pitting "trust," or "belief," against the legalistic goals of productive agriculture and a strong military defense, Feng in line with a statement by Confucius protested: "Belief is the great warp of the state. Adequate food, adequate military defense and belief of the people—none of these three should be lacking." If one cannot have all of them, Feng would rather do without military defense and food.[69]

Feng tenaciously maintained his faith in learning; but his weak and evasive defenses of learned discussions indicate how far the basis for that faith had deteriorated. Feng sensed that a belief in something was essential to the quality of human existence; but he had difficulty in defining the content of learning apart from political and social realities. Feng criticized the legalistic tendencies in Hsün Tzu and Wang An-shih—in particular, their emphasis on state wealth and power over learning. But Feng also acknowledged that prosperity could verify the value of learning. Feng felt touchy about the encroachment of the state on the moral leadership of scholar-officials. At the same time, he, like many legalistic thinkers, distrusted human nature. He believed that everyone had faults and that strict rules for the academies were therefore necessary. To preserve his sanctuary, the academies, Feng accepted that "learned discussions" should be circumscribed and that political topics should by all means be avoided. Feng had become captive of the very forms against which he was fighting.

The narrowing of Feng's vision sets in relief the thought of several of his contemporaries. Ku Hsien-ch'eng, whom Feng had met in 1582[70] and some of whose writings Feng admired

67. *FSHC*, 3:35b, 41a, and 7:26b.

68. *FSHC*, 3:41a–b. Feng also wrote an essay criticizing Hsün Tzu (*FSHC*, 14:15b–18a).

69. *FSHC*, 7:11a. See also 7:16a and 10:10b. In his comment on food, defense, and belief, Feng follows a statement by Confucius, *Analects*, in Legge, *Chinese Classics*, 1:254.

70. *Ku Tuan-wen kung nien-p'u*, 2:11a.

around 1612, found a way to break out of the boundaries that had trapped Feng.[71] Like Feng, Ku was disturbed that learned discussions had become vapid and pointlessly contentious; like Feng, Ku opposed the amoral tendencies in the learning of his day. But unlike Feng, who had instructed academies not to dabble in politics, Ku, who revived the famous Tung-lin Academy in 1604, found a justification for political involvement: an unusually severe moral crisis necessitated learned discussions through which the associates could save the world (*chiu-shih*).

Through a crisis mentality, one could draw strength from personal experiences without being limited by narrowness—as Yang Tung-ming had been. And through a crisis mentality, one could also build upon laws and regulations without becoming the captive of restrictiveness—as Feng had been. The implications of a crisis mentality will be illuminated by the writings of Lü K'un, who Feng believed would startle to their senses even those who "did not believe in learning." On reading Lü's *Groaning Words*, Feng felt he had obtained "a secret prescription;" more specifically, Feng admired Lü for his talent in "managing the world," or "statecraft" (*ching-shih*).[72] The following chapters will explore the relationship of this talent to a crisis mentality.

71. *FSHC*, 15:34a. In this letter, Feng notes that he had received and found very germane Ku Hsien-ch'eng's *Hsiao-hsin-chai cha-chi*.
72. *FSHC*, 13:12b–13b.

II

Lü K'un: New Avenues to Sagehood

5

As Doctor to Society

What scholar-officials did and what they thought worth writing about were not necessarily the same. Chu Hsi, Wang Yang-ming, and Lo Ju-fang energetically undertook such tasks as the organization of local granaries, *pao-chia*, and *hsiang-yüeh*. Wang and Lo even waged military campaigns. These men were active and effective administrators, but they devoted only a small portion of their writings to administrative plans.

A context for Lü K'un's statecraft

By the sixteenth century numerous scholar-officials filled page after page with meticulous calculations on such problems as financing the reconstruction of city walls, mobilizing labor for dike repairs, and allocating resources for post stations. The military strategist Ch'i Chi-kuang spelled out precisely how soldiers should be recruited, troops maneuvered, and even the type of banners to be used.[1] Hsü Kuang-ch'i (1562–1633) addressed at great length two areas that would strengthen the state. In his memorials he carefully itemized programs for military defense, and in his famous treatise on agriculture (*Nung-cheng ch'üan-shu*), he collected and evaluated information on fertilizers, plants and handicraft techniques.[2] Hsü Fu-yüan (1535–1604),[3] Ch'en Lung-cheng

1. See the biography of Ch'i Chi-kuang by J. F. Millinger and Chaoying Fang in *DMB*, pp. 220–24. See also James Ferguson Millinger, "Ch'i Chi-kuang: Chinese Military Official." Ch'i's two handbooks on training troops are *Chi-hsiao hsin-shu* and *Lien-ping shih-chi*.

2. Biography of Hsü by J. C. Yang in *ECCP*, pp. 316–19; and Lo Kuang,

(1585–1645),[4] and Ch'i Piao-chia (1602–45)[5] piled up detail upon detail on how grain should be stored and distributed for famine relief programs, on what kind of placards should be used for registering the participants in *pao-chia*, and on how medicine should be dispensed. The minutiae of practical matters thus loomed large in late Ming writings, always informed by, but often pushing to the side any discussion of moral concerns.

The impulse to use written records to routinize local administration had by the end of the dynasty become widespread and culminated in the compilation in 1638 of *Huang-Ming ching-shih wen-pien* [Writings on Statecraft of the Illustrious Ming Dynasty].[6] This impressively large work organized memorials and other administrative writings of over four hundred authors into 508 *chüan*. By collecting numerous materials on practical administration, the editors of this work legitimized and celebrated the tradition of statecraft.

Antecedents for Ming statecraft can be found in the Sung dynasty. Fan Chung-yen, Wang An-shih, Ch'en Liang (1143–94), and Yeh Shih (1150–1223)[7] wrote memorials to their emperors calling for institutional reforms. Some, like Ch'en Liang, abstracted general principles about institutions from past precedents. Others, mostly minor officials, wrote hand-

---

Hsü Kuang-ch'i chuan. For Hsü's memorials on military affairs, see *Hsü Kuang-ch'i chi, chüan* 3 and 4.

3. See, for example, the detailed instructions on the local administration of Fukien by Hsü Fu-yüan, *Ching-ho t'ang chi, chüan* 7 and 8.

4. Biography of Ch'en Lung-cheng by Julia Ching in *DMB*, pp. 174–76. Ch'en's collected works, *Chi-t'ing ch'üan-shu* and *Chi-t'ing wai-shu*, include numerous pieces on famine relief, grain equalization, *pao-chia*, and wall defense.

5. See the biography of Ch'i by Earl Swisher in *ECCP*, p. 126. For Ch'i's writings on famine relief, see *Ch'i Piao-chia chi, chüan* 5–6.

6. Ch'en Tzu-lung, Hsü Fu-yüan, and Sung Cheng-pi, eds., *Huang-Ming ching-shih wen-pien*, 30 vols. Hsü, the co-editor of this work, is not to be confused with the author of *Ching-ho t'ang-chi*, who was Feng Ts'ung-wu's teacher. Another noteworthy collection of writings on statecraft from this period is: Feng Ying-ching, *Huang-Ming shih-yung pien*.

7. For Fan Chung-yen, see Denis Twitchett, "The Fan Clan's Charitable Estate, 1050–1760." For Wang An-shih, see H. R. Williamson, *Wang An Shih: A Chinese Statesman and Educationalist of the Sung Dynasty*. For Ch'en Liang, see Hou Wai-lu, *Chung-kuo ssu-hsiang t'ung-shih*, vol. 4:2, pp. 692–739. For Yeh Shih, see ibid., pp. 740–82, and Winston Wan Lo, *The Life and Thought of Yeh Shih*.

books on local administration.[8] But an obstacle prevented the writing of statecraft from truly flourishing. The pursuit of statecraft implies an appreciation that institutions, laws, and regulations, no less than moral leadership, played a vital role in good government. However, the very preoccupation with rules and regulations that characterizes statecraft threatened the official's self-image as moral leader. As one bibliographer commented on a Sung dynasty handbook, those who gave priority to rules over education were nothing but "common clerks."[9]

This bias against laws in favor of moral suasion discouraged many officials from taking pride in or writing down administrative plans. Yeh Shih, who was deeply concerned with practical matters, vehemently attacked laws as encouraging amoral behavior.[10] His bias deterred him from writing detailed regulations for practical matters. In a ten-point program, Fan Chung-yen prefaced his discussion of land-equalization and local militia with a call for eradicating favoritism and for selecting worthy men by reforming the examination system. Writers of Sung handbooks likewise stressed the selection of good administrators as the key to successful local government. With such a bias, they were inclined to lavish greatest care, not on intricate outlines of institutional arrangements, but on moral exhortations. Those who like Wang An-shih did unabashedly call for legal and institutional reforms were promptly criticized most severely for their harsh laws. Whatever the actual reasons for grievances against Wang may have been, it is clear that the distrust of laws was so strong as to provide his opponents with a powerful weapon. Some change in outlook was necessary if the tools of statecraft were to win respectability.

During the Ming, population growth pressed officials to use more efficiently the bureaucracy, which had remained constant, or—as the Wan-li emperor refused to assign new

8. See, for example, excerpts from Lü Tsu-chien, "Kuan chen," in Ch'en Hung-mou, ed., *Ts'ung-cheng i-kuei*, 1:1a–5a. Nothing is known of Li Yüan-pi, the author of *Tso-i tzu-chen*; and the authorship of *Chou-hsien t'i-kang* remains anonymous.

9. Peter Bol, "The *Tso-i tzu-chen*: A Twelfth Century Guide for Sub-prefects," p. 33.

10. Lo, *Life and Thought of Yeh Shih*, pp. 130–31.

officials to vacant posts—even diminished in size. Without question, the mounting sense of crisis, intensified by both the encroachment of Mongols and Manchus on the northern borders and the utter despair of accomplishing anything through court politics, contributed to the growing interest in statecraft. To standardize procedures and encourage efficiency, Ming officials sponsored the compilation of numerous handbooks. Recognizing that frequent administrative changes were disruptive and harmful, Lü and several other censors, including Sun P'ei-yang and Liu Tung-hsing, jointly published in 1594 *Hsün-fang tsung-yüeh* [A General Compact for Regional Inspectors] whose crowded columns in small print suggest a concern for economy. In the preface to that work, the censors explain that because uniformity was essential in establishing laws, they wished to standardize procedures.[11]

As Lü assumed various administrative posts in Shantung and Shansi, he further issued handbooks addressing many specific social problems. These were jointly published in 1598 as *Shih-cheng lu* [Records of Practical Government]. At that time, Lü's *Records* included seven broad chapters on: (1) the duties of provincial officials (*Ming chih*) with a preface written in 1592; (2) essentials for the people (*Min wu*); (3) supporting and instructing the people (*Yang min*); (4) governing the people (*Chih min*); (5) local sub-official personnel (*Hsiang-chia yüeh*); (6) surveillance officials (*Feng-hsien yüeh*); (7) prisons (*Yü-cheng*); and three chapters, no longer extant, on the duties of the governors. Each chapter is rich in specific information on such topics as using fertilizer, planting trees, constructing granaries, running welfare homes, dispensing medical care, and organizing the post stations, *hsiang-yüeh*, and *pao-chia*.

The frequent republication of this work testifies to its importance. Among the numerous editions were one, under the title *Chü-kuan pi-yao* [Essentials for Officials], with a pref-

11. Sun P'ei-yang, Liu Tung-hsing, and Lü K'un, eds., *Hsün-fang ts'ung-yüeh*, pp. 1a–b. Hsü Kuang-ch'i notes that the task of land equalization was especially urgent in Shensi, Shansi, Pei Chih-li and Honan; and that Sun P'ei yang had requested that officials be examined on practical government that would protect the people (*Nung-cheng ch'üan-shu*, 3:24b).

ace by Tsou Yüan-piao; one printed in 1797; another contained in *Lü-tzu i-shu* [Lü's Transmitted Works], published in 1827; and one edition which was commissioned in 1834 by the famous opponent to the British import of opium, Lin Tse-hsü.[12]

Records of Practical Government won much praise from later generations. Ch'en Hung-mou, who reprinted a section in his *Five Types of Transmitted Guidelines,* appreciated that Lü was exceptionally penetrating and that every word, every phrase, rang true.[13] In general, Lü's admirers praised him for his practical outlook and for his trenchant, concise style.[14] They marvelled that the policies Lü had outlined in *Records of Practical Government* could actually be put into practice,[15] and that his writings were so real that one could see his heart through his writings.[16]

Because *Records of Practical Government* came to occupy an important place in the statecraft tradition, Lü K'un's comments on his society and his own self-analysis both offer clues to the efflorescence of Ming statecraft.

Lü had complained that the people were "difficult to lead,"[17] and that "although a yamen had been established for every affair and officials had been placed in every yamen, governmental matters were daily deteriorating and the livelihood of the people worsening."[18] Disastrous famines in 1581–82 prompted Lü's plans for soup kitchens.[19] An increase in vagabondage aroused his concern that everyone have an occupation. The rampant spread of banditry brought forth his careful organization of mutual surveillance.[20] To this

12. *Shih-cheng lu chieh-ch'ao,* edited by Lin Tse-hsü, is available at the Toyō Bunka Library in Tokyo. *Chü-kuan pi-yao* (Wan-li ed.) is available at the Sonkeikaku Bunko, Tokyo. Chang Shen-yen (1577–1645) refers to Lü's *Pao-min shih-cheng,* which must have been a section of *SCL* (*Tzu-shui chai wen-ch'ao,* 3:3b).

13. Ch'en Hung-mou, commentary on the *Ming-chih* section of *SCL, Ts'ung-cheng i-kuei,* 1:35a.

14. Ch'eng Tsu-lo, "Preface" of 1822, in *Lü tzu i-shu.*

15. "Memorial" of 1826, in *Lü tzu i-shu,* p. 1b.

16. A-le-ch'ing-a, "Preface," *Lü tzu i-shu,* p. 1b.

17. *SCL,* 2:2a.

18. *SCL,* 1:1a.

19. For Lü's graphic description of the famines of 1581–82, see *SCL,* 2:16b–18b; for his instructions for running the soup kitchens, see *SCL,* 2:41b–47a.

20. *SCL, chüan* 5.

extent Lü's records may be understood as a response to the social and administrative problems of his time.

At the same time, a comparison between Hai Jui and Lü K'un will show that Lü's approach to administrative matters represents a significant reorientation that made the pursuit of statecraft more acceptable to those officials who also valued themselves as Confucian scholars. Lü had found ways to bridge the gap between office and learning, or between the preoccupation with regulations (which characterized the administrator) and the concern for moral leadership (which distinguished the scholar-official from the mere functionary). In particular, this chapter will argue that Lü's skepticism about claims to knowledge, prompted by the incessant wrangling among his peers, forced him to find an objective framework through which the official could work. Lü redefined the official as a doctor who could take pride in exercising his administrative talent as well as his standards of morality.

Chapter 6 will show that how Lü fulfilled his mission as educator was shaped by his cognizance of the world of objective facts. His vernacular didactic works cannot be understood simply in terms of the spread of literacy or the popularization of sagehood. Rather, they were, for Lü, one part of a two-way communication in which moral ideals (associated with the highly educated at the top of society) were exchanged for real experiences (associated with the ignorant at the bottom). Thus in contrast to Lo Ju-fang, who had simply disseminated the ideals of the sages among the common people, Lü also collected information from the people.

Chapter 7 will show that the organizing principles behind Lü's community projects, his concern for the economic self-reliance of the poor, and his preoccupation with crises, owed as much to his acquiescence to the world of objective phenomena as to his commitment to Confucian moral ideals. Chapter 8, on correcting faults, will show that Lü's method of self-cultivation often took as its point of departure, not abstract statements from the classics, but his personal experience of concrete facts. Thus in achieving the scholar-official's goal of establishing coherence between administrative and moral concerns, Lü used in his self-cultivation the vocabulary and conceptualization most suited to practical administration. That objective facts had become the common ground for administration and self-cultivation demonstrates their centrality in Lü's outlook.

Biography of Lü K'un

A composite of Lü's biographies in *Ming shih* [The Official History of the Ming] and *Records of the Ming Philosophers*—where Huang Tsung-hsi obscurely buried Lü in the miscellaneous category of "Various Confucians"—in short, the Lü K'un known to most Chinese, might read as follows:

Lü K'un [*tzu*, Shu-chien; *hao*, Hsin-wu] was born in Ning-ling in Honan in 1536. He passed the provincial examination in 1561 and the metropolitan examination in 1571. After receiving the *chin-shih* degree in 1574, he served as magistrate in Hsiang-yüan, Shansi, where he gained a reputation for outstanding government. From there he began his steady if rarely eventful rise in the civil service; he was transferred in 1575 to the magistracy of Ta-t'ung, Shansi; and subsequently promoted successively to Secretary in the Ministry of Personnel (1578–87); Administrative Vice-Commissioner of Shantung (1587); Surveillance Commissioner of Shansi (1589–91); Administrative Commissioner of Shensi (1591); Grand Coordinator of Shansi (1592–94); Assistant Censor-in-Chief (1592); and Vice-minister of Justice (1594).[21]

21. See the biography of Lü by Chaoying Fang in *DMB*, pp. 1006–11. Much useful biographical information can also be found in the following sources: *MJHA*, 54:5a–b; *Ming shih*, 226:2605–8; Ku Ying-t'ai, *Ming shih chi-shih pen-mo* (Shanghai, 1937), 67:110–22; *Ning-ling hsien chih* (1693), 9:10b–15b; Sun Ch'i-feng, *Chung-chou jen-wu k'ao*, 2:38a–40b; Sun Ch'i-feng, *Li-hsüeh tsung-chuan*, 23:1a–3b; T'ang Pin, *Lo-hsüeh pien*, 4:76a–79b. Yang Tung-ming mentions a chronological biography of Lü, but this seems to be no longer extant (*SCKK*, 9:8b). Useful secondary sources on Lü include: Hou Wai-lu, *Chung-kuo ssu-hsiang t'ung-shih*, 4:940–57; T'ao Hsi-sheng, *Chung-kuo cheng-chih ssu-hsiang shih*, 4:366–70; and Hsiao Kung-ch'üan, *Chung-kuo cheng-chih ssu-hsiang shih*, 4:542–60. Hsiao briefly contrasts Hai, who used government power to root out the evil influences of locally dominant families, with Lü, who reformed local organizations and used the power of the people to enhance the authority of officials. Hsiao concludes that Hai's approach intensified authoritarianism while Lü's more closely resembles [modern concepts of] self-rule (ibid., p. 560, n. 152). I would like to thank Frederick W. Mote for bringing to my attention and

In 1597 Lü submitted to the court a memorial on his fears for society ("Yu-wei shu"). In the memorial he courageously warned the emperor that the people were harboring rebellious thoughts. The harvests for every year from 1582 on, Lü noted, had been poor, while taxes supporting the extravagant expenditures of the emperor remained heavy. The memorial reached the emperor but received no answer, whereupon Lü asked in several consecutive memorials for permission to retire on account of illness.[22]

At that time, the Supervising Secretary, Tai Shih-heng, accused Lü K'un of plotting with the imperial consort Cheng to make her son the heir-apparent. In order to form a liaison with Cheng, the accusation ran, Lü tried to flatter her with a version of his *Kuei-fan t'u-shuo* [Illustrated Regulations for the Women's Quarters] that included a biography of an earlier consort who had been appointed empress. In fact, Cheng had herself added that biography along with eleven others, composed a preface, and commissioned her uncle Cheng Ch'eng-en to reprint it. It eventually also became clear that Tai Shih-heng had been encouraged to impeach Lü by Chang Wei. Chang Wei had formerly been investigated by Sun P'ei-yang but suspected that Lü K'un had issued the instructions for that investigation. The emperor recognized how far-fetched the accusations against Lü were. However the emperor was displeased by the critical memorial Lü had submitted earlier that year and therefore released Lü from service.

Lü retired to his native Ning-ling in Honan, where for over twenty years he studied, taught, and participated in local affairs. He died in 1618 in his eighty-third year and posthumously received the title of Minister of the Board of Punishments.

Several early experiences locked Lü into government service and strengthened his commitment to solving problems, or ironing out tensions, within the acceptable boundaries for

---

translating Hsiao's comment. The above paraphrase follows Mote's translation closely. See also K. Hidaka, "Minmatsu no ichi kanryō Ryo Kon [Lü K'un] no taisei hihan to 'Jishoroku' [Shih-cheng lu];" and Keiyū Hikita, "Ryo Kon [Lü K'un] no denki to 'Shingingo' [Shen-yin yü]." I would like to thank Linda Grove for bringing the Japanese articles to my attention.

22. *CWCWC*, 8:63b.

political behavior. In 1562, shortly after Lü won a *chü-jen* degree, his father summoned both Lü and his older cousin, a recipient of the *chü-jen* in 1549, to the ancestral shrine.[23] There Lü's father explained that whenever he read Fan Chung-yen's "I-t'ien chi" ["Record of Charitable Fields"] he felt ashamed that his own lineage lacked the means to support welfare activities. He warned the two young *chü-jen* not to monopolize wealth and prestige but to look after their lineage. In 1568 both Lü's father and cousin died, whereupon the full responsibility for carrying out his father's unfulfilled ambition to establish charitable fields shifted to Lü's shoulders. His father's warning against monopolizing "wealth and prestige" undoubtedly had deeply affected Lü, for in 1578 Lü used the salaries from his first years in office to buy five hundred *mou* of high-grade land for his lineage.[24]

Two other early experiences—exposure to an innovative magistrate and a regrettable absence from his mother's deathbed—cemented Lü's commitment to selfless government service. Just as Lü was maturing into a scholar, attitudes associated with the prosperity and the spread of popular education in the Kiangnan region began to penetrate Ning-ling. In 1564, three years after Lü received the *chü-jen* degree, Hsiung Ping-yüan, an energetic and innovative magistrate from Feng-ch'eng, Kiangsi, came to govern Ning-ling.[25] Magistrate Hsiung was clearly fired by that sense of mission to "save the world and aid the people" then so contagious. Worried about the neglect of education in Ning-ling, he established schools and engaged teachers. He rebuilt the official granary and successfully solicited charitable contributions of two thousand piculs for a community granary. To ease the burdens on the commoners, he discontinued the costly practice of receiving and sending off officials. To prevent bandits from taking advantage of an isolated swampy road, he ordered that pathways with a drainage system be constructed and urged people to move into the area. He also commissioned the building of a pavilion for commemorating good deeds, a school for *yin-yang* medicine, and a library

23. *CWCWC*, 8:63b. 24. *CWCWC*, 8:64a.
25. Hsiung Ping-yüan, "Preface," *Ning-ling hsien chih*, p. 16a.

holding 630 volumes. In addition to promoting education and welfare, Magistrate Hsiung touched the consciousness of the local inhabitants in another way. To commemorate Ning-ling, he sponsored the compilation of its first gazetteer; and he appointed as editor not one of the town elders, but the young *chü-jen*, Lü K'un.[26] Lü's later activities resembled Hsiung's so closely as to suggest that the flattering recruitment of Lü as editor reinforced Lü's commitment to Hsiung's beneficent policies.

The circumstances under which Lü passed the highest degree also strengthened his commitment to office. When Lü was about to depart for the metropolitan examination in 1571, his mother fell critically ill. Lü refused to leave her bedside, but his mother argued that he had already postponed taking the metropolitan examination for three years to observe the mourning for his father, who had died in 1568. Lü, being truly filial, feigned acquiescence while in fact secretly remaining home to attend diligently to his mother's medicines. One day his mother overheard Lü's voice and scolded him for deceiving her. Recognizing a conflict between his personal career and filial duty, Lü protested: "Working for fame is unimportant. You are still ill; how can I bear to go?" Lü's mother in response argued that she would like to see him earn the *chin-shih* degree before she died. Lü hastened to the capital to take the examination and returned home a mere thirty days later only to discover that during his short absence his mother had died. He grieved for many days. His biographer therefore could justifiably conclude, "It is evident that K'un was not in a hurry to achieve fame [and did not] put his mother second." But if the biographer felt the need thus to come to Lü's defense, can we imagine that Lü easily lived down his remorse?[27]

Having paid such a high price for passing the examinations, Lü could not easily abandon officialdom. Where others sought tranquility in Taoism or Buddhism,[28] or escaped

26. *Ning-ling hsien chih*, 7:5a–6b.
27. Ibid., 9:11a–b. See also *CWCWC*, 8:62b–63a.
28. See, for example, Rodney Leon Taylor, *The Cultivation of Sagehood as a Religious Goal in Neo-Confucianism: A Study of Selected Writings of Kao P'an-lung*.

to the private academies, Lü, committed to action, believed that one's skill in self-vigilance, for example, must be tested by dealing with the imperial court. Without such tests, even lengthy discussions of the concept would be meaningless, he declared.[29] At the same time, from the year he passed the metropolitan examination—the same year his mother died—Lü had to prove that he did not care for personal fame. Throughout his life he struggled to check his tendency to be selfish and proud.[30] As Lü acknowledged in a piece to be discussed later, the painful experience of his mother's death moved him to be unusually charitable and compassionate.[31]

Yang and Feng did most of their writing while in retirement; upon release from office they found the time, freedom, and energy to express themselves. But the narrow horizons of their writings suggest retreat—into the affairs of a single hometown, or into the almost bankrupt intellectual life of the academies. Lü wrote most of his significant works—*Groaning Words, Records of Practical Government*, and *Illustrated Regulations for the Women's Quarters*—while in office. That he could write so much as an official points to his creative imagination in rising above the constraints of office. By substituting didactic works for "learned discussions," for example, Lü found the permissible avenues for fulfilling his mission as educator. No wonder the next dynasty read Lü's writings far more widely than those by Yang and Feng. Lü successfully solved problems that had hampered his two friends and thus served future officials better.

The appeal of statecraft

Those who lost faith in the basic goodness of man turned from moral suasion to institutional restraints in order to insure a harmonious society. By carefully defining the structures according to which society should be organized, one could both check greed and selfishness and compensate for

29. *SYY*, 2:347.
30. See the revealing epitaph Lü wrote for himself (*CWCWC*, 9:47b–48a; 9:50a–b).
31. *CWCWC*, 7:65a–67a, especially 65b.

inadequate moral leadership. Thus Hsün Tzu, who had believed that men were basically bad, stressed the importance of rituals and laws controlling social behavior;[32] Wang An-shih, who maintained that average men predominated, and Hai Jui, who distrusted his peers, relied heavily on laws;[33] and Feng Ts'ung-wu, who distrusted those attending "learned discussions," believed that strict regulations for the academies were necessary. A concern for institutional controls thus often accompanied pessimism about human nature.

In theory, Lü K'un knew that "one thousand good people are worth less than one worthy local official."[34] To this extent he tenaciously held to the ideal of moral leadership. In reality, Lü recognized that "by and large eight or nine out of every ten people are average."[35] Surveying how extensive the bureaucratic and subbureaucratic personnel were, Lü reasoned that only a small percentage could actually be virtuous:

> When official duties are conferred on scholars selected through the examinations and when men are honored by rank and salary, how many of them swear to remain incorrupt? And how many of these undertake their duties honestly? Today not less than two to three hundred chiefs and deputies of lecture units (*yüeh*) are established in each hsien and *chou*. If one wished that each person behaved altogether unselfishly like a gentleman and that each abided by the rules of the magistrate without regard for their [private] grievances, one would be [expecting] commoners to be more worthy than the gentry. Is this possible? Today, all the chiefs, the deputies, and the lecturers on the histories are swindlers, [yet] the local authorities allow them to be recommended. The good and fearful hide away in obscure places while the braggarts and reckless rush forward to compete for advancement.[36]

32. Wing-tsit Chan, *A Source Book in Chinese Philosophy*, p. 129.
33. See the section on Hai Jui in chapter 2.
34. *SCL*, 5:13b. 35. *SYY*, 5:770. 36. *SCL*, 3:1a–b.

To maintain order where the mediocre prevailed, Lü standardized procedures, carefully outlined duties, and clarified laws. Doubting that officials and clerks would exercise good judgment, Lü strove to regulate and standardize activities by writing up "contracts" (*yüeh*)—which were verbal agreements without legal sanctions—for those in his charge. Rather than concentrate on either the methods of selecting worthies or moral reform, Lü compensated for inadequate moral leadership by carefully allocating duties among his underlings. To clarify the division of responsibilities, Lü wrote the section on "Illuminating the Official Duties":

> The court establishes officials and divides the duties, and the yamen attaches a title to each command. The hundred officials think of their duties [because] they care for their titles; and they fulfill their allotted responsibilities. [If] everyone carried out what is apportioned to him, then the world would be trouble-free.[37]

Lü then called upon his fellow officials to consider first whether they had fulfilled their duties satisfactorily and only secondly whether they had remained incorrupt.[38] Lü's bias was apparent to his eighteenth-century admirer, Ch'en Hung-mou, who commented that Lü believed that "officials are established according to duties (*shih*) and that duties await the management of officials."[39]

Others like Lü's little known contemporary, Fu Mei, shared the view that the allocation of duties was the basis for successful government. In his essay on three types of functionaries (*li*), Fu Mei claimed that only fifty or sixty per cent of those who follow documents (*wen*) will succeed; that only seventy or eighty per cent of those who follow others (*jen*) will succeed; but that a full one hundred per cent of those who follow duties (*shih*) will succeed.[40]

37. *SCL*, 1:1a.
38. *SCL*, 1:1a.
39. Ch'en Hung-mou, *Ts'ung-cheng i-kuei*, 1:34b.
40. Fu Mei, "Hsün-fang san ts'e," in *Ts'ung-cheng i-kuei*, 2:6b–7b. Fu Mei, from Hsing-t'ai (Chih-li), took office in 1607 after earning the *chü-jen*

Kao P'an-lung (1562–1626), who was acquainted with several of Lü's friends, tried, like Lü, to retain the ideal that moral example should move the people to goodness. "If [the officials of] the *chou* and hsien are virtuous," Kao argued, "then the people will be at peace; if [the officials] are not virtuous, then the people will not be at peace." At the same time Kao, like Lü, questioned whether the ideal could be realized. Given that "there are about 221 *chou* and 1166 hsien," Kao asked, "how can one exclusively employ worthies?"[41] Aware that the "average man" dominated the bureaucracy, Kao tried to eliminate the problem of the inevitably uneven moral character of the bureaucracy by supplementing moral education with verbal agreements, or "contracts" (*yüeh*):

> Those who govern select the worthy and talented, do away with the thieves of the people, and contract with the average man. Most men in the world are average. If one contracts with them by using laws, none will fail to be worthy. The prefects contract with the *chou* and hsien; the circuit officials contract with the *fu*, *chou*, and hsien; and the governors contract with them all. There will be none who are not brought under contract so that everyone will abide by the laws, just as peasants who have boundaries [between their fields] do not think of trespassing. Then the world will be [well] governed.[42]

Thus in Kao P'an-lung, too, the concern for laws and for the careful delineation of boundaries accompanied a recognition that mediocre men prevailed.

Hai Jui and Lü K'un shared certain character traits that account for the ease with which they turned to legal and institutional restraints. Both distrusted human relations, and both had internalized an authority independently of the support of friends or the guidance of teachers. Early in his career, Lü K'un had tried unsuccessfully to seek comfort in

degree. He served in Teng-feng, Honan (*Teng-feng hsien chih* [1696], 6:5b). See also, *Ming shih*, 241:2747–48.

41. Kao P'an-lung, *Kao tzu i-shu*, 7:27b. This memorial was drafted but not submitted. Reprinted in *Ts'ung-cheng i-kuei*, 2:1a–6b.

42. Kao, *Kao tzu i-shu*, 7:27b–28a.

numbers. In a letter to Feng Ts'ung-wu's friend, Tsou Yüan-piao, Lü recalled how as magistrate of Hsiang-yüan, he "had dreaded the difficulty of sustaining the Way of the world and [had sensed] how easily one fails in striving forward alone." Therefore he had made a pact with his companions and fellow officials. But, Lü continued, such camaraderie proved unacceptable: "Those who [disregarding the facts] chime in with and conform to the multitude are many; those who, true to their own hearts, dispute difficult points are few, with the result that people get carried away with their egotistical prejudices."[43] Lü so doubted the worth—or feared the implications—of such associations that he did not dare sign the pact and was later deeply embarrassed to learn that Keng Ting-hsiang had seen it. Nor did he wish the written agreement to circulate. "I thought," Lü explained, "that a great official should identify men of talent by listening to their words and by observing their actions; and that judging a person's worth prematurely on the basis of idle words was inappropriate. I feared that false people thenceforth would attach value to words and thus mar the clarity [with which] older [officials] know men."[44] Lü was so wary about joining groups that he suggested that men should remain intellectually isolated. One should strengthen the self not by banding together with others but by establishing with Heaven "an agreement [or bond] of which one alone is aware" (*tu-chih chih ch'i*):

> Extending one's [sphere of] dependence is inferior to selecting what one depends on. And selecting what one depends on is inferior to being independent. Those who are independent depend on Heaven and . . . enjoy a harmony of which they alone are aware. And although they stand alone (*tu*) in the world, they are not solitary (*ku*). A man who refuses to budge [even] when many [try to] overthrow and destroy him—that is called "being a man."[45]

43. *CWCWC*, 4:49b–50a.
44. *CWCWC*, 4:50a.
45. *SYY*, 2:198. *Tu* means "unattended," "single-handed," or "independent." *Ku* originally meant "orphaned."

Lü's independent spirit and willing isolation from peer support reflects his personality. Even as a young boy, Lü "did not like to play with other children;"[46] and in contrast to Lo Ju-fang, who throughout his life had deeply respected authority figures, Lü never acknowledged the influence of his teachers. Unsociable by temperament, Lü boldly insisted, "I am just a 'me.'"[47] At the same time, Lü's declaration of independence found fertile ground in his social and intellectual environment, which had brought other self-contained, masterless men into full view: Ku Yen-wu and Fang I-chih, to name only two.[48]

Also like Hai Jui, who had relied on the law to withstand pressures from those who were wealthy and powerful, Lü owed his own rise in part to legal sanctions. Early in his career when serving as magistrate in Ta-t'ung, Lü resisted the request of the powerful official, Wang Chia-p'ing, that Lü use his influence to overturn a case indicting Wang's nephew.

More important than the similarities in character that led Hai and Lü to appropriate legalistic structures are the contrasts that illuminate why Lü's use of institutions and laws proved more attractive to scholars. Unlike Hai Jui, Lü handled personal relations sensitively and tactfully. Thus even the rebuffed Wang Chia-p'ing came to respect Lü for his probity. When Wang rose to the Ministry of Personnel, he recommended Lü's promotion, enthusiastically declaring, "No one in the world can match [Lü K'un], the magistrate of Ta-t'ung, for refusing requests."[49]

Diplomatic and astute, Lü weathered political storms unharmed. When a treacherous attempt was made to implicate Lü for allegedly interfering in the heir-apparent case, Lü cleared his name of the far-fetched accusations and sagaciously withdrew from office. However, Lü was no time-server. During a politically tumultuous period he unhesita-

46. According to the biography of Lü by T'ang Pin, *Lo hsüeh pien,* cited in *SYY,* p. 9.

47. *SYY,* 2:220.

48. See the comment by Willard Peterson on the "masterless men" of the early seventeenth century (*Bitter Gourd,* p. 12).

49. *MJHA,* 54:5a. For a fuller account, see *Ning-ling hsien chih,* 9:12b.

tingly and forcefully memorialized his views concerning the excessive burdens imposed on the impoverished people.[50] Lü was a man of integrity with a strong moral sense, who carefully sought a path between the dictates of his conscience and the demands of a corrupt and unpredictable government. His avoidance of conflicts suggests not weakness but ingenuity and tact.

Hai Jui had outlined regulations in order to realize ostensibly Confucian values, but as an angry lone defender of justice, he frequently clashed with his peers. In his arrogance, Hai had lost the true spirit of Confucianism. Even his defense of the people was expressed as much in anger against the wealthy as out of sincere compassion for the people.

In contrast to the brashness of Hai Jui, Lü worked cautiously within the conventional boundaries and was sensitive and talented enough to find the acceptable means of responding to the extremes of his time. Hai Jui fiercely opposed expedient measures; Lü condoned those who bent rules of conduct to cope with emergencies.[51]

Both Hai and Lü blamed social discord on people's desire for profit. Pessimistic about human nature, they alike sought a solution in institutions and laws. But Lü differed from Hai in one fundamental respect. Lü had learned from the experience of Hai's generation that disputes were unproductive, and was perhaps even aware that the strongly opinionated Hai had alienated many. Therefore, Lü blamed contention

50. For Lü's famous memorial, "Yu-wei shu," see *CWCWC*, 1:5a–20b. A condensation is included in his biography in *Ming shih*, 226:2605–6; the memorial is written in a forceful and direct style but is long and covers numerous points. Lü warns, for example, that there had been droughts every year since 1582 (*CWCWC*, 1:5a); that military defense had deteriorated (1:8a–b); and that the mining taxes were a hardship on the people (1:10b). The memorial also displays Lü's analytical powers when, for example, Lü outlined four types of rebellious people: those who were driven to rebellion in utter desperation; those who were unemployed and joined bands to find opportunities to plunder and rape; those members of such heterodox sects as the White Lotus who felt such strong bonds of kinship that they quickly responded to a call to arms; and those who seditiously harbored political ambitions (*CWCWC*, 1:6a–b).

51. See, for example, Lü K'un, *Kuei-fan t'u-shuo*, 3:81b. For a discussion of Lü's call for flexibility in emergencies, see Handlin, "Lü K'un's New Audience: The Influence of Women's Literacy on Sixteenth-Century Thought," pp. 19–22.

among his peers more than their greed for the social disharmony. Speaking in one breath of profit and opinions, Lü wrote: "Struggles over profit arise from each person having desires; struggles over words arise from each person having opinions."[52]

Some scholars had always tried to remain aloof from the corrupting influences of office. Many had been reluctant to take office for fear of tarnishing their integrity. To dissuade a disciple from taking an examination, for example, one Sung scholar related the following experience: "Once I bought a servant and wanted to give her an examination. Her mother became angry and would not permit it. She said, 'My daughter is not something to be examined.' Now you seek to become a teacher by taking an examination. You will surely be ridiculed by this old woman."[53] It was in this spirit of aloofness and of confidence in his own worth that Hai Jui had refused to bow before the visiting education officials. In contrast, Lü, who was surrounded by bickering academies and factional disputes, lost sight of questions of servility, or submission, and focused instead on competition among his own peers as the main source of their debasement.[54]

Lü repeatedly warned against "considering the self right and others wrong."[55] He scorned those scholars who "from the Ch'in and Han [dynasties] on have fought to the death in disputing 'right and wrong.'"[56] He observed that debaters never resolved their conflicts but only grew more obstinate as they waged their battles. To illustrate how "considering the self right and others wrong" only crystallized antagonisms, Lü used the example of a chaste woman entering a motley immoral crowd: "If she just subtly praises others for their purity, everyone will be ashamed. If she proclaims her own purity, then who would want to give in? If she mocks others as disreputable, everyone will clench his teeth, point to the woman [saying], 'You dirt! You dirt!' and seek to de-

52. *SYY*, 3:443.
53. Cited in Chu Hsi and Lü Tsu-ch'ien, *Reflections on Things at Hand*, p. 196.
54. For a discussion of this problem, see Wakeman, "The Price of Autonomy," pp. 38–39. See also David S. Nivison, "Protest Against Conventions and Conventions of Protest," pp. 177–201.
55. *SYY*, 3:377. 56. *SYY*, 2:315.

stroy her."[57] Lü appreciated that silence could often be more powerful than speech.

Where Hai Jui was arrogant and outspoken, Lü humbly knew when to retreat into silence. He had witnessed how "considering the self right and others wrong" had created social discord and how Hai Jui's assertiveness had generated only rancor. In addition, Lü warned against speaking precipitously. "Nine out of every ten times," he observed, "words are responsible for disastrous deaths."[58] Both Hai and Lü were loners by nature, but where Hai demonstrated his independence by singlehandedly promoting his cause, Lü expressed his by spurning all claims to knowledge. He criticized joining groups specifically because they fostered "egotistical prejudices" and "idle words."[59]

While Lo Ju-fang and Feng Ts'ung-wu found their views gratifyingly confirmed by their large followings, Lü regarded the petty squabbles among the academicians with disdain. In an early seventeenth-century letter to Ku Hsien-ch'eng, Lü condoned the activities of the Tung-lin movement but criticized the frivolity and aimlessness of philosophical discussions. Even a temple setting would not, he scornfully asserted, elevate the participants to anything more than inept scholars.[60]

Lü observed that opinions could be so divisive as to prevent the smooth accomplishment of tasks. He took for granted that "when a gentleman and a petty man share duties, [the project] will certainly fail;" but then added: "Even when two gentlemen share duties, [the project] will not necessarily succeed. Why? [Because] their opinions are different."[61] Aware that egotistical opinions only led to divisiveness and destruction, Lü had two alternatives. On the one hand, he could look for a collective opinion. Thus he commented that when "five people—one who is humane, one who is righteous, one who is proper, one who is wise, and one who is trusting—share one task," the task will fail "if each of the five holds onto his opinion" but will succeed "if the five aid one another."[62] Similarly divorcing principles from individual

57. *SYY*, 2:220. 58. Lü, *Kuei-fan t'u-shuo*, 4:32b.
59. *CWCWC*, 4:50a.
60. *CWCWC*, 9:47b–48a. 61. *SYY*, 3:377. 62. *SYY*, 3:377.

leaders, Lü maintained: "One need not select men; just select the strong points of a hundred men gathered together in a market town crowd. Everyone must have [at least] one opinion; by bringing together the opinions of a hundred men, one can devise a great plan."[63]

On the other hand, Lü appreciated that opinions must be decided dictatorially if critical goals are to be accomplished. Thus, in concluding the passage on how tasks shared by opinionated men are bound to fail, Lü wrote: "In the military, the soldiers offer plans; the military aides plot policies; and the commanding general makes the decision. [Who] dares to contend [on the basis of his] opinion?"[64] In this authoritarian vein, Lü, in an essay on profit and power to be discussed later, explained that power, which "must be monopolized by one man," should not be revealed to others; if one "speaks of power, then it cannot be monopolized."[65]

Whether Lü looked for a collective opinion or an authoritative goal-oriented decision, the result was the same: he had discouraged the individual gentleman from asserting his opinion. Lü went so far as to maintain that "the sage does not have his own view,"[66] and at times Lü even celebrated silence. "The marvel of the silent bond [or meditation]," Lü stated, "is that one passes over the Six Classics and the thousand sages to discourse directly with Heaven. Furthermore one need not exchange one word with Heaven but need only respond, [whereby] the two minds [of Heaven and self] become one."[67]

Hai Jui's sage was bold, even abrasive. Lü's sage was often silent, apprehensive, and self-watchful. Appearing to command no political power or overt moral leadership, Lü's sage was merely responsible for touching off the mechanism by which the world rotated. According to Lü, the sage "operates the world" by sharing in and grasping the spontaneity (*tzu-jan*) that characterized "the principle of things and the feelings of the people." If the sage successfully participates in the spontaneity, "the people of the world will not feel that they are being manipulated by the sage." Even if the sage uses "restrictive and oppressive rules to discipline the peo-

63. *SYY*, 2:209. 64. *SYY*, 3:377.
65. *CWCWC*, 7:61b. 66. *SYY*, 4:552. 67. *SYY*, 2:316.

ple," he will simply be in tune with "the impartiality that is natural to the heavenly principle." Consequently everyone will "become enlightened and submissive." "This," Lü concluded, "is how the sage touches off the mechanism of spontaneity and encourages the spontaneous feelings [of the people]."[68]

Where Hai Jui had disdained only those who were greedy, unprincipled, and self-righteous, Lü reacted in addition against those who were opinionated. This forced Lü to grope for a concept of objectivity, as the following passage illustrates:

> The many disparate disputations of today and ancient times, the numerous litigations filling the courts, and the books piling up to the rafters—all arise because the teaching for the world is unclear and because those who are intelligent and talented in arguing stick to their opinions in order to seek supremacy. [But] those arguing about weights will stop when they come to a scale; and those arguing about lengths will stop when they come upon a measuring stick; those arguing about amounts will stop when they come upon a measure; and those arguing about right and wrong will stop when they come upon a sage. The middle way is the measure used by the sage. The Sage [Confucius] is gone; but the middle way remains. What need is there for all this argument to prove oneself right?[69]

Thus divorcing principles from personal models, Lü took "the mean as his teacher" and substituted for the moral support of comrades, "the six friends [instruments such as the measuring stick and scale] to select the mean."[70]

Where Hai Jui had opposed compromise, Lü highly regarded the concept of "the mean," or "middle way" (*chung*) precisely because it could serve as a guiding principle when other standards of right and wrong had been called into question.[71] Thus in the following passage Lü turned to a mid-

68. *SYY*, 5:763.
69. *SYY*, 1:168.
70. *CWCWC*, 4:10a. See also *CWCWC*, 7:61b–62a.
71. *SYY*, 1:168.

dle course in reaction to the moral relativism and intellectual diversity of his day:

> A sage is arguing with ten men, and his opinion is correct. Each of the ten men also obstinately considers his own opinion correct. None of them will give in. Observers approach. Some consider the sage correct; some consider the ten men correct. None can decide. Only when a [second] sage comes will they recognize that the [first] sage is correct. But the ten men and the on-lookers will not necessarily recognize the late-comer as a sage; and [if a sage comes] he will not necessarily consider correct the [second] sage's approval of the [first] sage. Then how are right and wrong to be determined? . . . By holding up the two extremes and choosing the mean.[72]

Overwhelmed by the confusing social and intellectual environment, Lü elsewhere concluded that "outside [the concept of] the mean, there is no Way."[73]

Conscious that flexibility and ingenuity were important, Lü insisted that "the mean is without fixed form." "If the mean is fixed," Lü argued, "then one need only draw a cross between north, south, east, and west; but if it is not fixed, then one can consult the six friends [that is, instruments such as the measuring stick and scale]."[74] The mean, according to Lü, was a dynamic principle that required his initiative and constant reevaluation.

Both Hai and Lü used laws and regulations, but very differently. Lü's reaction against opinionated people and his search for a concept of objectivity distinguish his perception of and relationship to impersonal standards. For Hai Jui, the ideal of sagehood consisted of a perfected subjectivity. Lü K'un in contrast was groping to define sagehood in terms of objective impersonal standards. Hai rigidly and coercively used laws and regulations to achieve his humanistic ends. Lü recognized that the clues to his ideals in part resided in the objective world and that the sage, therefore, must participate in a flexible relationship with those objective forms. Thus where Hai Jui had limited his discussion of *pao-chia* to

72. *SYY*, 5:706. 73. *CWCWC*, 4:10a. 74. *CWCWC*, 4:10b.

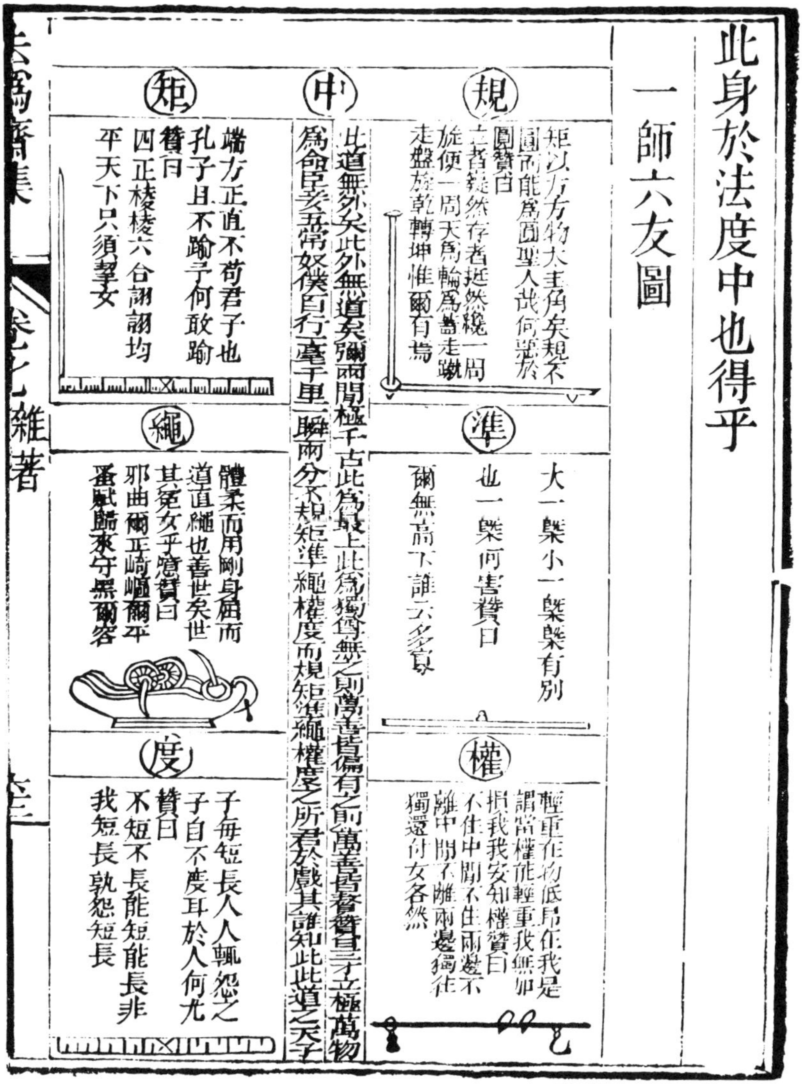

A Chart to Which Lü Gives the Title, "One Teacher and Six Friends" The center two columns comment on Lü's "teacher," "the middle way." To the right and left are illustrations of and comments on Lü's "six friends": the compass, the level, the scale, the square, the plumb-line, and the ruler. *CWCWC*, 7:62a.

(Courtesy of Harvard-Yenching Library, Harvard University)

problems of defense and surveillance, Lü insisted that the pragmatism of *pao-chia* and the educational values of *hsiang-yüeh* must be put into effect simultaneously. Otherwise, Lü warned the officials in his charge: "Even if you are clever, incorrupt, and able to keep records, you will not avoid being a common clerk. Why? Because you consider what is urgent as the end and do not cultivate the management of education."[75]

In the same spirit, Lü maintained that punishments should be used to supplement education rather than in lieu of education.[76] "How is it," he declared indignantly, "that the original instruction of the court was to mete out the five punishments without teaching a word?" He then concluded:

> If you include education in *hsiang-yüeh* and *pao-chia*, then litigation will naturally stop, taxes will naturally be paid in full, and records will naturally be accurate and will not need to be examined. Indeed, the methods of encouraging goodness and punishing evil are basically complementary, and *pao-chia* and *hsiang-yüeh* are basically inseparable.[77]

By insisting that the coercive methods of *pao-chia* and the suasive methods of *hsiang-yüeh* must be put into effect simultaneously, Lü overcame the criticism of a Sung dynasty handbook that those who stressed rules over education were nothing but common clerks.[78] And because Lü had successfully infused legalistic structures with a humanistic spirit, Feng Ts'ung-wu, who had specifically criticized both Hsün Tzu and Wang An-shih, could express praise for and maintain a friendship with Lü K'un.

Lü's perspective on society as outsider

Hai Jui and Lü K'un perceived their society differently. Hai Jui blamed greed and selfishness specifically on officials, clerks, and *sheng-yüan*, or "budding scholars" (*hsiu-ts'ai*). Lü, in contrast, detected signs of greed not only among officials and scholars, but all the way up and down the social hier-

75. *SCL*, 5:2a.
76. *SCL*, 5:1b.
77. *SCL*, 5:2a.
78. Peter Bol, "The *Tso-i tzu-chen*," p. 33.

archy. In a piece that at first glance echoes Hai's railing against *sheng-yüan*—to the extent that it was later erroneously attributed to Hai Jui—Lü K'un recalled a scene he had observed when living in the country in his youth: The elders of the hamlets and "small people" of the market places were banqueting and drinking together, laughing with great abandonment; but upon seeing a "budding scholar" approach, they suddenly donned serious expressions, stopped talking, and listened respectfully to what he had to say. Whenever a "budding scholar" passed through the market place, everyone stared and said, "This is the gentleman who owns such-and-such a library." Alas, Lü noted with exasperation, people find scholars so awesome. But the "budding scholars" are crude in mind and deed. They speak recklessly without regard for righteousness; and they do as they please without regard for propriety. When three or five gather together . . . they argue; when one or two travel about, they commit illicit deeds. Whenever one scholar is insulted by his village, his entire school rushes to complain to the local officials; and whenever one scholar is insulted by a local official, the entire school harboring a grudge, rushes to complain to the provincial governor. After attacking the behavior of young students, Lü, in contrast to Hai, commented on the behavior of all social groups. He wrote:

> No one in the world stands alone free of groups. When one person has been punished, the common people riot at the public hall; and when one soldier faces punishment, the troops riot at the general's quarters. [And so it is] on down to the artisans, merchants, clerks, soldiers, and village elders; all have their associations, and all without fail express their enmities. [The use of] power has certainly extended to private parties for perverse actions, and the recorded laws have all been abandoned. This is the way to great disorder.[79]

79. *SCL*, 1:17b–20a. The entire essay from which these passages are drawn (*SCL*, 1:17a–21b) is erroneously included with a few minor deletions (of the names of the *sheng-yüan*, for example) in *HJC*, pp. 19–22, with the note that the essay does not appear in Ming editions of Hai Jui's work. It is not, to be sure, in *Pei-wang chi* (photo reprint: Chia-ching ed.: Taipei, 1960).

Thus where Hai Jui had focused his social criticisms specifically on the upper strata, Lü had an outsider's view that took in and stressed the elements shared at all levels of society.

Associated with Lü's unusually wide horizons was his own humility. In particular his loss of confidence in the moral leadership of the opinionated bureaucratic elite had reduced his stature in his own eyes. "I'm afraid," he mused, "that if I were among one hundred men, I would not necessarily rise above them; so how can I disregard the common man and woman?"[80] Hai Jui, in allocating duties to clerks, had self-assuredly and insultingly exclaimed, "How those who are clerks today often brag about making a profit!" and then menacingly reminded his audience that clerks were often called "dog-clerks."[81] In contrast, Lü K'un avoided contention by humbly blaming himself and other high officials for the failings of their underlings. He explained: "In every case where a clerk governs poorly, the superior officials are responsible. Only after I [the superior] cleanse myself can I ask others to be pure; only after I love the people can I blame others for their stinginess; and only after I am diligent in government can I ask that others not be negligent."[82]

In his humility, Lü stressed those features that all social strata shared. Criticizing the practice of paying respect and honors to examination candidates at the expense of the people, Lü wrote: "There is no [distinction between] great and small among officials; one goes forward according to the commands. There is no high and humble in duties; one must follow and fulfill one's obligations."[83] Although members of his society enjoyed different statuses, they were alike in having important functions.

Lü further deflected attention from the distinction between officials and clerks by attaching importance to all sorts of external structures, such as laws and the division of responsibilities. By focusing on tasks—which constitute the objective world—rather than on questions of moral leadership, Lü could view high and low, clerks and officials, on the same plane:

80. *SYY*, 2:209.
81. *HJC*, p. 152.
82. *SCL*, 1:45a.
83. *SCL*, 1:9b.

> Alas! The officials generally despise the clerks; and the clerks also despise themselves. [But] in all the matters of the court, one never mentions officials without mentioning clerks. In sending despatches, one talks of transmitting orders down to the officials and clerks of such-and-such a yamen; in visiting superiors, one speaks of officials and clerks making obeisances; and in [issuing] proclamations, one talks of the officials and clerks and such people. What is lowly about clerks?[84]

Without losing sight of the principle of hierarchy, Lü had found a common ground—the responsibility to fulfill one's duties—that all social strata shared. In reference to external structures—such as the division of responsibilities—Lü could view high and low on the same plane. Contributing to Lü's unusual perspective was his capitulation to man's desire for profit, which a comparison between Lü and several of his contemporaries will illuminate.

Alternative responses to self-interest

The notion that competition for influential connections and fame lowered scholars to the level of merchants gained widespread currency during the sixteenth century. Around 1500, one outraged man exclaimed, "The examination center has become a trading place. Is that not shameful?"[85] Drawing an analogy between scholars and merchants, Li Chih, who hailed from the commercial port, Chin-chiang, Fukien, maintained that all personal relations resembled market relations and criticized those scholars who misrepresented themselves in the market place as sages.[86]

Lü K'un, from the less commercially developed province

84. *SCL*, 1:1b–2a. Lü also stated, "Although there are high and low positions, the tasks are alike" (*SCL*, 1:21a). Wen Huang similarly wrote: "Each man will rely on a salary. If high and low each maintain an occupation, great and small will naturally each produce some result" (*Wen-shih mu-hsün*, p. 6b).

85. Cited in Chang Hsüan, *Hsi-yüan wen-chien lu*, 45:2b.

86. De Bary, "Humanitarianism and Individualism," p. 188. See also Li Chih, "Lun chiao nan," *Li shih Fen-shu Hsü fen-shu*, p. 423.

of Honan and from a family of landlord-scholars, saw the resemblance between scholarly and commercial realms just as readily as Li Chih. "Those who like to study," Lü observed, "are like [those] pushing ahead in a bustling market place. Rubbing shoulders [in the crowd], the more strongly and firmly they stamp their feet and the further they advance, the more crowded it gets."[87] As commercialization spread and as competition for the examinations grew intense, the battle against those seeking profit and power mounted. The positions Hai Jui, Feng Ts'ung-wu, and Li Chih took in their fight against self-interest throw light on Lü's own adjustment to the concern for profit and ultimately to "the average man."

Hai Jui recognized that "principles and desires had long been in battle." Fearing that failure to overcome desires with principles would result in the destruction of the mind,[88] Hai stubbornly persisted in the combat. He often pitted "righteousness" (*i*) against "profit" (*li*) and "power" (*shih*),[89] and he derided those "self-righteous hypocrites" (*hsiang-yüan*) who had tried to strike a compromise with "righteousness."[90] Thus Hai Jui won fame—or notoriety—for his unswerving defense of justice; but he also failed to win adherents for his harsh policies, which failed to deal realistically with the changing social environment.

Feng Ts'ung-wu, like Hai, drew a line of battle between goodness (*shan*) and profit (*li*). In his "Shan li t'u" ["Chart of Goodness and Profit"] Feng demonstrated that very distinct paths led to sagehood, on the one hand, and to the evil of a bandit on the other. No middle ground, he argued, could be found between the two paths. Any attempt to compromise would eventually result in evil. The fierceness of Feng's warning against compromise suggests his heightened sense of conflict. Feng maintained faith in man's capacity to transcend self-interest, but he did so only by withdrawing into the academies far from everyday realities.[91]

Li Chih advocated another method of dealing with greed. He believed that those emulating the sages must "transcend [thoughts of] profit and power." But Li in fact could not completely rise above those thoughts to find tranquility of mind.

87. *SYY*, 3:339. 88. *HJC*, p. 105.
89. *HJC*, p. 95. 90. *HJC*, p. 106. 91. *FSHC*, 8:4a–8a.

Consequently he maintained that all relationships were market relations and that Confucius and his disciples had enjoyed a lasting relationship because "only Confucius had what the disciples wanted." Caught between his desire "to transcend [thoughts of] profit and personal influence" and his recognition that those thoughts in fact governed all relationships, Li Chih could mock his contemporaries and long for escape, but he could not find a *modus vivendi* for himself.[92]

Lü, too, was deeply concerned that economic changes had tarnished morality and disrupted social harmony. He observed that "when brothers disagreed, it was because of money,"[93] and that children were so selfish as to begrudge paying for the rituals for their deceased parents.[94] However, Lü was far more resigned to man's greed than the scholars discussed above, and he shaped his policies accordingly. In a jingle against greed in his *Tsung-yueh ko* [Songs for a Lineage Compact], Lü conceded, "In life, who turns his back on wealth?" before asserting that "there is a proper way to making money." The jingle, furthermore, abandoned moral arguments for other types of sanctions. Lü warned that obtaining wealth unfairly "will incur the wrath of the multitude . . . [and] will be punished by officials;" and he reminded his audience that "the advantages gained by harming others are [as uncertain as] a lamplight in the wind . . . and [as short-lived as] ice in a fire."[95]

Lü similarly accommodated greed in his "Warning against Ungratefulness." He opened the song with an appeal to humaneness—"who in the world does not rely on others?"—but capped it with an anecdote he thought "truly heartbreaking," but which ironically confirmed the inevitable cruelty of the competitive world: When men were closing in on a wolf in the mountains, a scholar magnanimously hid the wolf in his trunk. After the men left, the scholar released the wolf, who thanklessly observed: "I'm famished. It is better to save myself than to die of hunger. I should eat that scholar."[96]

92. Li Chih, "Lun chiao nan," *Li shih Fen-shu Hsü fen-shu*, p. 423.
93. Lü, *Tsung-yüeh ko*, p. 2a.
94. Ibid., p. 1a. 95. Ibid., p. 10a.
96. Ibid., pp. 11b–12a. This story is based on a play by K'ang Hai (1475–1541). See the biography of K'ang by Tilemann Grimm in *DMB*,

As tenaciously as Lü clung to the ideal of humaneness and as heartbreaking as he found the story of the betrayed scholar, in the final analysis Lü could not block out the cruel side of human nature. He knew that "the petty man often says, 'If you don't kill the poor guys, then you won't get rich.'"[97] And he likewise observed: "Although everyone likes to come out ahead, where in the world does one incident benefit both [sides]? If you win, he will lose. If you take advantage of the rich, you will invite their enmity. If you take advantage of a poor fellow, you will provoke his misery."[98] Thus while Lü argued that competition was harmful and mutual acquiescence beneficial, he conceded that "out of every ten men in productive [occupations], nine are greedy. From olden times, it has always been that the wealthy are malevolent."[99]

In a collection of parables entitled *Wu ju* [Disregard Comparisons], Lü again expressed his belief that greed and selfishness permeated the world. By arranging the parables in descending order from beggars, thieves, and courtesans to elephants and on down the ranks of the animal kingdom to birds and insects, Lü demonstrated that each stage in the descent provides examples of integrity and humaneness that surpass the behavior of many humans. The final anecdote concerns a tiny spider who availed himself of one strand of a large spider's web as a prop for his own small web. When the large web suddenly broke, the large spider decided to draw back the filament into his stomach to start afresh elsewhere. After hesitating, however, he relinquished the strand that was supporting the small spider's web. Lü commented: the thread is the "basic nature" (*hsing*), and "abandoning one's own thread out of concern for another [spider's] web is humaneness (*jen*)." Lü then described a man who "in disgraceful contrast to the large spider," had torn down the wall a neighbor had used to prop up his own house. "Alas!" Lü sighed, "How will the 'small spiders' survive?"[100] In short,

---

pp. 693–94. For the use of the fable by one of Lü's contemporaries, Ch'eng Ta-yüeh (1541–1616), see *DMB*, p. 214.

97. Lü, *Tsung-yüeh ko*, p. 14b.

98. Ibid., p. 15b. 99. Ibid., p. 19a.

100. Lü K'un, *Wu-ju*, in a composite edition of *Lü tzu i-shu* (1573?–

Lü doubted that humaneness—a concept which Lo Ju-fang had celebrated without reservation—was sufficiently powerful to protect those at the very bottom of society.

Again perceiving that selfishness was pervasive, Lü wrote: "The petty man is difficult to get rid of. If one attacks him too callously or tries to control him too abruptly, then it is like using sand to block up wildly swelling waters, or [like using] ashes to bury a fierce fire." Lü then proceeded to explain that although most people are average, "there are also numerous extremely evil and cruel people. If one abandons people as evil, thus encouraging them to lose their self-confidence and driving the average man to [become] a small man and the slightly petty man to become a very small man, then everyone will fight to his death without any reservations."[101]

Lü observed that the very thoughts of "personal advantage" (*pien*) stirred up destructive emotions: "People will hasten after profit, fall in love with beauty, and turn greedy upon seeing food and drink; they follow what is easy and cheat the ignorant and weak—all for personal advantage."[102] Lü urged gentlemen to prevent such behavior through instruction and legal restraints. At the same time he acknowledged, albeit reluctantly, that "prohibiting what is personally advantageous . . . is most difficult. . . . Throughout his life [the gentleman] combats 'personal advantage,' but in the end fails to vanquish it."[103] Despairing of eradicating desires completely, Lü tried to deal with them through the apportioning of "allotments," or "shares" (*fen*). Because "personal

---

162?), pp. 34b–35a. This edition is available in the East Asiatic Library of the University of California, Berkeley. Note also Wen Huang's observation that it is difficult for the poor to get ahead because they are always blamed for thefts (*Wen-shih mu-hsün*, pp. 3b–5a). Lü also bemoaned that the paternalism of earlier centuries had disappeared: "During the Liang and Sung, those with fields of a hundred *mou* did not cultivate [the fields] themselves but had to hire labor. The laborers were the hands and feet of the landowner, who, if frightened at night, depended on them for help and who depended on their labor for constructions. For a variety of matters, [the landlords] depended on [the laborers carrying out] orders. If [the landlords] did not take care of [the laborers], how could they live peacefully? . . . Now when tenants ask for help, the landlords ask for high interest" (*SCL*, 2:7b).

101. *SYY*, 5:770. 102. *SYY*, 5:641.

103. *SYY*, 5:642; see also, *SYY*, 5:702.

advantage" could not be vanquished, Lü concluded: "The sages rule men as they control the waters, which cannot be prevented from flowing downward [but] which can be divided so that they will not overflow; that is all. Even a Yao or Shun cannot dam them up so they will not burst forth."[104]

Capitulating to the "selfishness that naturally accompanies human desires,"[105] Lü reminded his fellow officials of their responsibility "to see that the things of the world obtain their due (*te ch'i so*)."[106] "If the ignorant men and women . . . do not fulfill their allotted desires (*fen yüan*)," Lü elsewhere warned, "then the world will not be peaceful."[107] Aware that "those who do not have enough will die by chasing after their shares," Lü called for the balanced and equitable distribution of goods.[108]

Lü, far more realistically than Hai Jui, Feng Ts'ung-wu, and Li Chih, tried to accommodate rather than conquer or escape man's greed. In his "Shih li shuo" ["Discussion of Power and Profit"], Lü designated emperors and kings as the omnipotent masters of power and profit and defined the role of officials in insuring the equitable allocation of profit. Even the ruling sages, Yao and Shun, Lü insisted, had monopolized power in order to pacify the world:

> If Yao and Shun could wear the clothes of the masses, stand in the market place, and summon the world to them; if they could establish officials and make [the officials] take them seriously; and if they could transform the world through instruction—then there would be no need for power. And if they could pacify the world and [see that] each obtain [his due] without [recourse to] laws and regulations, then there would be no need for power. Therefore the Son of Heaven uses power to control the hundred officials, and the hundred officials use the power of the Son of Heaven to distribute the local officials to carry out [the emperor's] virtuous intentions. And if everywhere the wise elders from

104. *SYY*, 5:642. 105. *SYY*, 5:763.
106. *SYY*, 1:26a. See also, *SCL*, 1:23a.
107. *SYY*. 5:629.
108. *SYY*, 5:712. For similar phrases, see *SYY*, 5:647; 5:657.

> among the people are instructed to uphold fearfully the laws, so that no one dares be reckless, then power is managed [well]. If power lies in the officials, then [the officials] will plunder; if power lies in the myriad people, then [the people] will be destroyed. Even Yao and Shun did not dare hand power over to the world. This is the effective instrument by which [all within] the four seas are united and [all within] the six directions pacified.

Lü thus examined the interdependence of personal profit and political power. Personal profit fosters life and should be evenly distributed among those below. Political power controls death and should be concentrated in one source above. Lü's discussion of power and profit in terms of the extremes of life and death reveals a sense of urgency. Lü was, after all, aware that "the poor who have no one to rely on will lose benefits and will gather together to seek what they desire, thus paving the way to disaster in the world." More important, Lü focused not on the sage rescuing the world but on the relationship between the exercise of power and the distribution of profit.

Lü was conscious that he had let the moral concerns of the sage recede from the written page, for he pursued in his "Discussion of Power and Profit" an imaginary dialogue with someone who remarked, "You do not speak of reputation and morality but speak of power and profit," and then asked, "Is that sagely instruction?" In defense, Lü responded that "the ancient sage-kings enriched life before they erected virtue." How, Lü further queried, would lectures on propriety and acquiescence, or instruction on humaneness and righteousness, benefit the starving? He then went so far as to argue that the various features of morality in fact "are put into effect through [the workings of] personal advantage." Thus while Lü insisted that "sages cannot be confined by [thoughts of] power and profit" (and a later chapter will show just how he enlarged his view), moral issues had in fact slipped into the background as considerations of power and profit came to occupy a central place in his view.[109] This is further apparent in three ways.

109. *CWCWC*, 7:58b–62a.

First, Lü sympathized with the interests of merchants and opposed the ruthless taxation of goods brought to market.[110] He also criticized the officially fixed prices. These, he explained to his underlings, harmed the people by discouraging them both from selling their livestock in the markets and from keeping their shops open. Lü then suggested methods by which "each merchant will obtain his share."[111]

Secondly, Lü K'un defended the redistribution of tax burdens on the grounds that over the long run even the wealthy would benefit. Hai Jui had wrested land from the wealthy on the grounds of justice for the poor small landowners. For his principles, he had sacrificed his own self-interest and died almost penniless. Lü K'un found an argument which would serve rich and poor alike and which thus freed him to exercise his social conscience without any sacrifice to his own well-being. He explained that on retiring to his native Ning-ling, he had been shocked to discover that many formerly wealthy families had grown poor.[112] Showing that laborers and clerks of one period might become great families or tax collectors in another period, and that even the most illustrious families might fall, Lü argued that the tax burdens on the commoners of Ning-ling should be reduced.[113] Equalizing the burden would, he argued, insure long-term stability for all. Unlike Hai Jui, whose policies had expressed anger towards the wealthy, Lü stressed that the fortunes of rich and poor alike were cyclical, and he dispassionately analyzed in a chart the principles by which families rise and fall.[114]

Thirdly, accompanying Lü's accommodation of man's selfishness was a sharp recognition of the contribution that talent, distinct from moral leadership, could play. Aware that "in the final analysis it is easy for the gentleman to withdraw and difficult to get rid of the small man," Lü concluded that "it is better for the gentleman to control the policy and select talent to execute it."[115] Cynical about the efficacy of moral suasion and acquiescent to man's selfishness, Lü took

110. *SCL*, 1:5a. 111. *CWCWC*, 4:34b–35a.

112. *CWCWC*, 5:42a. According to the editor of *CWCWC*, this essay had formerly been separately printed as *T'ien-jih yü chi*.

113. *CWCWC*, 4:19b–20a. 114. CWCWC, 6:16a–17b.

115. *SYY*, 5:770.

advantage of the profit motive. He explained: "I hold up remunerative sanctions and show them the goal, saying, 'If you are like this, you will be wealthy; if you are not, you will be poor.'" Lü thus let moral sanctions give way to remunerative ones. He had perceived: "The talents [of the petty men] can ruin the world, but they also can accomplish merit in the world. One can provoke them to incite disasters and can also nurture them to produce benefits."[116] Not only did Lü draw strength from man's selfishness by using remunerative sanctions constructively; in addition, he went so far as to redefine the official in terms of talent, as the following section will discuss.

Talent and morality

By providing structures for the careful division of responsibilities and allocation of benefits, one could, Lü believed, protect society. However, once these structures are set, human initiative in governing society is ruled out, and officials risk becoming the servants of the organization, mere functionaries. Thus, although Hai Jui reserved for himself the right to clarify each official's "share in protecting the proper Way,"[117] his domineering effort to enforce a static ideal threatened to diminish the stature of other officials.

In contrast, Lü K'un's conceptualization of the bureaucracy left room for the dynamic involvement of all. Lü considered not only whether officials were moral, but also whether they were talented. While never completely ignoring moral values, Lü concentrated his attention on the goals of effective and practical administration and concomitantly on employing men with the talents for carrying out specific duties. Just as Lü believed that one could devise a great plan by pooling the strong points of a hundred men of different and imperfect opinions, so he believed that one could bring about good government by coordinating people with different powers; the key was not in selecting moral men, but in matching talents to tasks:

116. *SYY*, 5:770. 117. *HJC*, p. 48.

> The world has long been without a perfect talent. [Therefore] each person should be employed according to his powers (*shih*). The eyes cannot hear; the ears cannot see; the nose cannot eat; and the mouth cannot smell—[because they have different] powers. Today those who employ people haphazardly confer [office] on them without inspecting their talents and qualifications. [Consequently] the man in charge of accounts attends to criminal law; and the Ministry of Personnel controls the military.[118]

Lü, in contrast to Hai Jui, envisioned a broad range of bureaucratic types rather than the simplified categories of virtuous and corrupt officials. Taking both character and talent into account, Lü defined the following eight permutations: (1) those who are highly compassionate and work hard on behalf of the people; (2) those who "do everything they must" but conform to the Way with a "slightly forced" effort; (3) those who do good on behalf of their reputation; (4) those who mean well but, lacking talent, are "ineffectual in government"; (5) those whose hearts are in the right place but whose actions fail to benefit the people because they understand matters superficially; (6) those who are manipulative and do not really love the people; (7) those who fail in "practical government" and "feign goodness"; and (8) those who are greedy and competitive.[119] Thus concerned with both talent and morality, Lü's categories fan out to take into account many types of people.

For Lü, talent had a special value. Thus, separating the issues of morality and talent, he stated: "The order and disorder of the world is related to man's talent. And whether man's talent is corrupt or correct is related to the schools. Compare this to products: the school is where they are produced; and the court is where they are used."[120] Even when discussing how women should behave, Lü agreed with a Sung scholar who said: "To die for something in the world is

118. *SYY*, 5:724. See also *SYY*, 5:722–23. Yang Ch'i-yüan (1547–99) also believed that "most people were average" and that one should therefore pay attention to how the average men were daily employed (*Yang Fu-so hsien-sheng chia tsang wen-chi*, 3:22a).

119. *SCL*, 1:26a–27a. 120. *SCL*, 1:35b.

easy; to accomplish something in the world is difficult." "Accordingly," Lü explained, "the sages value virtue, but more than that, they value virtue accompanied by talent."[121] Similarly Kao P'an-lung, who, like Lü, stressed that "most men in the world are average,"[122] let the criterion of performance modify considerations of morality. He acknowledged that a number of types served the bureaucracy:

> The worthies regard the ruler as heaven and do not dare deceive him; they regard the people as their children and cannot bear to harm them. They respect the law and perform their official duties because they refuse to let their own faults have any effect. Next are those who desire and force themselves to be good and who are fearful and dare not commit evil. The lowest are those who do not know what the performance of duties or [respect for the] laws are; they give rein to their passions and that is all. They are the thieves of the people.[123]

Because Lü focused on tasks and talent rather than on the moral leadership that distinguished the officials from commoners, he could easily imagine diffusing responsibilities among the common people. Encouraging widespread participation in community affairs, he suggested that any who had good methods of distributing grain should be given awards. "Thus everyone will be able to present his ability, and the methods of putting humaneness into effect will flourish."[124] Lü also diffused responsibilities among the people to check the corruption of the mediocre bureaucrats. He lamented that laws had become so complicated that students and commoners could neither master their many ramifications nor personally manage them.[125] To persuade the people of the advantages of *hsiang-chia*—that is, the inseparable *hsiang-yüeh* and *pao-chia* institutions—[126] Lü argued that orderly mutual surveillance would secure the people against unwarranted investigations by the yamen, and that public

121. Lü, *Kuei fan t'u-shuo*, 3:28b.
122. Kao, *Kao tzu i-shu*, 7:27b–28a.
123. Ibid., 7:27b.
124. *SCL*, 2:42b.
125. *SYY*, 5:755–56.
126. *SCL*, 3:1a.

knowledge of the assessed land taxes would prevent the clerks from falsifying records in favor of the wealthy.[127] For Lü knew well that officials often tried to cheat the illiterate by collecting taxes according to the old system.[128]

Lü was also willing to spread legal knowledge among the common people. Lü believed that "the downfall of good government began with the rise of legal codes," but he also regretted that students and common people did not have access to the codes.[129] On at least one occasion he advised widows to consult the law codes to defend their property rights.[130] In his search for objectivity, Lü granted importance to outlines of tasks and legal forms and had thus enlarged the ground shared by the officials and the common people.

In giving primacy to tasks, Lü also gave officials a new identity. He defined magistrates and other provincial officials not only as moral leaders but also as doctors making out prescriptions for specific social ills.[131] He believed that the official should be judged on his efficacy in prescribing the correct cures for society, as well as on his integrity. Carried away by the metaphor, Lü once even disparaged abstract moralizing as a most inadequate cure: "If one is sick with vomiting or diarrhea, even daily food and drink will fail to cure one's illness. Learning that [simply] goes in the ear and comes out the mouth, even with daily explanations and research, will fail to benefit body and mind."[132]

As the official assumed the guise of a doctor, he also took on medical tasks. Lü himself read over a thousand *chüan* on medicine,[133] and wrote a work on measles.[134] Not surprisingly, he advised magistrates to treat doctors like members of the

127. *SCL*, 3:5b–6a. See also 3:42a.

128. *SCL*, 3:34b. 129. *SYY*, 5:755–56.

130. Lü, *Ts'ung-yüeh ko*, p. 15a. According to the *Ta Ming hui-tien*, women could inherit property when there were no male heirs (cited in Chao Feng-chieh, *Chung-kuo fu-nü tsai fa-lü shang chih ti-wei*, pp. 13–14). Also see *SCL*, 3:26a for regulations on inheritance for widows. For other information on the legal status of women, see Ch'u T'ung-tsu, *Law and Society in Traditional China*, pp. 102–10.

131. Sixteenth-century writers often used medical imagery; cf. the title of Yao Shun-mu's *Yao yen* [Medicinal Words].

132. *SYY*, 2:313. 133. *CWCWC*, 3:45b–46a.

134. For Lü's preface to his work on measles, *Chen k'e*, see *CWCWC*, 3:47b–48a.

officialdom.[135] The distinction between doctor and official, who alike applied their skills to an objectified world, had become blurred in Lü's view.

As the official turned doctor, his relationship to the people changed. The official, like the doctor, was hired by the people and received a salary in exchange for his efficacious treatments.[136] Accordingly, Lü compared prefects and magistrates arriving at their posts to doctors undertaking the care of the sick. The local officials should "examine the symptoms of the prefectures and capitals" just as a doctor "examines the pulse and breath" of the patient. If the doctor fails to cure his patient, then "when he leaves with his medicine bag, who would on seeing him off ask that he return to the host?" According to Lü, the official, like the doctor, is subject to evaluation by the people. Thus, when the local officials leave, the people "count their deeds and praise them."[137]

In this manner Lü had redefined the official. As a doctor, Lü's official participated in an objectified, frequently immoral world without experiencing the degradation of a functionary subordinated to administrative regulations. Rather, by diagnosing society and administering cures for social ills, the official turned doctor could take pride in performing tasks effectively.

In his search for an objective framework through which one could overcome conflicting claims to knowledge, Lü made room for the delineation of laws and regulations, for the definition of tasks, for the selection of talent, and, as chapter 7 will further demonstrate, for the consideration of concrete affairs in general. In so doing, he let the concern for "principle"—which had dominated so many philosophical discussions—recede into the background. Thus where others had based their authority for moral leadership on their claims to understanding "principle," Lü maintained, in the passage cited below, that the understanding of "principle"

135. *SCL*, 2:48b.

136. *SCL*, 1:21a; 1:24b; 1:27b.

137. *SCL*, 1:24b. Lü's concept of the people as host to the officials anticipates Huang Tsung-hsi's declaration that the ruler is the people's guest (see Wm. Theodore de Bary, "Chinese Despotism and the Confucian Ideal: A Seventeenth-century View," p. 171).

was too simple to warrant lengthy discussion. Instead the coordination of affairs deserved most attention:

> Although there is [only] one principle [governing] what one studies at home and what one does in office, there are many affairs (*shih*). Therefore in regard to talent, one values thorough coordination (*t'ung*) rather than uniformity; and in regard to affairs, one values practice rather than deliberation. . . . [Accordingly] the urgent task for scholars entails more than discussions of nature and heaven, principle and ether. Now, the mind is able to grasp principles but has difficulty grasping affairs. It is possible to unify principles but difficult to unify affairs.[138]

Lü thus shifted his focus from abstract philosophizing to concrete affairs. At the same time he shared the sense of mission as moral leader and educator that characterized the Confucian tradition. Thus he prefaced the above passage on principle and affairs with the comment that "office and learning had become separated ever since the teaching of *The Great Learning* had ceased to be clear," and that it was his desire to reunite office and learning that had prompted his concern for the concept of *t'ung* in accommodating the diversity of tasks or affairs. *T'ung* can variously be translated as "to coordinate," "connect together," or, as in this case, to articulate the disjointed sectors of his society. It can also mean "to communicate" and "to provide access to." How Lü used records, manuals, and didactic literature to "coordinate rather than make uniform" will be the subject of the next chapter.

138. *CWCWC*, 4:57a–58b.

6

By Writing for Women, Children, and the Poor

Lü wrote no less than ten didactic works and handbooks for women, children, and the poor. These genres had existed long before the Ming dynasty, but the writing of so many works by one man who was also a noted scholar-official was unusual if not unprecedented. Lü's willingness to write so extensively for the uneducated again reflects his outsider's perspective on society. While liberating, or detaching, himself from the fruitless "learned discussions" of his peers, Lü could nonetheless fulfill his mission as educator by writing didactic works. And disdainful of philosophical disputations, Lü perceived that the views of the upper and lower social strata were equally valuable and should be exchanged, through disseminating didactic works and collecting information.

In his didactic works, Lü made numerous concessions to semiliterate and illiterate audiences. Unlike one contemporary, who responded to the social flux by rigidly maintaining distinctions between the refined language of the officialdom and the vulgar language of the streets,[1] Lü often forsook the classical style for the language of the market place. On occasion he advocated the use of "very simple and common words" and the exclusion of classical phrases "so that women and children would all understand."[2] His *Kuei chieh* [Precepts for Women] consists of thirty-seven verses composed in the same meter and therefore easy and pleasurable to memorize. His *Illustrated Regulations for the Women's Quarters* brought arcane biographies of women to life for his sixteenth-century

1. Wen Huang, *Wen-shih mu-hsün*, p. 2a.
2. *SCL*, 2:34a.

readers. Lü based this collection on *Lieh nü chuan* [Biographies of Model Women], a Han dynasty work that took its present form—various categories of biographies of women, each followed by a brief encomium—by the beginning of the thirteenth century.[3] Lü made the biographies more attractive for poorly educated female readers in a number of ways. To explicate obscure characters that might confuse his readers, he provided brief glosses and indicated the proper pronunciation by inserting two characters to represent the initial and final sounds. He condensed the original biographies, almost always deleting allusions to difficult classical texts. He played to his reader's emotions. And he had the work richly illustrated with a woodblock print for each brief anecdote.[4] He also replaced the laconic encomiums of the *Biographies of Model Women* with his own. An opinionated and powerful editor, Lü freely departed from the original accounts to raise questions and explore problems that preoccupied him. To Lü's alterations, sixteenth-century readers responded with enthusiasm: *Illustrated Regulations for the Women's Quarters* went through many editions even before the end of Lü's life.[5]

Similar concessions to popular taste can be found in the works for children. These include two collections of songs composed by Lü's father and published by Lü—*Hsiao-erh yü* [Words for Children], and *Nü hsiao-erh yü* [Words for Girls]—and two works by Lü K'un, *Hsü Hsiao-erh yü* [A Sequel to Words for Children] and *Yen Hsiao-erh yü* [Acting Out Words for Children] (preface, 1593). Appended to many of the songs or interspersed among their lines are explanatory asides such as: "You will know how your parents viewed you by looking at

3. See the preface, written in 1214, to Liu Hsiang, *Lieh nü chuan*, ssu-pu pei-yao edition. For a translation of the *Lieh nü chuan*, see Albert Richard O'Hara, *The Position of Woman in Early China*.

4. Lü, "Preface," *Kuei-fan*, p. 2a. For a fuller discussion of how Lü modified the *Lieh nü chuan* [Biographies of model women], see Joanna F. Handlin, "Lü K'un's New Audience: The Influence of Women's Literacy on Sixteenth-Century Thought."

5. In a postscript to a memorial in which Lü pleaded innocent to charges that his *Kuei fan* had some nefarious intent in the heir apparent controversy, Lü listed four editions of the work and remarked that the gentry were circulating it among themselves and that merchants were selling it everywhere (*CWCWC*, 2:33b).

your own children; if you failed to treat your parents with filiality, then your children will also act that way."[6]

By making concessions, Lü tried to reach even the illiterate poor, for whom he wrote *Hao-jen ko* [The Song of the Good Person]—a list of proscriptions in twenty-four stanzas of four five-syllable lines each, concluded with a seven-syllable couplet exhorting the avoidance of evil.[7] Although tedious to read, this list, set to music, undoubtedly was a catchy patter song. More engaging and richly textured is Songs for a Lineage Compact (preface, 1599), which Lü composed for his lineage. This collection includes eighty-five songs on numerous aspects of family and village life: ancestor worship, filial duty, neighborliness, education of children, working diligently, frugality, planting trees, drinking, profligacy, cruel jokes, litigation, guidelines for merchants and labor brokers, fortunetelling, and eating cattle. In numerous ways, Lü shaped these songs to reach his uneducated audience. While advocating such values as neighborliness, hard work, and humaneness, the songs show that Lü was in touch with the harsh realities—self-interest, greed, and competitiveness—of rural life. Lending veracity to his songs are such comments as: children will certainly claim they lack money for maintaining their parents' tombs—but they'll spend money on entertaining guests;[8] brothers disagree over money;[9] merchants cheat the simple-minded;[10] and wives enjoy their guests while letting their mothers-in-law do the cooking.[11]

Further engaging his audience, Lü asks numerous provocative questions such as "How do you compare to Confucius?"[12] and "How many lazy people are good?"[13] To arouse his audience, he reminds them that "the man in the cangue

6. *Hsü hsiao-erh yü*, p. 1, in *Lü shu ssu-chung* in *Lü tzu i-shu*. This and the other didactic works by Lü Te-sheng and Lü K'un are to be found in *Lü shu ssu-chung*. Chou Tso-jen, who like his brother Lu Hsun, promoted the writing of vernacular language, took an interest in Lü K'un's sequel to *Hsiao-erh yü* (see "Lü K'un te 'Yen hsiao-erh yü'" in *T'an lung chi*, pp. 285–90). See also Chu Chieh-fan, "Lü K'un te *Hsiao-erh yü*," pp. 191–93; 218–20.

7. *Hao jen ko* is included in *Lü shu ssu-chung*.

8. *Tsung-yüeh ko*, p. 1a. 9. Ibid., p. 2a. 10. Ibid., p. 8b. 11. Ibid., p. 9b. 12. Ibid., p. 1b. 13. Ibid., p. 5a.

was originally a good person;"[14] that those who shirk work will die;[15] and that Heaven has its eyes on those merchants who deceive the naive. Finally, to facilitate use of the text for these songs, Lü encloses the characters for textual asides in diamonds and indicates those lines that should be repeated with circles.

Lü wrote so many of his didactic works in verse because he understood that even the illiterate could easily master and orally transmit songs.[16] In the preface to his *Songs for a Lineage Compact*, Lü expressed regret that his lineage was large, and its members poor. Whenever they went to the market town for clothes and food they failed to understand anything that had the slightest trace of literary style. But, Lü explained, because they were capable of singing three hundred stanzas, he wrote for them didactic verses that were "very shallow, clear, and colloquial."[17]

In addition to the works described above, Lü wrote a collection of parables, *Disregard Comparisons*, discussed in chapter 4, guidebooks for fortunetellers and storytellers, which unfortunately are no longer extant, and *Ssu-li i* [A Supplement to the Four Rituals] (preface, 1573), a guide to bringing young children up properly.[18]

For writing and editing didactic works, Lü found inspiration in his father, Lü Te-sheng. In a 1558 preface to his *Words for Children*, Te-sheng had rejected as dull and meaningless the outdated children's songs from the Liang and Sung dynasties and defended the "harmlessness of unrefined words." He had boldly declared that because his verses were instructive and principled, he need not be ashamed of using "shallow" words to win the attention of his young audience.[19] Lü K'un greatly admired his father for "writing [songs] as though he were speaking, with the result that everyone who recited them was moved to clap and dance."[20] Lü K'un had

14. Ibid., p. 2b. 15. Ibid., p. 4b.
16. Lü, "Preface," *Tsung-yüeh ko*, p. 1a. 17. Ibid.
18. On the guidebooks, see *CWCWC*, 7:65b. For *Ssu-li i*, 4 *chüan*, see *Tsang shu shih-san chung*, edited by Chu Shih, (1736), *ts'e* 44.
19. Lü Te-sheng, "Preface," (1558) *Hsiao-erh yü*, p. 1a.
20. Lü K'un, "Afterword" (1593), *Hsiao-erh yü*, p. 1a.

learned from his own writing efforts how difficult mastering the vernacular style was.

Lü K'un was aware that his didactic writings were most unconventional. In the afterword to his father's songs for children, Lü expressed some fears: some people might think that the words, whether in the colloquial or literary style, were "empty talk" and might therefore question why one should bother substituting them for the traditional children's songs.[21] Similarly, in his preface to the songs for his lineage, Lü expressed apprehension that his use of "incorrect characters and local expressions" would provoke literary types to ridicule him.[22]

Lü defended writing in the colloquial style several times. In his preface to *Precepts for Women,* he declared that even at the risk of committing stylistic errors he would not substitute literary for colloquial phrases, because he wished to facilitate reaching the listeners.[23] Similarly, in the preface to his *Illustrated Regulations for the Women's Quarters,* Lü noted that because the ancient didactic works for women were difficult to understand, a change in style was necessary. Lü further argued for the use of colloquial language on the grounds that the songs should be enjoyable and moving. Committed to pleasing his audience, Lü feared that his sequel to his father's verses for children would sound stilted and bookish.[24] And in writing songs for his lineage, Lü contended that he must use "local expressions" in order to "please the listeners" and "startle them to enlightenment."[25]

Lü further defended indulging the popular demand for pleasure on the grounds that improving education was critical to mending his degenerate society. Thus in the preface to *Illustrated Regulations for the Women's Quarters,* he noted that women who had been educated by female teachers in an-

21. Ibid., p. 1b.
22. Lü, "Preface," *Tsung-yüeh ko,* p. 1a.
23. Lü, "Preface," *Kuei chieh* in *Lü tzu i-shu,* p. 1a.
24. Lü, "Afterword," *Hsiao-erh yü,* p. 1a. Elsewhere, Lü rejected Wang Ken's celebration of pleasure, which Lü maintained was as insipid as a sweet melon that had never been bitter. Lü instead advocated "being encouraged through fear" (*SYY,* 2:346).
25. Lü, "Preface," *Tsung-yüeh ko,* p. 1a.

cient times had behaved dutifully. With the recent decline of instruction, however, the behavior of women, Lü observed, has deteriorated. Village women have grown accustomed to hearing vulgarities, and wealthy women have grown lax and arrogant, extravagantly flaunting their jewels, "almost like prostitutes"—"all because instruction is lacking."[26]

In the preface to *Precepts for Women,* Lü confided that he worried night and day that "the wives of peasants, artisans, and pedlars, and the girls from villages and remote places never throughout their lives hear one fine phrase." Under the circumstances, it would be wrong, Lü argued, to forbid didactic songs. Then, once again slipping into the role of doctor to society, Lü remarked that one could compare the circulation of didactic songs, which have the power to startle listeners, to treating a chronic stomach ailment, for which acupuncture is far more effective than drugs. "Those who worry about the Way of the world," Lü concluded, "must know with what bitter heart I speak."[27] In short, the urgent need to cure his degenerate society pressed Lü to use the most effective means available for instructing others.

In his impulse to popularize education, to use a simple, colloquial style, and to make learning pleasurable, Lü resembled the followers of Wang Yang-ming, in particular the members of the T'ai-chou school, which included Wang Ken and Lo Ju-fang. But the resemblance is partial and fails to take into account Lü's departures from the T'ai-chou school. Lü had read Wang Ken's "Song on the Enjoyment of Learning," but was skeptical of Wang's view that learning produced happiness.[28] Wang's kind of learning was like a sweet melon that has never been bitter,[29] and his happy-go-lucky attitude was too superficial for Lü K'un. Where Wang Ken had communicated an exhilarating sense of oneness with the masses, Lü looked in two directions. He wished to accommodate and please the uneducated, but he also felt compelled to justify his popularized songs to his peers. He valued information from the masses, but also struggled to impose his ideals on troublesome realities. Where Wang Ken

26. Lü, "Preface," *Kuei-fan t'u-shuo*, pp. 1a–b.
27. Lü, "Preface," *Kuei chieh*, pp. 1a–b.
28. *SYY*, 2:351. 29. *SYY*, 2:346.

and Lo Ju-fang had expressed their missions as teachers by giving lectures, Lü pursued his mission as educator not by lecturing or joining suspect study groups—and conspicuously absent from his large corpus are any recorded dialogues—but by writing didactic works. By communicating in print to anonymous audiences, Lü remained free from politically suspect learned discussions. Indeed, both Lü and his father perceived that the availability of didactic songs would minimize the importance of the student-teacher relationship. Lü Te-sheng remarked that any child who had learned the songs could then spread them to other children.[30] And in a similar spirit, Lü K'un advised that old blind female beggars be trained to perform the songs from his *Precepts for Women* so that they could spread them to the female quarters of elite households, from which men were barred.[31] For Lü, vernacular didactic works were the means by which the ideals associated with the top of society could be exchanged for real information from below. To understand Lü's position as mediator between top and bottom, an examination of his response to the masses will be useful.

The feelings of the people

Early in his career Lü learned how powerful the feelings of the people could be. When he was transferred from the magistracy of Hsiang-yüan to that of Ta-t'ung, a boisterous gathering braved a heavy snow and muddy roads to send him off. They were so reluctant to see their cherished magistrate leave that they followed along for miles carrying incense and clinging to his carriage. Women knocked their heads against their doors and lost their voices wailing; children kowtowed by the roadside; and musicians wept so profusely at the farewell feast that they could not perform. The author of Lü's biography in the gazetteer concluded, "The people are ignorant but perceptive; how could there not have been reasons for their cheers?"[32] Such descriptions appear so often in tra-

30. Lü Te-sheng, "Preface," *Hsiao-erh yü*, p. 1a.
31. Lü, "Preface," *Kuei chieh*, p. 1a.
32. *Ning-ling hsien chih*, 9:12a.

ditional biographies that one might well doubt the veracity of this report were it not for Lü's own testimony. He was clearly touched by "the several thousand people in sixty-one clusters along the roadside;" and he marvelled at "the generosity of the people's feelings."[33] He was also flattered that the people of Hsiang-yüan later erected a shrine and tablet in his honor.[34]

If Lü found his relationship with the people of Hsiang-yüan exhilarating, he, like many officials of the sixteenth century, also felt alarmed by the power of the people, who were frequently participating in uprisings or simply congregating into ominously large crowds.[35] In frustration he commented that the common people were often unruly, touchy, demanding, volatile, and "comparable to spoiled sons."[36] He compared their emotions to the uncontrollable rush of water after dikes have burst,[37] and he noted that "when the feelings of the people overflow, restricting them is difficult . . . and as unbearable as cutting two toes joined together or a tumor."[38] Thus Lü felt both paternalistic towards the common people and also feared them. He both warned against those "troublesome laws . . . which provoke the reckless anger" of the masses,[39] and established rules to prevent "disturbing the people."[40] He criticized those who joined rebellious bands and sects for heterodox or seditious reasons; at the same time he understood that some had been driven to rebellion by desperation and unemployment.[41] As a solution to social unrest, Lü, like Hai Jui and many other fair-minded officials, urgently called for the equitable redistribution of wealth:

> If Heaven does not establish a ruler and the ruler does not establish officials, then the benefits of the

33. *CWCWC*, 8:59b; *Ning-ling hsien chih*, 11:12a.
34. *CWCWC*, 8:59b.
35. *SCL*, 1:20a. Note also Lü's suggestion that the size of charitable kitchens be kept small to discourage young wanderers from forming gangs (*SCL*, 2:44b).
36. *SYY*, 4:656. 37. *SYY*, 5:734. 38. *SYY*, 4:647.
39. Lü, *Kuei-fan t'u-shuo*, 2:26b. See also *SYY*, 4:757.
40. *SCL*, 5:4a. 41. *CWCWC*, 1:6a–b.

> world will revert to the bravos, the greedy, and the cruel. . . . The poor, who have no one to rely on, will lose benefits and will gather together to seek what they desire, thus paving the way to disaster in the world. Therefore benefits must be equitably distributed . . . and the Son of Heaven should collect just enough taxes for clothing and food, just enough to provide for the needs of the army and the state, and that is all.[42]

The restlessness of the masses and the fragility of social relations brought into sharp focus the wide gap between the common people and the bureaucratic elite and challenged in particular the magistrates to mediate between local interests and the imperial government. Hai Jui, who had served as magistrate before rising to high office, observed that the people felt closest to the provincial officials and feared most those of high status.[43] He further recognized that "the voice of the people is small; they have a public opinion (*kung-i*) which cannot of its own accord reach the top;"[44] that "lofty plans are remote from human feelings;"[45] and that "stopping up the voice of the people is more difficult than preventing a river flood."[46] But because Hai viewed society from the top, he rarely made place for details about the common people and never incorporated their outlook into his writings.

Lü was more deeply awed than Hai by the volatile emotions of the common people and allowed their views to intrude into his own consciousness. Opening Lü to influences from the common people was his exasperation with the often irrelevant scholarship of his peers. Criticizing those scholars who wasted time on abstruse debates, Lü wrote: "From the Ch'in and Han [dynasties] on down, [scholars] have been fighting to the death in disputing 'right and wrong' with others. This is already very laughable; how much more laughable if, on hearing that you are clever, you become proud and unwilling to descend among men."[47] "I'm afraid," he further mused, "that if I were among one hundred men, I would not

42. *CWCWC*, 7:60a. 43. *HJC*, p. 212. 44. *HJC*, p. 105.
45. *HJC*, p. 28. 46. *HJC*, p. 276. 47. *SYY*, 2:315.

necessarily rise above them; so how can I disregard the common man and woman?"[48]

Consequently, in contrast to Hai Jui, Lü stressed that the channels through which the people could vent their frustration and anger—in short their differences—must be kept open. Lü observed that repressing the emotions of the masses was not only difficult but would in fact provoke unmanageable outbursts: "The feelings of the people should not be blocked up at all. If you dam up water for embankments, then once [the dikes] burst, [the water] will carry rooms afloat and move mountains. If you pack in ammunition for a ballista, then once [the bullet] is shot, it will shatter rocks and bring down trees."[49] He moreover observed that the villainous rulers "Chou and Chieh had blocked up the feelings of the people," but that the worthy "T'ang and Wu had let them pass through (*t'ung*)." "This," Lü concluded, "is the great device [that determines] survival and destruction; and it is what those who rule the world work hard at from dawn to night."[50]

In his concern to reunite society, to eliminate feelings of separateness, Lü maintained that gentlemen should "cause others to be like the self"[51] and that "empathy," or "feelings of sameness" (*t'ung-jan*), were important.[52] "The enlightened king," he stated, "promotes spontaneity and establishes feelings of sameness."[53] Apprehensive that the people might rebel, Lü further advocated that "the ruler and people should be [united] in one body" and that "the hearts of the people must be firmly bound together."[54] He praised "those good at putting themselves in the place of others,"[55] and specifically the first kings, who strove to eliminate their selfishness in order to "identify with others."[56]

At the same time, Lü acutely felt that "the myriad things of heaven and earth were disconnected, purposeless, and unrelated to the self."[57] Ever since the three dynasties, Lü complained, "upper and lower have failed to connect for a long time. This is because each person has a separate body

48. *SYY*, 2:209. 49. *SYY*, 5:734. 50. *SYY*, 5:734.
51. *SYY*, 2:207. 52. *SCL*, 1:13b. 53. *SYY*, 4:653.
54. *CWCWC*, 1:6a. 55. *SYY*, 6:805. 56. *SYY*, 4:649.
57. In a letter to Ku Hsien-ch'eng, *CWCWC*, 5:7a.

and everyone has separate feelings."[58] In one passage, Lü stubbornly protested that all things should be "undivided, expansive, and boundless."[59] In another passage, he declared that "the single word, 'separation,' is most disastrous for human feelings."[60] Nonetheless, Lü was painfully conscious that everything was disconnected and that "people of the world all make divisions between things and the self."[61] The reality Lü perceived was at sharp variance with the ideal of undividedness.

Although Lü vociferously called for sameness, he could not share in the euphoric affirmation of the oneness of all things that characterized Lo Ju-fang's thought or Chang Tsai's *Western Inscription*, which had inspired Lo Ju-fang.[62] Lo had acknowledged but left little room for exploring or dwelling on the differences that individuated society. He had assumed that all his listeners, even if of different social statuses, would alike reach for the values to which he pointed. Lü responded to the differences, not by overlooking or striving to eradicate them, but by opening up channels of communication that fully acknowledged them. He entertained a vision of society that left salient, even while finding disturbing, the differences among men.

In a letter to a friend, Teng I-tsan, Lü kept alive both his belief that "others and the self should have empathic experiences and feelings" and his recognition that each person was different.[63] Failing to resolve the tension between his desire for oneness and his recognition that differences are inevitable, he used two words: "embody" (*t'i*), which he defined as "regarding others like the self," and "comprehend" (*hsi*), which he defined as the exercise of imagination to understand those who are different. To illustrate his point, Lü told of a southerner who could tolerate the summer heat and who did not realize, therefore, that his perspiring inferiors craved for permission to use the fans they timidly kept in their sleeves. Lü criticized the southerner for his "failure to

58. *SYY*, 4:652; see also *SYY*, 4:658.
59. *CWCWC*, 10:4b. 60. *SYY*, 1:81. 61. *CWCWC*, 10:5a.
62. For Chang Tsai's "Western Inscription," see Wing-tsit Chan, *Source Book*, pp. 497–98.
63. *CWCWC*, 4:9b.

comprehend," and concluded: "Regarding others like the self while realizing that others are not necessarily [like] the self is 'comprehension.'"[64]

For Lü, social differences, in particular the distinction between upper and lower, was more than a method of organizing society; in addition it was a paradigm for the exchange of elite ideals and information about the real world. On the one hand, Lü realized that the elite were masters of refined language and subtle arguments, which, as he observed in the following passage, the multitude could not understand:

> The multitude can see a small mustard leaf. [But] if you place the small mustard leaf one hundred *li* away, then only the Black Dragon can see it. One wonders whether [even] a worthy can make out what seems to be the truth. As for righteousness (*i*) refined to the point of divinity, only a sage can discriminate. Now to speak to a worthy about what the sage alone can understand will deepen his doubts. How much more so [when speaking to] the multitude! Accordingly, subtle words do not enter the ears of ordinary people of the world.[65]

On the other hand, Lü associated real experiences, "the things seen and heard," with the lower reaches of society. Thus in a passage that highlights the importance of magistrates, who of all officials were closest to the "true feelings" of the people, Lü commented:

> The higher one is, the more one is deaf and blind, and many are the things concealed. The lower one is, the truer are the things seen and heard. Therefore if one discusses "seeing and hearing," [one could say that] the ruler knows less than the prime minister, and the minister knows less than the provincial intendants; the provincial intendants know less than the prefects and magistrates, who in turn know less than the people. If one discusses concealment, then [one could say that] the prefects and magistrates conceal [information] from the provin-

64. Ibid., 4:9b. 65. *SYY*, 3:360.

cial intendants. . . . A pity! The true feelings at the very bottom cannot be made known to the one at the very top.[66]

Hai Jui's worry that the common people were unable to express themselves was limited specifically to his desire that they be defended against their oppressors. Lü's interest in communication between "upper and lower" was related to the value he placed on information about the real world.

Hai Jui was specifically concerned with the tensions between rich and poor. Lü's concern for communication also extended to other hierarchical social relations: adult and child, man and woman. That Lü's attitude toward the common people coincided with his attitude toward other examples of "inferior" status is apparent in his *Supplement to the Four Rituals*, a guide to raising children.[67] Here Lü maintained that the explications of books should be as simple as the language of villages and market places. He believed that "only if lecturing on *Chung-yung* [The Doctrine of the Mean] and *The Great Learning* moved male servants and female cooks to clap and dance could it be considered true textual explication."[68] Lü thus used an imaginary audience of female cooks and male servants as a model test even for teaching children who were undoubtedly of the elite—if one judges from the references to book-learning and the proper care of writing utensils.[69] Where Wang Ken and Lo Ju-fang had extended their educational efforts to fellow scholars and the poor, Lü extended his to women, children, and the poor. All examples of inferior social status—women, children, and the poor—were merged together in Lü's mind and were associated alike with the verification of real facts.

This association is again apparent in the preface to Lü's *Chiao-t'ai Rhyme-book*, where he explained that he had rejected the authority of established schools of thought on

66. *SYY*, 5:732–33.

67. Lü's preface to this work was written in 1573 (see the edition with the commentary by Chu Shih). This work should be distinguished from *Ssu-li i* [Doubtful points on the four rituals].

68. Lü, *Ssu-li i*, ed., Chu Shih, p. 5a.

69. On book learning, see ibid., p. 5a. On the care of writing implements, see pp. 2b–3a.

rhyme and followed instead what he heard directly from women and children. Lü described how difficult he had found the method for determining finals for the purpose of writing verse. Lü devoted the bulk of his preface to a debate with a friend about the proper method of incorporating the tones when using the *fan-ch'ieh* system of spelling out rhymes. The friend finally acknowledged that Lü's system was best and excitedly asked, "What school [of historical phonology] do you follow?" Lü replied, "I am not affiliated with a school; I trust my voice." The friend persisted in asking, "Who is your teacher?" Lü replied, "Women and children are all my teachers." Lü's friend was distressed. He had struggled for thirty years to master the rhymes, whereas Lü understood the principles of rhyme directly and effortlessly. Lü reassured his friend that the conventional approach was not entirely wrong. His friend simply did not perceive that the old rhyme-books, patterned on the speech of former centuries, served the present poorly. Accepting that words were first written to represent sounds that come from nature, Lü criticized the rhyme masters who failed to make alterations as the sounds changed. In sum, he explained to his friend, "I sought [the pronunciations] nearby and you looked for them afar; I took what was easy, and you took what was difficult."

The title of Lü's rhyme-book suggests what inspired him to develop a novel method. *Chiao-t'ai* is a phrase taken from a passage in the *I ching*, which states: "In the world of man it is a time of social harmony; those in high places show favor to the lowly, and the lowly and inferior in their turn are well disposed toward the highly placed. There is an end to all feuds." The phrase, *shang hsia hu ying*, with which Lü concluded his preface, might also be translated "upper and lower shouting and responding." In short, Lü turned away from established schools of phonology and recognized instead the value of learning from his own experiences—which he associated with the experiences of women and children, those at the bottom of the social hierarchy.[70]

Lü consciously accepted the differences that constituted

70. *CWCWC*, 3:12b–13a. Richard Wilhelm, tr., *The I Ching, or Book of Changes*, p. 50.

society, and he believed that "upper" and "lower" each had a cognitive as well as social value. It is in this light that his efforts to communicate to the lower social strata must be understood. Where Hai Jui had taken it upon himself to speak on behalf of the people, and Lo Ju-fang had tried through *hsiang-yüeh* to inculcate his values in the people, Lü K'un was concerned not with such one-directional communication but with the mutual exchange between "upper and lower," between the ideals of the elite and the real information associated with the experiences of the common people.

Lü's view that the top and bottom of society must participate in a reciprocal relationship is apparent in many ways. Desiring to communicate the ideals of the elite to the common people, Lü used simple language; simultaneously accepting the actual tastes of the common people, he tried to find a justification for the circulation of popular songs:

> The commoners like to hear popular songs and new tunes. But the licentious words and sounds are extremely pernicious to the customs of the people. If there is an old teacher or scholar, a writer of *tz'u* or a poet, who can transform the recent and fashionable tunes into constructive words, he will be rewarded one peck (*tou*) of grain for each tune.[71]

Lü also willingly shaped policies to suit the actual practices and economic needs of the people. Hai Jui, adhering to the proper rules of behavior, had forbidden even working women from going out onto the streets;[72] Lü advocated that laws be bent to accord with local customs, or the feelings of the people:

> The men and women in poor families easily mix; and the commoners take their reputations very lightly—unlike the gentry families, who strictly separate the inner and outer [parts of their households] and who use propriety and righteousness to cultivate their minds. Therefore one should not force the Way of the sages on the ignorant and poor people; and when making judgments on this sort of illicit be-

71. *SCL*, 2:33b. 72. *HJC*, pp. 445–46.

havior, one cannot adhere to the letter of the law but must get at the essential meaning behind the law.[73]

Acknowledging the differences that constitute society, Lü, unlike Hai Jui, could mediate between the actual behavior of the common people and the values of the bureaucratic elite.

Because Lü entertained the outlooks of both the upper and lower reaches of society, an admixture of realism and idealism often resulting in contradictory statements runs throughout Lü's writings. For example, in one instance Lü adheres to the optimistic view that all men are educable. He tells of a king "who used virtue to transform others." An arrested cattle thief asked that his case not be reported to the king, whereupon the king sent the thief a roll of cloth and explained to his puzzled retainers that the thief's fear of exposure demonstrated his sense of shame and hence his capacity for moral improvement. "Therefore," concluded the king, "I used this [reward] to give him strength." To be sure, when someone later lost a sword on the road, the reformed cattle thief returned it to the original owner.[74]

Elsewhere Lü expressed a cynical view of a similar case. He tells of a governor who used rewards to foster goodness. When a man returned a lost lamb to its owner, the governor praised the finder for his honesty and gave him a reward worth twice the value of the lamb. Some time later the finder connived with an acquaintance: "You lose some money, which I'll pick up and return." When the governor heard that the lost gold had been returned to its owner, he rewarded the finder two taels. The finder ecstatically said: "I am greedy. I usually make profit at the expense of my reputation. Today I both made a profit and earned a good reputation. What will I not dare do?"[75]

Similarly contradictory, Lü urged the common people to attend the community schools by asking rhetorically, "How often have you seen literate people become thieves?"[76] but elsewhere despaired that educated children were often rebellious and that one might as well, therefore, exchange books for grain to aid the starving.[77]

73. *SCL*, 6:16a. 74. Lü K'un, *Wu ju*, 1:4b–5a. 75. *SYY*, 5:769.
76. *SCL*, 3:8a. 77. Lü K'un, *Tsung-yüeh ko*, p. 17a.

Paper work

With Lü's view of communication, bureaucratic paper work took on a new significance. Paper work sometimes exasperated him. He complained that "the downfall of good government began with the rise of the legal codes; and harm set in with the complications of record-keeping."[78] He often felt overwhelmed by the task of imposing order on the papers that stacked up day after day,[79] and repelled by "the thousand items and the hundred [book] cases, gnawed at by mice and dampened by rain . . . and the divergent bits of information."[80] Such tedious and endless paper work more closely characterized clerks, or petty functionaries, than moral leaders.

At the same time, Lü perceived that extensive paper work, which opened up channels of communication, could benefit the people. He thus found a way to rise above the mentality of the functionary. When a friend criticized Lü for wasting too much vermilion ink,[81] Lü conceded that he could save much over the days and years by accumulating the small bits wasted on writing each character. "Of course," he added, "one should not use the 'fat of the people' negligently." But, he concluded, because some matters were more important than waste, he was not economical with paper. When Lü later served as governor, he instructed his clerks in the usefulness of paper work. In contrast to the profligate spending of wealthy lads, he argued, the liberal use of paper and ink within the yamen would benefit the people.[82] Lü, who elsewhere carefully calculated that minute savings pile up to significantly useful amounts over long periods of time,[83] here defended extravagance because his own sense of purpose had become bound up with voluminous paper work.

In addition to the more conventional records of registration of the population and loans to the poor, which were written simply to regulate, codify, or preserve a memory of certain arrangements, Lü imaginatively applied the concept of record-keeping and handbooks to other areas.

78. *SYY*, 5:755.
79. *SCL*, 3:42b.
80. *SYY*, 5:756.
81. *SYY*, 2:294.
82. *SYY*, 2:294.
83. *SCL*, 2:16b; 2:19b.

First, Lü wrote manuals to spread information. He designed guides both for members of *hsiang-yüeh* and *pao-chia*, and for the subbureaucracy. He printed military manuals,[84] and he planned to write a medical treatise to be distributed to all lecture units (*yüeh*), for he feared that those in distant villages might not have ready access to doctors.[85] Complaining in his *Records of Practical Government* that there had been numerous books on "teaching the Way" but few on "methods of supporting the people,"[86] Lü also disseminated information on fertilizers, planting trees, building rat-proof granaries and other practical matters.[87] Moreover, as mentioned in the previous chapter, he spread information among the people for their protection against oppressive and rapacious bureaucrats.

Secondly, Lü used records for the collection of information which was then to be tested against new data. He advocated, for example, that all student doctors should keep records of their treatments so that they might better assess the various medicines administered.[88] Similarly, elaborating on a practice that dates back to the eleventh century, Lü instructed the members of *hsiang-yüeh* to keep track of their moral progress. Both the collection of medical data and records of reform were qualitatively different from more conventional record-keeping: rather than subordinating behavior to an institutionalized routine, they involved men in a continual process of sharing, evaluating, and acting upon information. Records, for Lü, were the tools through which men could collect information from and assert control over their objective world.

The collection and dissemination of information—of useful facts—played an important role in Lü's vision of local government and his definition of the worthy official. At a time when increased reliance on paper work and regulations in the pursuit of efficiency threatened to diminish the status of officials, Lü also provided them with a new ennobling way to relate to their society and environment.

84. *SCL*, 1:44a. 85. *SCL*, 2:51b. 86. *SCL*, 2:4a.
87. *SCL*, *chüan* 2. 88. *SCL*, 2:49b.

7

In Search of Crises

In the eighth month of 1547, Lü reported some forty years later, his mother suddenly woke up to discover that she was blind. She knocked her head, screamed, and refused to eat. On the third day, the family invited a famous eye doctor who upon examining Lü's mother avoided everyone's eyes and went through his paces quickly; he could not cure her. Consequently, the family called a blind woman to entertain Lü's mother with music and songs, and gradually Lü's mother recovered her spirits. When one singer had run through her repertoire, the family hired another, and sometimes they invited storytellers as well. Any famous lute player, whether from near or far, had to come.[1]

Just as in Lü's later life, when the urgent need to educate the common people justified departing from the convention of writing in the literary style, then, too, a crisis—his mother's blindness—excused a deviation from the norm. Lü's father had always warned against letting such women as matchmakers and storytellers enter the gates, but, according to Lü's account, "On this occasion, he bent the rule and tolerated the emotions of women and children."[2]

Sights and sounds

This event, which others might have left dangling in isolation in faint memory, Lü took as the point of departure for a lengthy essay, "Chia yüeh chieh" ["An Explanation of Family Music"], a full forty years later. Around the traumatic experi-

1. *CWCWC*, 7:65a. 2. *CWCWC*, 7:65a–b.

ence of his mother's blindness crystallized not only Lü's feelings of compassion but an entire program for action, for Lü turned from the dramatic account of his mother's sudden loss of sight, with which he had opened the essay, to a deep appreciation of the power of music and even to a plan for helping beggars.

Lü explained that from 1571 on, the memory of his mother's loss of sight moved him to feel compassion for blind beggars. Therefore he hired a blind teacher to instruct and drill the beggars in telling stories and fortunes and edited two manuals, *Tzu-p'ing yao-yü* [The Essentials of Astrology] and *Ch'üan-shih ko-tien* [A Songbook for Exhorting the World] to guide the teachers. In addition, he provided musical instruments so that the beggars would eventually be able to clothe and feed themselves and get married. Taking pride in the effectiveness of his program, Lü noted, "And I have heard that some have ceased to become beggars."[3]

Lü also defended music at great length in his essay by addressing those who might argue that "one should not let women from all over enter the women's quarters," or that "the sounds of singing should not be heard in the women's quarters."[4] To his imaginary critics, Lü conceded: "These objections are made to defend the home; how dare I say they are wrong?"[5] However, Lü then proceeded to cite various examples from respectable ancient texts, such as *Nü hsün* [Instructions for Women], that sanctioned the participation of women in music.[6] The quality of the sound, Lü argued, depends on the attitude of the listener rather than on the instrument. Thus the filial son will grieve on hearing his sick parent groan, while others will cover their ears. "And when cicadas chirp, what is it that actually moves people?" Lü asked, and then responded that most people would be deaf to the sound, but that a woman longing for her mate would grieve. "Therefore," Lü concluded, "it is said that [the quality of] sounds arises from people's minds. My home draws the line at prostitutes and forbids lewdness but has never forbidden popular music."[7]

3. *CWCWC*, 7:65b. 4. *CWCWC*, 7:65b–66a. 5. *CWCWC*. 7:66a.
6. *CWCWC*, 7:66b–67a. 7. *CWCWC*, 7:67a.

In Lü's essay on family music, numerous seemingly disparate themes coalesced: his mother's horrifyingly sudden loss of sight, the power of music, his compassion for and instruction of beggars, and his concern that the poor become self-reliant. Bringing these themes together was not the event of Lü's mother's blindness but the way in which Lü, forty years later, organized his perceptions of past experiences. Lü's conceptual framework as well as the actual events determined which facts he retained. Shaping Lü's concerns was a general pattern, which appeared in many contexts other than the isolated event of Lü's mother's blindness. The same themes—crisis, sense-perceptions, and self-reliance—frequently clustered together when Lü wrote about topics other than his mother's blindness. The same themes also appeared in the writings of Lü's predecessor, Ch'i Chi-kuang. Finally, both crises—of which illness was only one type—and each person's capacity to be self-reliant played a special role in the struggle not only of Lü but also of some of his contemporaries in dealing with the confusing array of experiences. Only by looking at the recurrent clustering of these themes rather than the isolated fact of Lü's mother's blindness, can one understand why Lü went far beyond treating blind beggars charitably to instruct them to become self-reliant.

Conflict between mind and senses

Lü repeatedly expressed his fear of "getting mired in the present," or, more literally, "in what is before the eyes" (*niu yü mu-ch'ien*).[8] Vulnerable to the impact his complex environment made on his senses, and annoyed that a change of scene or of views expressed in print easily threw him off balance, Lü complained:

> When living in a village, one's vision is limited to several ten *li*; obstinately one preserves [the vision] and a hundred attacks will not destroy it. [But] when one wanders into a large city and sees the affairs

8. See, for example, *SYY*, 3:410.

> (*shih*) of one thousand *li*, one confusedly loses oneself. Living today, one's vision is limited to a thousand or ten thousand people; narrow-mindedly one keeps to it, and one hundred attacks will not destroy it. [But] when one reads the ancient classics and sees the events (*shih*) of a thousand or ten thousand years, then one confusedly loses oneself.[9]

The mind and the environment had become so thoroughly separated that they were almost in battle. How one should withstand the onslaught of sense perceptions through mental discipline deeply concerned Lü.

Lü persistently tried to resist the powerful lure of sights and sounds but could not. His difficulty might in part be traced to the rich material environment of the flourishing urban centers. There was no phenomenon that could not be seen or heard, the late Ming preface to a survey of technology declared: "We are fortunate to be living in an era of enlightened rule and great prosperity, when the carriages from Yunnan may be seen traversing the plains of Liao-yang [Southern Manchuria] and the officials and merchants from the southern coast travel about freely in Hopei."[10] The diversity of eye-catching fashions and products, generated by commerce and travel, made self-discipline difficult.[11]

However, men are not susceptible to external influences unless they are internally conflicted, unless some internal soil is accommodating. Thus in the following passage Lü presents a disturbing argument against the "obstacles of seeing and hearing." On the one hand, he struggles against getting mired in the present. On the other hand, he paints in the vision he wishes to overcome as vividly as the one to be grasped:

> [I asked] "If one threw a beautiful piece of fruit into urine, cleansed it and presented it to you, would you

9. *SYY*, 3:401. *Shih* can mean both "event" and "affair." In other contexts, it can also mean "duty" and "task."

10. Sung Ying-hsing, *T'ien-kung k'ai-wu, Chinese Technology in the Seventeenth Century*, p. xiii.

11. For a description of the rapidly changing fashions during the late Ming, see Fu I-ling, *Ming-tai Chiang-nan shih-min ching-chi shih-t'an*, pp. 106–7. On the frequent neglect of sumptuary regulations, p. 102.

eat it?" He replied, "I would not eat it." I said, "If you had not seen [it thrown into urine] and ate it, would you get sick?" He said, "I would not get sick." "If someone behind a mountain pointed and cursed at you, would you hear him?" He said, "I would not hear him." "If he faced you and pointed and cursed at you, would you get angry?" He said, "I would get angry." [I said] "These are the obstacles that seeing and hearing present. Now, if one could be made to look at it and eat it, hear it and not get angry, one could even brave the dark sea and tread on a bare blade. This is what those who wish to discipline the mind should know."[12]

The experiences of "seeing and hearing" can be upsetting, Lü observes, but rather than deny those experiences, rather than repress the senses, one must learn to discipline the mind to handle them with equanimity.

In his "Hsing-mi yin" ["Preface to Awakening the Deluded"], Lü again explored the problem. He observed that most men were "deluded by their eyes," but at the same time he recognized how valuable sense experiences were.[13] He reasoned:

These days, a child about four feet [tall] can distinguish between north, south, east, and west, but once confused by a forked road, he will go to Ch'u via Yen. The harm done by confusion is great indeed.

Now, nine out of ten are deluded by their eyes and one out of ten are deluded by their minds. Everyone is clear of mind but befuddled by the eyes. Therefore the mind becomes the slave of the eyes, fails in its function, and just tags along. The fact that the whole world is blind is the fault of the eyes.

There was a person who called the east south. Two enlightened people said, "Look at the sun. How could it possibly rise in the south and set in the north?" The confused one said, "I certainly know

12. *SYY*, 1:45. 13. *CWCWC*, 3:34a–35a.

> that the sun does not rise in the south and set in the north, but today it has." The enlightened ones said, "Would you call your eyes correct? Or your mind correct?" The confused one said, "If my mind stopped trusting my eyes, then how could I direct my feet?" The enlightened ones said, "You are unable to overrule your sight in order to follow your mind; moreover, you are duped by today's [experience]. We truly have no great expectations for you."[14]

Lü then bemoaned that people fail to overcome "their overwhelming and captivating desires" even when they know the difference between right and wrong.[15] Both the passage on the fruit dipped in urine and the "Preface to Awakening the Deluded" leave the reader's mind reeling. How can one erase the vivid picture of the tainted fruit when asked to discipline the mind to overcome "the obstacles of seeing and hearing"? And on what grounds should one determine that the sun has not risen in the south? In neither passage could Lü block out the experiences of the senses. Sight is, after all, necessary to walking in the correct direction. At the same time, Lü appreciated that the mind must be disciplined through some objective framework to impose order on the experiences of the senses. Names such as "north" and "south" referring to that objective framework may be arbitrary, but they are useful nonetheless.

The onslaught of perceptions—or the impact of his environment—was sometimes so fierce as to prove paralyzing. A rapidly changing society and an overwhelming sense of diversity had made it increasingly difficult to discipline the mind to make choices and find stability. Numbed by the dazzling multitude of choices, Lü craved for a sense of direction and a means of making choices. Accordingly, he wrote: "Confusion is my only fear. . . . If I enter the mountains with their multitudinous scenes, I can wander about, [but] if I want to go somewhere, then I must not wander aimlessly. If I enter the valleys with their many flowers, I can survey them

14. *CWCWC*, 3:34a. 15. *CWCWC*, 3:34b.

all, but if I want to break one off, then I must not let my eyes get dazed."[16]

Lü struggled to gain some mastery over his environment through study. Foreshadowing the famous agronomist, official, and Christian convert, Hsü Kuang-ch'i,[17] Lü treated his environment objectively. He recognized that man could act upon and even alter his environment. Refusing to accept faulty harvests passively, Lü argued that "rotting things can be transformed into rarities"[18] and that fertilized soil "can produce a myriad of things."[19] He was distressed that those living in distant rustic villages simply let their livestock defecate in the fields without realizing that fertilizer could be made more effectively by processing it.[20] Repeatedly, Lü exhorted others to act upon their environment. He observed: "When grain is piled up in a granary, one above all fears the damp ground and leaking roof, and one in addition fears that swallows will enter and rats will bore their way through." He then asked rhetorically: "How is it that the defense against these does not lie in the power of men?"[21] Similarly Lü observed of the ancients: "They blamed the earth and rejected the power of the earth. In good years, they tolerated hunger passively; and in lean years, they starved to death. But it was not all the fault of the harvest," Lü explained, and then advised: "Use of manure and diligent hoeing will produce greater yields from small plots of land."[22]

To assert some control over, or impose order on his bewildering environment, Lü used methods that fully acknowledged the centrality of affairs or events (*shih*). Accordingly, to determine what was important, Lü did not simply reaffirm the ideals of the classics, but thought in terms of crises; to eliminate conflict, Lü did not urge that people abandon their greedy ways but assumed a long-range view that embraced

16. *SYY*, 2:350. Around 1598, some years after the publication of *SYY*, Kao P'an-lung observed that the mountains and waters in the world were so numerous that one was "incapable of passing them all each day." Therefore, Kao explained, "I pick out one that is sufficient to hold my aspirations and I rest." Cited in Taylor, *The Cultivation of Sagehood as a Religious Goal*, p. 29.

17. Biography of Hsü by J. C. Yang in *ECCP*, pp. 316–19.

18. *SCL*, 2:4a. 19. *SCL*, 2:4a. 20. *SCL*, 2:4a.

21. *SCL*, 2:12a. 22. *SCL*, 2:2b–3a.

and mediated among the interests of all; and to achieve a sense of mastery over the multitude of events, Lü compiled lists. We turn now to Lü's methods of finding order by these means.

In search of crises: illness and warfare

Taking warning from those who "seeing that what is before their eyes is pleasing, simply leave it at that,"[23] Lü savored illnesses, crises, battles, and "critical junctures" (*kuan*) —in other words, concrete situations that forced him to make choices.[24] To determine, for example, what the scholar should value most highly, Lü conjured up crises: "When you rush to the city gate at sundown, if you are one step late, you will be locked out. Where will you stay the night? Therefore scholars value being on time. When hanging from a precipice, clinging to a lonely tree, if you let one hand go, you will fall. Where will you fall? Therefore scholars value exertion of strength."[25] Similarly, the test whether the fruit dipped in urine would indeed make one ill helped Lü pinpoint the obstacle of seeing; and the critical situation of confronting a forked road tested one's knowledge of direction. In the same spirit, Lü maintained that "the sage's [ability to] empathize with others is tested even more in times of difficulty;"[26] and he acknowledged: "Ordinarily nothing special happens and you think you are a completely good person. . . . [But] when you confront a great difficulty, you will discover what kind of person you [really] are."[27]

To arouse himself out of his state of numbness, Lü craved for pain. Accordingly, he complained in a letter to Ku Hsien-ch'eng that he "felt nothing" because "there was no ache or pain."[28] Elsewhere he argued that "only words deriving from mental hardship are cutting and flavorful"[29] and that: "everyone knows that one must do good and get rid of evil; but in the end they do not do good or get rid of evil because the

23. *SYY*, 3:364. 24. For example, *SYY*, 1:40; 1:48.
25. *SYY*, 2:350. 26. *SYY*, 4:646. 27. *SYY*, 2:334.
28. *CWCWC*, 5:7a. 29. *CWCWC*, 4:8b.

meaning does not ring true. Why? . . . Because their knowledge is not trenchant (*t'ung-ch'ieh*)."[30]

Lü's emotional need for crises fastened on real situations, in particular, illnesses and military battles. In his "Plaque for the Temple for the Medicine Sage," Lü recalled in vivid details several serious illnesses his parents had experienced. In 1554 his mother felt such acute pain that her screams reached the next village and she prayed for death. A few years later, Lü found her sick again, curled up in agony "like a lizard shedding its skin." His father died of dysentery in 1568; and his mother followed soon after in 1571.[31] This passage would not deserve attention if it did not fit into a larger pattern: the theme of illness not only remained a life-long interest for Lü but preoccupied other sixteenth-century writers such as Lo Ju-fang, Chou Ju-teng (*chin-shih,* 1577), Yüan Hung-tao (1568–1610), Li Chih, and Lin Chao-en. The filter of Lü's adult outlook had determined which childhood experiences were to remain important. Some writers distinguished between mental and physical illness, but most accepted that the two often converged, and used the vocabulary of medicine to describe remedying their malaise. "Medicine is the will, and the method rests firmly in your own mind," a teacher had instructed Lin Chao-en.[32] For thirty years, Lü kept a record of his thoughts, later published as *Groaning Words,* with the hope, he explained, of curing himself.[33]

Lü lacked confidence in a cure. Citing the *Tso chuan,* he initially took comfort in the knowledge that a good physician can cure an arm broken in three places; but Lü then quickly despaired: his arm had been broken in nine places. Lü had so little confidence in the efficacy of self-cultivation that he decided only half-heartedly to publish *Groaning Words* when persuaded to do so by a friend. The friend's argument reflected Lü's own doubts. "Even if you do not get better," he told Lü, hardly reassuringly, "you can use *Groaning Words* to cure others, and is that not already a lot?"[34]

Lü K'un was not alone in his conviction that good health

30. *CWCWC,* 4:39b. 31. *CWCWC,* 8:61a–63a.
32. Cited in Berling, *The Syncretic Religion of Lin Chao-en,* p. 69.
33. Lü K'un, "Preface," *SYY,* p. 22. 34. Ibid., p. 23.

was unattainable. Yüan Hung-tao observed that the desire for sensual pleasures was so compelling as to infect and deprive everyone of a sense of control:

> Question: When sick, how does one gain control?
> Answer: You should not consider illness as illness. Today all good people are sick.
> Question: How is it that good people are also sick?
> Answer: The eyes desire beauty; the ears crave for sounds; and one also desires food and clothing—everyone has this illness. In the midst of this, it is difficult to gain control. How much more true of chills and fevers and such illnesses—once they penetrate the body, how can you gain control![35]

Illness had gained a special value. Some of Lü's contemporaries recognized that through sickness they could overcome their numbness. Just before Lü first published his *Groaning Words*, Li Chih wrote: "The ancient worthies and sages did not write unless they were exasperated. To write without being exasperated is like trembling without being cold and groaning without being sick."[36]

Chou Ju-teng, one of Lo Ju-fang's admirers, went so far as to glorify the hidden benefits of illness:

> When I was sick in bed for three years, a guest came by to inquire about my illness. I was then spread out, dishevelled, groaning, impoverished, and pitying myself on account of my illness. The guest said: "Illness is your good fortune; how can you consider it misery?" I, taking exception to his words, asked for an explanation. The guest asked, "Have you heard the saying . . . 'without an enemy country and outside worries, you will constantly forget the state?' You often drink wine, indulge in sex, are bad-tempered, and boastful. When you are not ill, you indulge yourself freely and do not know when to stop. Now I see you [are extremely careful] trem-

35. Yüan Hung-tao, "Shu t'an," in *Yüan Chung-lang sui-pi*, p. 34.
36. Li Chih, *Li shih Fen shu*, p. 130.

> bling as though walking on spring ice or overlooking a precipice. Music and women, personal advantage, and superficial formalities are all forgotten, just as though you are throwing off an illness. Are you blind to [this hidden benefit]?"[37]

Chou's guest then told two parables to illustrate the benefits. In the first parable, a thief was about to steal jewels when a raccoon scavenging for food broke a plate, scared away the thief, and woke up the owner. The owner was so upset over the broken plate that he failed to realize that a raccoon had prevented a theft. In the second parable, just as a candle carelessly left burning was about to ignite a pile of firewood, a thief entered the room, extinguished the candle for fear of being illuminated, stole some valuables, and left. When the owner awoke, he was angry about the theft without realizing that the thief had prevented a fire. "Your illness [which discourages overindulgence in sex and drink]," the friend instructed Chou, "[resembles] the disturbances made by the raccoon and the thief. . . . You can decide whether these are misfortunes or not."[38]

The benefits of illness again figure in an account of Lin Chao-en, who was famous for his view that the three religions, Buddhism, Taoism, and Confucianism, originated from the same source—a view that displayed his responsiveness to the culture of the common people. Lin was acquainted with Yüan Huang and Chou Ju-teng, and his proselytizing was defended by two of Lü's acquaintances, Tsou Yüan-piao and Keng Ting-hsiang.[39] To some extent, then, Lü and Lin shared the same milieu. A teacher advised Lin on how to compensate for the lack of official status. Lin—who as a mere commoner would have difficulty in converting others—asked his teacher: "With what shall I verify it to bring others to believe?" The teacher responded: "Verify it with illness. If the illness is cured, they will believe."[40] Curing an

37. Chou Ju-teng, "Ping yen chi," in *Tung-yüeh cheng-hsüeh lu*, 11:10b. Chou wrote a biography of Lo Ju-fang that included details about Lo's mental collapses (*Chin-hsi tzu chi*, 1:13b–19b).

38. Chou Ju-teng, *Tung-yüeh cheng-hsüeh lu*, 11:11a–b.

39. Berling, *The Syncretic Religion of Lin Chao-en*, p. 84.

40. Ibid., p. 69.

illness had a role in determining what was most valid, in giving legitimacy, or value, to ideas. The account of Lin is also important both for implying that the legitimacy of ideas was closely identified (in the eyes of the masses, at any rate) with official status and for suggesting that overcoming crises, in this case curing an illness, was an alternative to following an authority in defining values.

To jolt himself out of lethargy, Lü struggled to keep a sense of urgency alive in times of leisure.[41] Lü directly opposed "urgency" to sensual pleasures, as in his statement, "All those things that are not urgent and that please the ears and eyes are impractical."[42] Consequently just as one entangled in worldly pleasures overlooks important issues, so do healthy people, Lü noted, forget what it is like to be ill.[43] Likewise perceiving that the healthy tend to be negligent, Chou Ju-teng concluded his essay on illness with the following words: "I was afraid I would turn my back on my guest's words when I got better, so I wrote them down and made them my guiding motto."[44] Chou Ju-teng thus warned himself in healthy times that overindulgence in wine and women would lead to illness. Similarly, Lü summoned specters of danger to admonish himself against slipping into the absorbing world of the present. In short, Chou and Lü, like so many of their contemporaries, generated a mood of fearful alertness both to ward off the temptations of their attractive environment and to select what was most essential from the confusing array of choices.

Lü's penchant for crises found real form not only in illness but in military emergencies. In 1609, after retiring from office, Lü composed *Chiu-ming shu* [A Book on Saving Lives], a guide for defending his home town, Ning-ling, against bandits. Lü wrote this book for several reasons. He had noted that the disintegration of the regular army necessitated the organization of a local militia.[45] He also feared the ubiquitous roving bandits and heterodox sects. And he knew that the frequent floods in the Ning-ling area, which was a low plain

41. *SYY*, 3:424. 42. *SYY*, 5:630.
43. Lü K'un, "Preface," *SYY*, p. 22.
44. Chou Ju-teng, *Tung-yüeh cheng-hsüeh lu*, 11:11b.
45. *Chiu-ming shu*, in *CWCWC*, 7:49a.

between two rivers, made necessary the safe storage of grain within the city walls.[46] Still fresh in the minds of the natives of Ning-ling, furthermore, was the devastating famine of 1595, which could have been alleviated if the officials had not just a year previously distributed the grain extravagantly among the people.[47]

Finally, Lü's interest in fortifying the city walls reflected a widespread late sixteenth-century concern for military problems. Shortly before Lü first assumed office, the famous general Ch'i Chi-kuang wrote several manuals on warfare in response to the incursions of the Japanese pirates (*wo-k'ou*). Lü never acknowledged a debt to Ch'i. Yet he was so interested in military manuals, even writing a preface to *Hsing-chün hsü chih* [What the Infantry Should Know] by Meng Feng (1456–1526),[48] that it seems most likely that he was familiar with Ch'i's popular work. Lü's calculations on unifying the energies of large military forces often resembled Ch'i's. Ch'i, for example, wrote: "If each [soldier] has the strength [to lift] 100 catties, then 1000 [soldiers] have the strength [to lift] 100,000 catties. . . . How can one make [the soldiers] act with one mind?"[49] Lü, calculating along similar lines, stated: "Those good at using strength lift 100 *chün* as they would one feather; those good at using the multitude train 10,000 troops as they would one man."[50]

Lü was inspired to expand and fortify the wall when an estate owner, fleeing bandits, begged to enter the city and promised to finance strengthening the wall in return for protection. After laborers had already been recruited, the estate owner reneged on his promise, whereupon Lü devised a plan which, he argued, would essentially cost the people nothing: by investing in a well-planned construction project, they would save the many miscellaneous services and fees that would otherwise be exacted for piecemeal upkeep over the long run.[51]

46. *CWCWC*, 7:20a.
47. *Chiu-ming shu*, in *CWCWC*, 7:37a.
48. *CWCWC*, 3:10b–11a.
49. Ch'i Chi-kuang, *Lien-ping shih-chi*, p. 65. For a discussion of similarities between the outlooks of Ch'i and Lü, see Joanna F. Handlin, "Definitions of Community by Ch'i Chi-kuang and Lü K'un," pp. 18–25.
50. *SYY*, 3:458. One *chün* equals thirty catties.
51. *CWCWC*, 7:32b–33a.

Shortly after Lü's death, when bandits attacked Ning-ling, the inhabitants marvelled at Lü's foresight.[52] In the light of Ch'i's popular work and later events, Lü's manual appears to be nothing more than an obvious response to the challenges of his time. In fact, however, the urgency of fortifying the city wall became apparent only when bandits subsequently attacked Ning-ling. Initially most of the local inhabitants had fiercely opposed the plan and belligerently asked, "Why bother with building walls in times of peace?"[53]

What impelled Lü to write up a plan for city defense was not the objective situation—which others had faced unresponsively—but Lü's outlook. His interest in crises, his caution and alertness, and his fear of unsuspected enemies—as much as the conditions of Ning-ling—shaped his plan for fortifying the wall. Thus even as young as fifteen *sui*, long before the publication of Ch'i's works, Lü had brought together in a poem, "Chao liang-hsin" ["A Summons to My Conscience"], the very themes that years later again merged in his *Book on Saving Lives*. "If my home is without a master," the young Lü had written, "the enemy will fill the surrounding fields. . . . The body should value proceeding cautiously; otherwise it will be too late to regret."[54] In short, Lü K'un had already adopted in the area of self-cultivation an outlook that was particularly conducive to writing about military preparedness. Drawing again on the image of the surreptitious approach of thieves, Lü warned: "Before the event, the body is negligent and the spirit confused. When the event comes, one is flustered; when the event has passed, the mind is at peace and one's attention is relaxed. These are the thieves of events." And then, illustrating the ease with which Lü had come to share a military general's outlook, Lü concluded, "This [type of person] is especially unsuited for the military."[55]

Foresight and fear of regret

By generating a sense of crisis, Lü imposed order on the confusing array of affairs, thereby confirming their central im-

52. Wang Yung-jui, "Appendix," *Ning-ling hsien-chih*, p. 6a.
53. *CWCWC*, 7:21a. 54. *CWCWC*, 10:15b. 55. *SYY*, 3:458.

portance. Similarly by assuming a long-range view—which Lü expressed through his fear of regret and call for foresight —Lü avoided getting "mired in the present" while keeping his eye on concrete facts.

Lü's preoccupation with regret and foresight stresses a temporal dimension to his thoughts and indeed Lü often mentioned "facts and times" (*shih shih*) simultaneously.[56] Dreading regret, which results from being "caught up in what is before the eyes," or being "mired in the present," Lü promoted a sense of urgency about time. In the following passage, Lü resigned himself to the inevitability of aging, and the impossibility of "recapturing each breath that has passed," but believed that one could take precautions against feeling regret:

> This is called truly cherishing one's time. Those who say, "I won't experience this day again" and "[wasting] this day would be regrettable" are all thinking [in terms of urgencies such as] putting out a fire and saving [those about to] perish. . . . Alas! Do not worry about not having enough time, but worry about wasting time. If you do not throw away your time, and if your mind is at ease and satisfied, what will there be to regret?[57]

In line with his penchant to savor crises, Lü feared that even one event, or one minute, might prove critical. "There is a famous couplet," he observed, "'One slip will cause ten thousand years of regret; if one turns back again, all will be well for one hundred years.'"[58] Apprehensive that one mishap might cause permanent regret, Lü gave the following advice: "When happy, examine it once; when angry, examine it once; when lazy, examine it once; when lax, examine it once. These are the major items of an examination. When people confront [the examination], they cannot remember or pay attention to most of it. Once they go wrong, then it is too late to regret."[59]

Regretfulness points to a consciousness of choices, or alternative plans—an awareness that one might have acted

56. *SYY*, 2:334. 57. *SYY*, 2:335.
58. *SYY*, 2:270. 59. *SYY*, 2:232.

otherwise. Thus Lü stated, "Before [feeling] regret, nothing is better than being cautious about how one begins; after [feeling] regret, nothing is better than changing one's plans."[60] Foresight, according to Lü, distinguished the sage from the ordinary man. Lü admired those sages and worthies who "from beginning to end are single-minded." Such men "confront [events] with sure minds. When they act, they are correct from the start. After they act, what have they to regret? Even in misfortunes and calamities and during the time of action, they are generally like this."[61] To avoid regret, Lü argued, one must prepare for future events. "Deliberation," he maintained, "is necessary to prevent what might happen."[62] "[If] the wise scholar just applies effort to the unexpected, then each time all will be perfect and there will be no worries afterward."[63]

Lü contrasted the expansive outlook of the sage with the nearsightedness of petty men. "The awareness of most people," he complained, "is the same throughout the world: shallow, unenlightened, and perverted by what is before their eyes."[64] "[People with] commonplace feelings," Lü further observed, "utterly fail to be farsighted; and petty men rise up in destructive bands whenever [the plans] fail to serve their selfish [desires]."[65] The common people "are not economical and do not know how to manage their lives," Lü further noted, but then added, "there is an art to coming to the rescue in disasters and a Way to prepare for disasters."[66]

In contrast to the nearsighted common people, Lü sought to cope with his complex environment by enlarging his view. Thus when Lü complained, in a passage cited earlier, that he had lost his balance when entering a city with a villager's outlook, he concluded that "a confined view must not be cramped; if it is cramped . . . and narrow, it will be inadequate for doing good in worldly affairs."[67] Analogously, in the essay on influence and profit discussed in chapter 5, Lü did not try to transcend influence and profit—as had Li Chih—but counseled instead that the sage "must not be con-

60. *SYY*, 3:401. 61. *SYY*, 3:441. 62. *SYY*, 3:364.
63. *SYY*, 3:406. 64. *SYY*, 3:410. 65. *SYY*, 3:357.
66. *SCL*, 3:41b.
67. *SYY*, 3:401. See also *SYY*, 4:516; 4:521; and *CWCWC*, 7:60b.

fined by [thoughts of] influence and profit."[68] Lü tried to embrace such thoughts rather than eradicate or block them out. With an enlarged view, Lü could gain perspective on a wide range of experiences and heterogeneous social groups. By focusing on future events, by taking as his major points of reference urgent projects involving life and death, Lü could deflect attention from current social conflicts. And social conflict within his community, as much as the fear of banditry from without, prompted him to propose a plan for the city wall.

An anonymous circular voiced widespread opposition to Lü's plan to rebuild the city wall. The circular is no longer extant, but Lü's itemized response to its criticisms gives us an unusual glimpse of local politics even though the picture is sketchy. Although Lü's response fails to delineate just how power was distributed in Ning-ling at that time, it does reveal a sharp conflict between the city dwellers and those living on the estates. Lü noted that homes within the walls cost many times more than the most extravagantly constructed estates. To some extent, he explained, the protection which the city walls provided was responsible for driving up the prices of town homes; but Lü also observed incidentally that the city dwellers could conveniently open shops.[69] By promising the laborers—drawn from the common people living beyond the city walls—the right to seek protection within the gates in exchange for their cooperation, Lü, who was conscious of the growing tension between town and country, sought to knit back together a rapidly disintegrating community. Lü's selflessness was apparent to the author of the colophon to Lü's *Book On Saving Lives*, who observed that "the lives of all, not simply the lives of Mr. [Lü's] own person or family" were being saved.[70]

Lü believed that farsightedness, preparedness, and alertness for urgent emergencies—qualities that acknowledged

68. *CWCWC*, 7:61b. 69. *CWCWC*, 7:31b.

70. *Chiu-ming shu*, in *CWCWC*, 7:52a. In this respect Lü resembles the famous playwright and official, Ch'i Piao-chia (1602–45) who designed a system that would, according to Philip A. Kuhn, "have the advantage of providing for defense against bandits from outside the village at the same time as it would neutralize class antagonisms inside the village," (*Rebellion and Its Enemies in Late Imperial China*, p. 33).

the centrality of facts—distinguished the true scholar from the petty man. Even as concrete events loomed large and threatened to throw him off balance, Lü retained a steadfast commitment to certain ideals. Defining the limits of Lü's foresight were his high regard for life and desire for a harmonious, united society. Thus he defended the large project of repairing the city wall in terms of the value of life. Accordingly, he opened his *Book On Saving Lives* with the rhetorical questions: "Is there anything more urgent than life? . . . Is there anything more urgent than saving lives?"[71] Again, committed to humaneness, he apologized that the strict "military law," which was necessary to insure that all cooperate,[72] left little room for "human feelings." Lü was aware that the plan was harsh, but he could justify the strict organization in terms of the value of life. He argued that "the city depends on [this] in order to survive;"[73] and that "the ten thousand lives within the walls depend on those guarding it."[74] By generating a sense of crisis, by calling for foresight, Lü had enlarged his view just enough to define that point where his humane concern for the survival of all could intersect with the inhumane demands of a successful military organization.

Humaneness similarly infused Lü's discussion of the military in *Records of Practical Government*. He held military leaders responsible for thousands of lives,[75] and displayed, in the following passage, remarkable sympathy for the lone soldier's life:

> Think of those military expeditions to the north and south: how could one person with one horse [have succeeded]? They could not [have succeeded] with less than a thousand troops and ten thousand horses advancing together to kill. The officials receive promotion upon promotion according to how many decapitated heads they get. And if they die in battle, they receive posthumous honor upon honor. As for the troops, there are countless [ones] who, sacrificing their lives, advance to confront the enemy and die. But which one is known by name? Which one is

71. *Chiu-ming shu*, in *CWCWC*, 7:34a.
72. Ibid., 7:39a.
73. Ibid., 7:41b.
74. Ibid., 7:39a.
75. *SCL*, 1:44a.

> mourned for his valor? Who sympathizes with his descendants? Who searches for his bones? What one general accomplishes [is based on] the strength of the many soldiers; and his ancestors enjoy the favors of the soldiers. A T'ang poem says, "Death belongs to the fighter; merit belongs to the general."[76]

This passage comes from *Records of Practical Government,* whose purpose is effective administration. Yet much more than Lü's goal of efficient military strength has determined its content. Simultaneously Lü expressed compassion for the fate of the individual soldier and appreciation for the sacrifice the soldier must make for the larger collectivity. His outlook made room for both humaneness and necessity.

Also defining the range of Lü's foresight was the ideal of social harmony. The following passage, in which Lü again criticized the ignorant for being shortsighted, shows that Lü extended his vision just far enough to prevent any inequitable distribution of wealth that might provoke social conflict.

> One person covered his roof with tiles. Another person, who covered his roof with thatch, said to the one who used tiles, "You spent ten times the amount I did, but [the tiles and thatch] are alike in protecting against the wind and the rain." The one who used tiles said: "Thatch will rot within ten years, but tiles will not break in a hundred years. You will have to change [the thatch] ten times in one century, and you will [therefore] waste much more labor. This is the toil of repeated changes." Alas! Nothing in the world is more calamitous than long-lasting expenditures resulting in the labor of repeated change. This is called laboring in futility and harming the profitable. Nothing is more benighted in the world than confining [one's interest] to the immediate future while forgetting the long-term security. This is called wanting quick results and eyeing petty profit. Therefore the way by which the sage regulates things and uses them efficaciously

76. *SCL,* 1:41b–42a.

> consists of simplicity and thorough strength. Those who like ornament consider simplicity shameful and make luxurious things that are easily destroyed. [This is] very unwise. Someone asked: "Is it all right to make the thoroughly strong luxurious?" I replied: "If it is already thoroughly strong, why make it luxurious? If one uses the funds [that were intended] for luxuries to aid what is thoroughly strong, wouldn't it get even stronger?" Therefore the gentleman, in doing something beneficial, treats one thousand [pieces of] gold lightly; and in doing something useless begrudges one small bit. Even if it costs not the slightest bit, the gentleman will not do anything that is not beneficial. Why? [Because] he does not dare indulge pleasures of the senses to spark off such calamities as the impoverishment of the people and the exhaustion of wealth.[77]

Lü has chosen the figures arbitrarily. Can one really assume that tiles, which cost ten times as much as thatch, also lasted precisely ten times as long? Lü offered such a neat equation because it suited his purpose, which was less to evaluate the relative merits of tiles and thatch than to press on to pose the question, how should surplus funds be handled? Using tiles is, after all, a way of saving, of absorbing to advantage a surplus that might otherwise be wasted. Looking beyond "petty profit" and "the pleasures of the senses," Lü called for a long-range view through which people could iron out the uneven experiences of individual years and so avoid calamities.

The long-range view enabled Lü to resolve social conflicts between the wealthy and the poor even while maintaining social differences and indulging the self-interest of the wealthy. Lü was concerned about "the impoverishment of the people," to be sure. But in giving the wealthy the opportunity to abandon the luxurious for the strong, Lü defined a way that they might save for their own advantage without being socially irresponsible. Through the concept of foresight, Lü

77. *SYY*, 3:387–88.

found that point where self-interest and social conscience intersected. Just as in his military plans in *The Book on Saving Lives*, foresight here allowed Lü to iron out social tensions without denying the differences that constituted society.

The same principles—the use of foresight to avoid social conflict—operated when Lü addressed the poor, whom he advised to save toward bad harvests rather than waste money worshipping spirits.[78] Thus in one passage, after demonstrating that landowners of common status who consume two to three hundred *tan* of rice in good years could in fact survive on much less, Lü queried, "How will that poor fellow manage to save?" and then, once again conjuring up a sense of crisis by opening with the phrase, "If one indeed values life," Lü reasoned:

> There is a method by which the poor can calculate. When poor, you cannot manage on less than two meals a day. [But] once you did buy a jug of wine and a *catty* of meat; or you spent one or two hundred cash on litigations; or you spent three to five hundred cash joining meetings, offering incense, and building temples. I urge you: if in one day you must eat food [worth] ten cash, then eat only [food worth] nine cash; you will not starve to death and by saving one cash a day you will save 360 a year. . . . Think of those famines of the ninth and tenth years of the Wan-li reign [1581–82].[79]

Lü's emphasis, on strengthening and saving, echoes earlier writings on frugality; but the focus of his efforts is new. Perceiving how depersonalized landlord-tenant relations had become,[80] Lü departed from the traditional forms of charity, which made the needy dependent on the wealthy, and stretched his imagination to find a way to bolster the self-reliance of the poor. Thus the goal of one long-range project was to deprive the wealthy of their power over the destitute. He suggested that the wealthy contribute to educating the handicapped to be street singers and storytellers. By en-

78. *SCL*, 2:18b. 79. *SCL*, 2:16a–b.

80. *SCL*, 2:7b. For a description of traditional forms of charity, see Hsü I-t'ang, "Social Relief during the Sung Dynasty," pp. 207–215.

abling the poor to be self-reliant, Lü argued, the wealthy would save many expenses for charity over the long run.[81] Lü's plan for community-sponsored charity derived from the same vision of society—a long-range view that benefitted rich and poor—that also inspired his project for fortifying the city walls of Ning-ling.

Through the specter of crises, Lü found ways of mediating the interests of various social groups. Inherent in his efforts was a keen consciousness that society was constituted of distinct social groups and isolated persons. Accordingly, Lü observed that in crises even members of a family cannot always depend on one another: "One can rely on one's father and older brother, but if one loses one's virtue and disgraces one's name, then father and brother cannot provide protection. Birth and upbringing come from one's father and mother, but catching diseases and falling into dangers do not."[82] Similarly underscoring a sense of isolation during crises, Lü declared: "Hunger, cold, and pain, I alone shall feel; even my parents will not feel them [for me]. Senility and death, I shall face alone; even my wife cannot take my place. If one neglects the Way to self-love and self-preservation, on whom can one rely?"[83] Lü, subscribing to the ideal of oneness, tried to eradicate the distinction between himself and others[84] and repeatedly warned against the practice of "considering oneself right and others wrong" (*shih-chi fei-jen*). Nevertheless he let slip the following statement, which again associated a sense of crisis—this time military—with the view that antagonisms between the self and others are in fact inevitable: "Knowing others and knowing the self is not only the method of the military. In managing people and managing affairs, it must not be the least bit lacking."[85]

Lü's focus on concrete affairs entailed a conception of society that markedly differed from that held by Hai Jui and Lo Ju-fang. Hai and Lo focused their writings on the ideals of justice and humaneness. Even in his lengthy regulations, Hai Jui aimed at defining a static and ideal order. Lü's view of society worked better with a sense of urgency. Critical situa-

81. *SCL*, 2:34b–35a. 82. *SYY*, 1:90. 83. *SYY*, 3:471.
84. *CWCWC*, 4:9b. 85. *SYY*, 1:137.

tions not only enabled Lü to define what was important; they also commanded the participation of all social strata, and served as points of reference that educated and uneducated alike could share. Hai Jui and Lo fought against or tried to transcend the corrupting influences of sense perceptions. Lü avoided losing himself in the present, neither by transcending nor by fighting against mundane concerns, but by taking a larger view of the surrounding circumstances and stretching his imagination to mediate among the conflicting interests of all social strata.

Because there are many ways of responding to emergencies, Lü's choice of large-scale projects is significant. By centering everyone's attention on tasks, rather than on personal obligations, and by generating an atmosphere of urgency—which forced people to realize that their own survival depended on their cooperation—Lü gave practical expression to his vision of a highly individuated but cooperative society.[86]

The pattern behind the cluster of themes in Lü's "Explanation of Family Music" should now be clear. Every theme can be traced back to Lü's feeling that the senses through which one could explore and collect information about the real world were important. As Lü turned part of his attention from the affirmation of abstract ideals to the collection of actual facts, and as his confidence in humaneness weakened, Lü became concerned that others be self-reliant. This led him to focus on crises.

A way of looking at the world brought Lü's themes of crisis and self-reliance together. The very same constellation of concerns appears in the writings of the military strategist Ch'i Chi-kuang, whose manuals were published several decades before Lü's. Like Lü, Ch'i Chi-kuang perceived that society was individuated and that "men's minds are as different as their faces."[87] Ch'i repeatedly pondered, therefore, "How can I make them have one mind?"[88] To unify the common

86. For some interesting parallels to Lü, see Ray Huang's illuminating discussion of Ni Yüan-lu. Huang shows that much of Ni's thought is based on concepts from the *I ching*. A similar argument could be established for Lü ("Ni Yüan-lu: 'Realism' in a Neo-Confucian Scholar-statesman," pp. 415–48).

87. Ch'i Chi-kuang, *Lien-ping shih chi*, p. 170.

88. Ibid., p. 65.

people, Ch'i, foreshadowing Lü K'un, imagined communicating with the people through the corporals. He compiled two handbooks which, he instructed, were to be read aloud to each platoon and memorized by the troops. In addition, he purposely wrote in a simple, often vernacular style,[89] and spoke in concrete terms that all shortsighted, self-centered men could understand. Ch'i maintained, for example, that banners should not be labelled "north, south, east, and west"—terms that would only confuse the ignorant—but should be labelled "left, right, forward, and back" so that all could identify the directions with "their own bodies."[90]

Ch'i Chi-kuang was so resigned to man's self-centeredness that he argued that military skills should be mastered for self-defense rather than out of public-mindedness.[91] A critical essay published in 1782 on Ch'i's *Chi-hsiao hsin-shu* [New Manual of Effectiveness] observed that men during the Ming dynasty were cooperative only "if the self were in the center of the affair," and that self-centeredness accounted for Ch'i's habit of explaining in such detail just how the rank and file would profit by cooperating.[92]

Acknowledging that men were inevitably disconnected and self-centered, Ch'i tried to establish cooperation among them, not by appealing to common ideals, but through reference to external objects. Even Ch'i's explanation of the meaning of "regulations" (*chieh-chih*)—a compound that includes the character for "segment" (*chieh*)—reflects his desire to coordinate people who were separate but alike. Ch'i compared regulations to bamboo, which, although hollow, can extend into a strong, straight shoot because it has segments, or regulated spacing. Drawing an analogy to bamboo, Ch'i noted that regulations can guide countless soldiers to fight as though they were one man.[93] Similarly, in viewing regulations as con-

89. Ch'i, "Directions to the Reader," in *Lien-ping*, p. 1. See also *Lien-ping*, p. 172; and Ch'i Chi-kuang, *Chi-hsiao hsin-shu*, p. 33.

90. Ch'i, *Lien-ping*, p. 78; *Chi-hsiao*, p. 40.

91. Ch'i, *Chi-hsiao*, p. 48; *Lien-ping*, p. 81. See also *Lien-ping*, pp. 127, 131.

92. *Ssu-k'u ch'üan-shu tsung-mu, ch'in-ting*, 99:23b–24a. The comment also calls attention to Ch'i's emphasis on "trust" or "faith" (*hsin*). The description to some extent also fits Yang Tung-ming.

93. Ch'i, *Lien-ping*, p. 151.

crete forms, he elsewhere compared regulations to the rope men used to coordinate their strength for pulling large stones or trees. External objects had replaced humaneness as the primary bond.[94] As in the case of Lü K'un, an appreciation of the role that objects and regulations could play in coordinating the efforts of a large collectivity accompanied Ch'i's willingness to write handbooks for the uneducated.

The same cluster of concerns—a keen consciousness that society is individuated, an emphasis on objects that even the uneducated can perceive through their senses, and critical situations (whether real, as in the case of Ch'i, or imagined, as in the case of Lü)—appears in the writings of both men. The cluster of themes also distinguish Ch'i and Lü on the one hand from Hai Jui on the other, even though all three men devoted much of their writings to practical concerns. Hai Jui did not dwell on the differences that individuated society nor was he preoccupied with crises. He wrote handbooks to standardize administrative procedures but never felt the need, as did both Ch'i and Lü, to adjust his style to a semiliterate or illiterate audience. That adjustment, as the preceding chapter has shown, accompanied the recognition that information about the real world was important. Practical as Hai Jui was, his orientation was entirely different. Where Hai Jui had tried to regulate his world to conform to his ideals of justice, Lü and Ch'i acknowledged the reality of objective phenomena and the importance of the senses in grasping that reality.

94. Ibid., pp. 65–66.

8

By Correcting Faults

Two types of records of self-cultivation reflect sharply different ways of viewing the world. Recorded dialogues and reading notes took ideas from the Classics as their point of departure and furthered moral perfection through the mastery of scholarly learning. This will be called the "ideal-centered" method. Records of merit and demerit and diaries took personal experiences or concrete events as their points of departure and advanced moral perfection through the scrutiny and correction of faults (*kai-kuo*). This will be called the "fact-centered" method.[1] The two approaches were not mutually exclusive. The examination of specific deeds was informed by, even if not concentrated on, the values of the Classics; and some who, like Lo Ju-fang, practiced the ideal-centered method as adults had started with the easy fact-centered method as youths. Nonetheless, that Lü's generation debated the relative merits of the two methods shows that the methods were distinct.

The scrutiny of facts best suits administrative concerns. But even in his self-cultivation—an area far removed from the objective problems of banditry, plague, and starvation—Lü

1. Other scholars have discussed this shift from angles different from my own. See in particular the following articles: Tadao Sakai, "Confucianism and Popular Educational Works;" Wei-ming Tu, "Yen Yüan: From Inner Experience to Lived Concreteness;" Hellmut Wilhelm, "Chinese Confucianism on the Eve of the Great Encounter;" Pei-yi Wu, "Self-Examination and Confession of Sins in Traditional China;" *Liang Ch'i-ch'ao, Intellectual Trends in the Ch'ing Period*, pp. 19–48; and Irene Bloom, "On the 'Abstraction' of Ming Thought: Some Concrete Evidence from the Philosophy of Lo Ch'in-shun." Covering some of the same territory on self-disciplinary record-keeping as I do is Chün-fang Yü, *The Renewal of Buddhism in China: Chu Hung and the Late Ming Synthesis*, chapter 5, which was published after I submitted my own manuscript to press.

favored the fact-centered method, which was disparaged by many of his peers. Not increased severity of social problems, of which every dynasty had its share, but his orientation—which centered on concrete facts, which anticipated crises, and which dwelled on, or regretted past events—brought such practical concerns as city defense, medical care, and famine control into the foreground of his writings.

A context for Lü's Groaning Words

Organizing his thoughts around concrete events and focusing on his errors, Lü K'un experienced numerous swings between restraint and laxity, and between self-confident efforts to improve himself in events of the future and remorseful feelings about events of the past. At fifteen, Lü felt so "bitter about the mind easily letting itself go" that he composed a poem, "A Summons to My Conscience," in which he "suddenly became ashamed of past wrongs."[2] Elsewhere Lü admitted that he periodically lost his self-control. "When I was young," he reminisced, "I struggled to restrain myself [by keeping] *Hsing-hsin chi* [A Record of Self-Examination]; and after my middle years, I gradually freed myself. No sooner had I freed myself than I became lazy and dissipated, and no sooner had I restrained myself than [I felt] cramped."[3]

Throughout his life, minor errors, which others would have failed to notice, dominated Lü's thoughts. Dredging up and analyzing at length errors undoubtedly long forgotten by his friend Tsou Yüan-piao, Lü wrote: "In one meeting, I committed three errors. First, when we met, I spoke lofty and high-flown words as though no one was around. Second, I was unreceptive and considered myself right and others wrong; my manner was crude and my words overbearing. Third, I did not restrain my laughter and derisiveness and I acted totally out-of-hand."[4] Even in his epitaph, written just before his death, Lü again self-effacingly called attention to past wrongs: "Regretting that I was formerly defiled, I

2. *CWCWC*, 10:15a–b.
3. *CWCWC*, 4:25a. For *Hsing-hsin chi*, see *CWCWC*, 3:26b–32b.
4. *CWCWC*, 4:49a.

styled myself 'New Me' (Hsin-wu). But the cleansing was ineffective, and in the end it is the old me speaking."[5]

Lü had led a successful and humanitarian career, and had committed no major mistakes that justified his regretfulness or his gnawing apprehension of creating reasons for future regret. Therefore his feeling regretful should be understood in terms of his manner of perceiving the world rather than in terms of the external features of his life. Lü's compulsion to itemize three errors in the letter to Tsou cited above is only one example of how complicated and diverse events dominated his thoughts. To cultivate himself, Lü only rarely elaborated on abstract values or commented on the classics. More often he kept track of and assessed his behavior in specific events. His errors loomed large and became the central focus of his writings.

Abstract principles transcend events. Therefore those who pursued the ideal-centered method conveyed a sense of continuity or constant identity through disparate experiences. In contrast, those who followed the fact-centered method punctuated the records of their lives with daily entries and monthly reckonings. "Throughout the day," Lü instructed, "simply check off things about oneself."[6] "At the close of the evening, check off your list of whatever words you have spoken during the day."[7] Concentrating on discrete events, Lü was often disturbed that his feelings were disjointed. Just as he forgot during healthy moments what it was like to be sick, so he forgot during times of leisure what it was like to deal with a special event. In a characteristically disjointed mood, Lü observed: "In times of leisure, I am lazy. In busy times, I am frantic. Being frantic produces errors." Responding to Lü's plight, someone advised:

> This is losing [the sense of order] between before and after. If you would [concentrate on] checking things off before the event, you would save yourself from checking things off afterwards. And you would also save yourself regret. If you would apply thoughts

5. *CWCWC*, 9:47b–48a.
6. *SYY*, 2:213. See also *SYY*, 2:196.
7. *SYY*, 2:217.

> of urgency to times of leisure, you would save yourself mistakes and would also save yourself anxiety.[8]

The friend then explained that it was "not the event that tires one's mind but the mind that tires itself."[9] Only by being cautious and diligent at every turn can one judge events correctly. By concentrating on and anticipating events or facts, or by generating a sense of urgency, Lü could avoid errors and regret.

To keep track of his behavior in numerous disconnected events, Lü advocated the method of "checking off lists," or "taking inventory" (*tien-chien*). The term *tien-chien* had also evolved to mean self-cultivation. However, even when translating *tien-chien* simply as "self-cultivation," one should keep in mind that the etymology indicates the observation of discrete phenomena, and that Lü's use of the term clearly perpetuated that original meaning of checking items off lists. For example, Lü rhetorically asked, "These two matters, Heaven and Man—how can one keep watch over their many complications?" And then answered, "There is a simple method, which can be applied to the self. One keeps a list of every thought, word, and action, until the last blemish has disappeared."[10] Elsewhere Lü distinguished the specific act of checking off lists from the general concept of self-cultivation: "Try keeping track of what you say throughout the day and whether there are a few appropriate phrases. Then you will observe the extent of your self-cultivation."[11]

Further illustrating Lü's method of keeping lists is his *Record of Self-Examination*, which he decided to keep in 1580. The metaphorical language of its preface forcefully conveys Lü's fact-centeredness, his perception of even abstract processes in concrete terms. Apprehensive that numbness might set in, Lü, who frequently used the metaphor of bandits to connote deception or unsuspected dangers,[12] kept the record in a spirit of fearful alertness. Thus he explained:

> The ten thousand principles all lie within the mind; and the ten thousand evils all arise from the mind's

8. *SYY*, 3:424–25. 9. *SYY*, 3:425. 10. *SYY*, 2:225.
11. *SYY*, 2:233. 12. *SYY*, 2:317; 1:34–35.

> being unsettled. For this reason, [just as] bandits attack men by taking them by surprise, and the enemy states make surprise raids by taking advantage of one's being unprepared, so do wrongs attack people by taking advantage of their ignorance. If the mind is always on the alert, sometimes edgy, sometimes fearful, then how can faults emerge? Faults emerge from carelessness when the mind is ignorant and unsettled. . . . [But if] the mind is pure . . . [then] evil thieves and oppressive desires will shrink back, looking on for a time but not daring to encroach upon [the mind].[13]

For his record, Lü drew up a chart consisting of numerous columns, one for each type of error. Because his self-examination concentrated on numerous discrete events, Lü found it necessary to break the conventional three categories of errors—mental (*hsin*), verbal (*k'ou*), and physical (*shen*)—down into numerous finer categories. Even "one hundred categories," Lü explained, would not exhaust all the possibilities.[14]

Lü also outlined principles for keeping the record: he should check off how many faults he had committed during the course of each day and enter each misdeed in the appropriate column; at the end of each month, he should examine which type of errors he had committed most often and concentrate on correcting those; improvement in his behavior would verify that he had been studying diligently enough.[15]

It was in the same spirit that Lü published, in 1593, *Groaning Words*, the very title of which again indicates the perception of self-cultivation in concrete terms. This time, however, Lü conceived of the work not in terms of military preparedness, but, as the metaphorical title indicates, in terms of illness—which so often alternatively conveyed Lü's sense of crisis. Both the *Record of Self-Examination* and *Groaning Words* illustrate the cluster of themes—discrete events, periodic (daily and monthly) evaluations, and, to be discussed later, independence from teachers—that characterize the fact-

13. *Hsing-hsin chi*, in *CWCWC*, 3:26b–27a.
14. *Ibid.*, 3:28b. 15. *Ibid.*, 3:27b.

centered method of self-cultivation. Lü compiled *Groaning Words*, like the *Record of Self-Examination*, to keep track of his behavior. Commenting on his proclivity to intemperate speech, for example, Lü wrote, "Every time I commit this error, I make a record to warn myself."[16] In spirit, in concentration on specific deeds and in the goal of self-scrutiny, the two works are similar. In execution, however, *Groaning Words* departs from the *Record* and from contemporaneous works that resemble Lü's *Record*. In the *Record*, Lü simply outlined a lean skeletal plan defining the categories and drawing up blank columns for scrutiny. In *Groaning Words*, he fully displayed in six substantial *chüan* the numerous minute details of his self-doubts and everyday activities. Lü has, albeit with some feelings of misgiving and uncertainty according to the preface, made public his innermost thoughts. In this respect Lü differed markedly from Lo Ju-fang who also kept a daily record but took care to burn it before his death.[17] Where Lo had taken care to eliminate his doubts and emotional struggles from his final self-image, Lü willingly exposed and shared his feelings with others. Through his mature years, Lü continued to practice a method of self-cultivation that Lo had outgrown.

The entries in *Groaning Words* are pithy and on the whole brief, sometimes only two phrases of four or five characters. They are loosely organized under such categories as "preserving the mind and heart" (*ts'un-hsin*), "actualities and names" (*hsing-ming*), "self-cultivation" (*hsiu-shen*), "learning," "heaven and earth," and "the way of government."[18] Neither a philosophical system nor a discernible chronology governs the order in which the passages appear within each category.

Groaning Words played the same role in Lü's self-cultivation that keeping records of what one read or recording discussions had long played for others, but Lü's orientation was entirely different. Those who kept reading notes, or recorded

16. *SYY*, 3:456.

17. The editors of *Lo Ming-te kung wen-chi* report that Lo burned *K'o chi jih-lu*, his diary of 1532 (prefatory *chüan*, p. 13b).

18. For *ts'un hsin*, see *Mencius* in Legge, *Chinese Classics*, pp. 333 and 449.

dialogues, took passages from the Classics as the point of departure for their comments. Lü, who as a young student had found wading through the abstruse commentaries tiresome,[19] usually moved from concrete examples or actual experiences to general moral points. Lü believed that with experiential understanding (*t'i-jen*) "one need not read all the ancient and contemporary books." Those equipped with experiential understanding will not use up the contents of one book even in a lifetime. And those without experiential understanding will be nothing more than erudite scholars even if they read widely.[20]

Attaching importance to experiential understanding, Lü moved from the specific example of "spoiling children with tasty foods" to the general statement that "nine out of ten [people in the world] end up killing themselves by spoiling themselves;"[21] from the specific example, "In printing books one must first have fine wood blocks" to a general warning that one should avoid using crooked officials to promote officials;[22] and from the vivid example of cutting pieces evenly with a knife to the general value of treating people evenhandedly.[23] Sometimes Lü's comments were unabashedly autobiographical, as when he extracted a moral lesson from his father's reprimand for divulging a secret.[24] Sometimes—but even then only incidentally—Lü appropriated phrases from the Classics to express his own experiences. But his primary focus was on his personal experiences, as was clear to Tsou Yüan-piao. On reading one volume of *Groaning Words,* Tsou reported, "I began to believe that the Six Classics were all commentaries on the self."[25]

The informal colloquial style of *Groaning Words* further underscores its personal, non-bookish tone. Lü freely uses such phrases as "*Wo hsien-tsai kan hsieh shemma shih?*" for "What should I do now?"[26] and "*li-pu-liao ssu-ko tzu*" for "one must

19. *CWCWC,* 9:48b. For a discussion of the long-standing debate on whether to read books or not, see Yü Ying-shih, "Some Preliminary Observations on the Rise of Ch'ing Confucian Intellectualism."

20. *SYY,* 2:314. 21. *SYY,* 3:468. 22. *SYY,* 5:677.

23. *SYY,* 1:91. 24. *SYY,* 3:431.

25. Tsou Yüan-piao, *Yüan-hsüeh chi,* 2:14b.

26. *SYY,* 2:217.

never lose sight of these four words."[27] The concrete examples, the pithy metaphors, the colloquialisms, and the autobiographical touches lend a vitality and immediacy to each entry apart from the whole and, in the absence of threads connecting the entries into a grand scheme, accentuate the sense that human experiences are fragmented and multitudinous.

Practice and criticisms of the fact-centered method of self-cultivation

The fact-centered method of self-cultivation had been practiced long before Lü's time. Even *The Analects* fleetingly mentions it. One of Confucius's disciples daily examined himself "on three points,"[28] and Confucius commented, "To have faults and not to reform them,—this indeed, should be pronounced having faults."[29] Keeping records of merits and demerits again surfaced among the Taoists, first in the fourth-century text, *Pao-p'u-tzu* and then in the Sung.[30] Early signs of it can also be found in village self-government in the Yuan dynasty. According to the instructions preserved in the *Yüan shih* [History of the Yuan Dynasty], bad deeds were to be recorded on the door of the wrongdoer's home. If the wrongdoer completely reformed himself by the end of the year, the record was to be erased. Those who failed to reform themselves were to be punished by serving in the *corvée* labor of the village.[31]

Before the Ming period, however, the fact-centered method found expression primarily on the periphery of the scholar-official's world—among the common people in their practice of Taoism and Buddhism, as a method of discipline in local government, and by children in their early training. During

27. *SYY*, 1:50.
28. Confucius, *Analects*, in Legge, *Chinese Classics*, 1:139.
29. Ibid., 1:302.
30. Sakai, "Confucianism and Popular Educational Works," p. 341. In his *Chūgoku no zensho*, Sakai finds antecedents for the practice of keeping records of merit and demerit in the late Han (p. 359).
31. Cited in Wen Chün-t'ien, *Chung-kuo pao-chia chih-tu*, p. 163.

the Ming, the practice of the fact-centered method trickled into the writings of serious and mature Confucian scholars. In his *Tu-shu lu* [Record of Reading Books], Hsüeh Hsüan (1389–1464) not only commented on passages by great thinkers of the past but carefully evaluated his own daily activities.[32] He declared, for example, "All the things I do each day, I must understand experientially (*t'i-jen*);"[33] and he warned himself: "Every night when I go to bed I must think over the deeds of the day; if my actions were principled, I can sleep peacefully; if they were unprincipled, I restlessly toss and turn and wonder how I can change the errors. Because I want to start being diligent and to put an end to my laziness, I am keeping a record to warn myself."[34] Thus Hsüeh Hsüan's writings reveal the very cluster of themes that were later to be found in Lü's writings—the emphasis on personal experiences, the daily self-evaluation, the restless anxiety about one's errors, and the use of a record as a warning.

It was on reading a passage by Hsüeh Hsüan in 1531 that Lo Ju-fang, still a young boy, felt inspired to burn incense, to swear he would become a sage, and to start keeping a record in order to examine his faults.[35] However, the fact-centered approach to sagehood surfaced only fleetingly in Lo's writings and apparently took second place in his thought to the method of concentrating on such ideals as humaneness.[36] Unwilling to be known through his efforts of self-examination, Lo burned his diary.[37]

By the next generation, the practice of keeping records of merits and demerits—after having circulated among the masses for several centuries—figured visibly in the writings of many important scholar-officials. Yüan Huang (1533–1606), who incidentally was one of Lo Ju-fang's many fol-

32. See the biography of Hsüeh Hsüan by Cze-tong Song and Julia Ching in *DMB*, pp. 616–19. For a discussion of Hsüeh's thought in the context of Ming Confucianism, see Wing-tsit Chan, "The Ch'eng-Chu School," in *Self and Society*, ed., de Bary, pp. 29–51; and Hellmut Wilhelm, "On Ming Orthodoxy."

33. Hsüeh Hsüan, *Tu-shu lu*, p. 2a.

34. Ibid., p. 3a.

35. *HTCC*, 2:37a.

36. For two rare occasions when Lo refers to *kai-kuo*, see *HTCC*, 1:69a–b; 2:11b.

37. *Lo Ming-te kung wen-chi*, prefatory *chüan*, p. 13b.

lowers, had been inspired to pursue the fact-centered method when he received from a Taoist recluse a morality book, *Kung-kuo ko* [A Ledger of Merit and Demerit], which stressed the evaluation of deeds.[38] A fortune-teller had previously predicted that Yüan would enjoy little success in officialdom and would fail to produce a son. By keeping a record of his merits and demerits, Yüan became master of his fate, passed the metropolitan examination, and even fathered a son. Chou Ju-teng, also a follower of Lo Ju-fang, wrote a preface to Yüan's "Li-ming pien" ["Essay on Establishing One's Destiny"] and found inspiration in Yüan's work to start his own diary.[39] Chou Ju-tang insisted that daily self-scrutiny was as important as washing one's face. "How can you face others," Chou asked, "if you don't wash your face?" Even after washing it, he elaborated, one can still clean it further; and certainly one must wash it every day.[40] In the same spirit of daily self-evaluation, Chu-hung wrote *Tzu-chih lu* [The Record of Self-Examination] (preface, 1604).[41]

As the fact-centered method took hold, its merits became a topic of debate. Those who supported the ideal-centered method believed that the fact-centered method was inferior and compromised the concept of sagehood. That two distinct approaches had come into sharp conflict is especially apparent in an exchange of views between Lü K'un and Tsou Yüan-piao.

Lü greatly admired Hsüeh Hsüan. He advised Tsou to put aside the metaphysical discussions of men like Wang Yang-ming and to concentrate instead on the works of those like Hsüeh Hsüan who "do not deviate one bit from the correct road of Confucius."[42] Tsou, in a letter to Lü K'un, argued that one should concentrate on settling the basic issues in learning rather than dissipate energies on disparate minor battles. He

38. See Sakai, *Chūgoku no zensho*, chapters 4 and 5; and "Confucianism and Popular Educational Works," pp. 341–43; 348. See also Liu Ts'un-yan, "Yüan Huang and His 'Four Admonitions.'"

39. Chou Ju-teng, *Tung-yüeh cheng-hsüeh lu*, 7:19a–22b.

40. Ibid., 3:2a.

41. Kristin Yü Greenblatt (Chün-fang Yü), "Chu-hung and Lay Buddhism in the Late Ming," pp. 116–21.

42. *CWCWC*, 4:49b. In this passage Lü also warns against the thought of Ch'en Hsien-chang and urges an interest in Hu Chü-jen.

questioned the efficacy and wisdom of daily record-keeping.[43] Tsou clearly was addressing Lü's position, expressed in *A Record of Self-Examination*, that one should take pains to guard against even the smallest errors, which often insidiously lead to large wrongs.[44]

Also participating in the debate was Yang Tung-ming, who observed that "correcting faults is done after the slip," and then asked, "Is it not better not to slip?"[45] And in analyzing three methods of learning, Yang placed the method of correcting faults last. Yang explained that the first method, emphasizing reverence (*chu-ching*), was like walking calmly on a straight path without wandering off into detours; the second method, examination of incipient activity (*yen-chi*), was like hesitating on a crooked path and trying hard to figure out the correct way; and the third method, correcting errors (*kai-kuo*), was like backtracking after becoming aware that one has already made a wrong turn.[46] Meng Ch'iu, commenting on a letter Lü K'un had written to Tsou Yüan-piao, argued that one should concentrate on achieving goodness rather than on correcting faults.[47]

The debate on the relative merits of the methods of self-cultivation is also apparent in the writings of Lü Wei-ch'i (1587–1641), who embraced and wrote elaborately on the correction of errors. Lü Wei-ch'i lived in Hsin-an, Honan, just west of Lü K'un's hometown. He had grown up in the shadow of Lü K'un's social circle and shared Lü K'un's cultural milieu. Wei-ch'i made at least one reference to Lü K'un[48] and had also associated with several of K'un's friends: Feng Ts'ung-wu, who had attended study meetings held by Wei-ch'i,[49] Yang Tung-ming, and Tsou Yüan-piao. Wei-ch'i also greatly admired his fellow townsman, Meng Hua-li, who was close to Lü K'un's friend Meng Ch'iu.[50]

43. Tsou Yüan-piao, *Yüan-hsüeh chi*, 2:13a.
44. *Hsing-hsin chi*, in *CWCWC*, 3:27b.
45. *SCKK*, 6:40b. 46. *SCKK*, 6:28a.
47. Meng Ch'iu, *Meng Wo-ch'iang hsien-sheng chi*, Wan-li edition, 1:28a–29a. See also ibid., 27a.
48. Lü Wei-ch'i, *Ming-te hsien-sheng wen-chi*, 15:4a. See the biography of Lü Wei-ch'i by Søren Egerod in *DMB*, pp. 1014–17.
49. Lü Wei-ch'i, *Ming-te hsien-sheng wen-chi*, 8:10a.
50. For a discussion of the mutual influences among these men, see Pei-

After earning his *chin-shih* degree in 1613, Lü Wei-ch'i proved to be a conscientious and energetic official with wide-ranging talents. He discussed philosophical principles with students at the Chih-ch'üan Academy, which he established in 1622; and also promoted famine relief, the *pao-chia* system, and compiled regulations for a guild. His integrity and selfless devotion to service stood the test of severe crises. He generously distributed his own grain to the famine-stricken of 1637; and he defended Loyang, albeit unsuccessfully, against rebels in 1641. For refusing to capitulate to the rebels he was eventually decapitated.

Lü Wei'ch'i wrote detailed regulations for several study societies that focused the practice of self-cultivation on the examination of errors.[51] He urged those who joined the study groups to encourage one another to do good deeds and avoid faults[52] and to keep records of their behavior.[53] Good deeds, Lü Wei-ch'i instructed, should be made public and, if verified, should be recorded to encourage others. Misdeeds should be corrected in private, and if the wrongdoer failed to reform, the group leader should make a record of it to warn others.

In one discussion on the proper approach to sagehood, Lü Wei-ch'i disagreed with and, according to his own testimony, finally converted Feng Ts'ung-wu to the fact-centered outlook. Feng had claimed that understanding "humaneness, filiality, sincerity, and respect"—in short, concentrating on abstract ideals—was the key to eliminating all difficulties. Lü Wei-ch'i in response explained that one should use actual experiences to corroborate received opinion: "When I studied in my youth, I tested [the contents of] each book against my actual experiences. I understood only about one-half [of what I read and therefore] I recklessly said that the half I found unintelligible was the 'empty theories' of the sages. But gradually I understood their significance and with daily re-

---

yi wu, "Self-Examination," p. 24. Also note that Lü Wei-ch'i was directly familiar with some of Yüan Huang's work (*Ming-te hsien-sheng wen-chi,* 12:16b).

51. Several "meeting agreements" (*hui-yüeh*) are included in Lü Wei-ch'i, *Ming-te hsien-sheng wen-chi,* chüan 21 and 22.

52. Ibid., 21:2a. 53. Ibid., 21:7a.

newal [of effort] I came to recognize experientially (*t'i-jen*) every word in actual fact."[54] Again the themes—personal experience, daily effort, and actual facts—have been clustered as a contrast to bookish learning.

Scholars like Yang and Feng were uneasy about the correcting-faults method for several reasons. Above all, the method often disintegrated into the mechanical and amoral use of merits to cancel out demerits. An example of this approach appears in *Records of Practical Government*, where Lü K'un instructed: "Today, I am starting a record for good deeds performed by the members of the *hsiang-yüeh*. . . . All good deeds, whether performed by rich or poor and . . . whether large or small . . . should be recorded."[55] Lü then listed various types of deeds, ascribing to each a large, medium, or small merit. Finally, he outlined various equations by which one could use merits to cancel fines and punishments owed for bad deeds.[56]

Similarly, for his study group, Lü Wei-ch'i maintained that a good deed, or reformed behavior, could cancel out an error and that one should not, therefore, speak of "recording errors" but simply of "correcting" them. According to Wei-ch'i, initial offenses should not be recorded; those who commit three errors in a row should be warned after the meeting adjourns; but warnings should stop once the wrongdoers perform good deeds.[57]

If Lü K'un and Lü Wei-ch'i sometimes appeared to approach self-cultivation mechanically, their goals were ultimately moral. Lü K'un explained that he had instructed the members of the *hsiang-yüeh* to evaluate their merits and demerits because he wished to encourage good behavior. He also argued that by commemorating the good deeds of the people, one could arrest the recent decline of education.[58]

Others, however, took advantage of the opportunity to let a good deed cancel out an evil and consequently condoned, or at best, seemed to condone, wrongdoing. The extreme

54. Ibid., 23:6a. 55. *SCL*, 5:22a–b.

56. For the list of good deeds, see *SCL*, 5:23b; for the bad deeds, see *SCL*, 5:27a–33b.

57. Lü Wei-ch'i, *Ming-te hsien-sheng wen-chi*, 21:7a.

58. *SCL*, 5:22a.

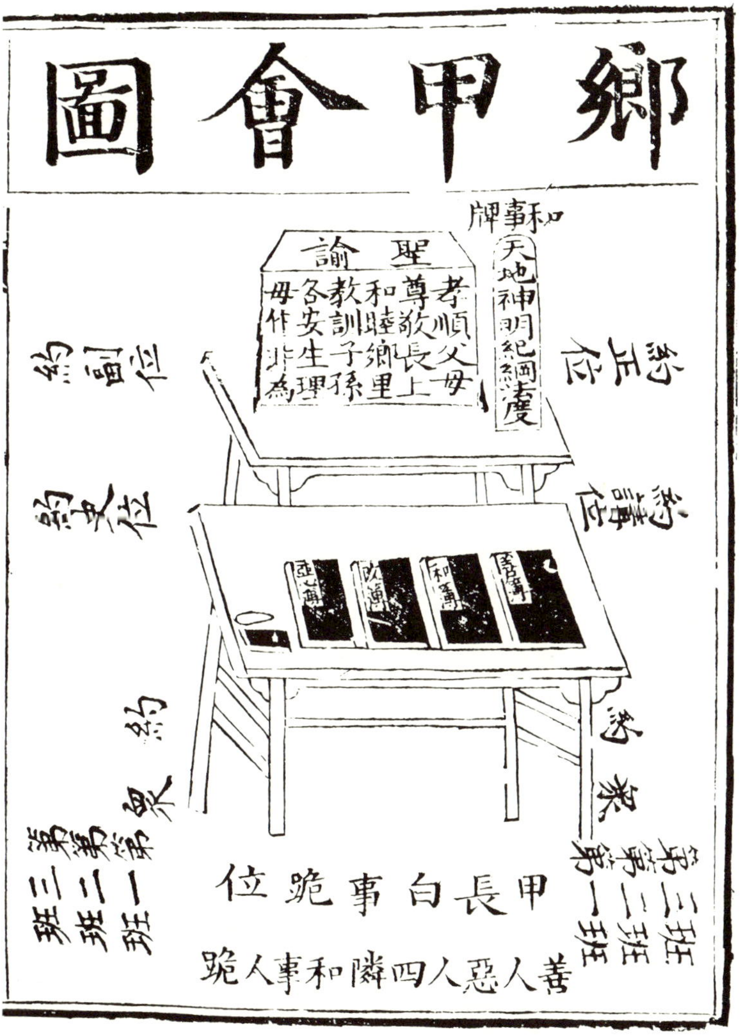

Lü K'un's Floor Plan for the *Hsiang-chia* Meeting
To the right and left of the upper table Lü designates seating for the chairman, assistant chairman, clerk and lecturer of the lecture unit (*yüeh*); below the lower table, to the right and left, Lü designates seating for the participants of the lecture unit; immediately in front of the lower table, Lü designates places where the head of the *chia* reporting on cases and those being reviewed should kneel. On the upper table are the Six Imperial Injunctions; on the lower table are four volumes for recording those who have earned merits, those who are accommodating, those who have promised to reform, and those who have earned demerits. *SCL* (1797 ed.), 5:19a.

forms that such immoral calculations could take are evident in the short stories by the prolific seventeenth-century writer, Li Yü (1611–80).[59] Asserting that "one good deed can expunge a hundred evil ones," Li Yü lightheartedly allowed a swindler to pay for a lifetime of misdeeds by establishing—through trickery and deceit no less—a Buddhist shrine.[60] Li Yü similarly excused a group of scholarly companions who had selfishly tricked a friend into moving back to their neighborhood. The group leader later easily redeemed himself because he was willing to listen to criticisms of his faults.[61]

The method of weighing merits against demerits could also lead to viewing moral cultivation in crass economic terms, as a work, albeit from around 1830, usefully illustrates:

> The expense of one hundred copper cash counts as one meritorious deed. If the same good deed is performed by a poor person, the number of merits increases in proportion to the degree of poverty. In the case of a really poor man, even if he incurs an expense of no more than five or ten coppers, it is counted as equal to one hundred coppers spent by the rich.[62]

Offended by the materialistic overtones of keeping ledgers of merits and demerits, Liu Tsung-chou (1578–1645), who had associated with Feng Ts'ung-wu at the Shou-shan Academy, criticized Yüan Huang for advocating a self-serving approach to self-cultivation.[63] In contrast to Yüan Huang, who had tallied up merits as well as demerits, Liu believed that one should concentrate only on the faults, so as "to put [thoughts] of profit at a distance."[64]

Another reason for considering the fact-centered method inferior might have been that it accommodated mediocre people who would find the more difficult ideal-centered method

59. Biography of Li Yü by Man-kuei Li in *ECCP*, pp. 395–97.

60. Li Yü, "The Swindler" ("Kuei-cheng lou") in *The Twelve Towers*, pp. 37–38.

61. Ibid., pp. 122, 131.

62. Cited in Tadao Sakai, "Confucianism and Popular Educational Works," p. 350.

63. Liu Tsung chou, "Preface," *Jen-p'u*, signed 1634.

64. Ibid., 1b.

discouraging. That the fact-centered method suited average men was observed by Chou Ju-teng, who had been inspired by Yüan Huang's "Essay on Establishing One's Destiny" to start his own daily record.[65] When asked about the phrase from Confucius's *Analects*, "To err and not change,"[66] Chou Ju-teng responded: "This is how Confucius showed men an easy way to sagehood. Most people believe that sages are too high [to emulate] and themselves too low. They believe that only sages can occupy errorless ground, and since we cannot avoid making errors, [they ask] how can we share the ranks of sages? Therefore, as soon as they have committed an error, they give up."[67] Chou then explained that many have misunderstood the meaning of "error." Those who promptly correct their errors have done no real harm; only those who have consciously let their errors stand are truly at fault. In conclusion, Chou declared: "All those who change will occupy a faultless ground. What the sage called faultless was also like this—which is to say, how can anyone have been born without the slightest fault?"[68] In the same spirit of adjusting standards to those who were untalented or lacked determination, Chu-hung maintained that the fact-centered method of self-cultivation best suited people of medium quality.[69]

To encourage all to persist in their cultivation of sagehood, some, like Chou, stressed that everyone had faults. Thus Feng Ts'ung-wu, who must have indeed acquiesced to Lü Wei-ch'i's arguments favoring the fault-correcting method, declared, "People are not sages" and then asked, "Who is without faults?"[70] Others who endorsed the fact-centered method went farther than Feng to point out that even the sages had faults. Meng Hua-li, in the "Preface to the Record of Errors for His Three Sons," allowed that the sages were not faultless.[71] And Lü Wei-ch'i, to encourage members of one

65. Chou Ju-teng, *Tung-yüeh cheng-hsüeh lu*, 7:20a. See also 7:19a.
66. Confucius, *Analects*, in Legge, *Chinese Classics*, 1:302.
67. Chou Ju-teng, *Tung-yüeh cheng-hsüeh lu*, 5:6a–b. Signed 1601.
68. Ibid.
69. Chün-fang Yü, *The Renewal of Buddhism*, pp. 116-17.
70. *FSHC*, 6:4a.
71. Meng Hua-li, *Meng Yün-p'u hsien-sheng*, 4:12a. See also Pei-yi Wu, "Self-Examination," p. 23.

study group to seek moral improvement, rhetorically asked, "Who is without faults?" and then reassured his audience: "Faults can be corrected. . . . From ancient times, all sages and worthies have had faults."[72]

The fact-centered method, with its mechanical amoral calculations, its adjustment to men of mediocre talents, and its emphasis on the universality of flaws was, some sixteenth-century writers believed, clearly inferior to the ideal-centered method. Nonetheless, Lü and other well-educated, successful officials turned to the fact-centered method. Feng Ts'ung-wu, who had debated the merits of the two methods with Lü Wei-ch'i and who rarely gave a place to the correcting-faults method in his recorded dialogues, seems to have changed his opinion in time. Accordingly, he once stated that "learning begins with correcting faults";[73] and he tried to combine the two approaches in his "Chart of Goodness and Profit" ("Shan-li t'u").[74] In the chart itself, Feng—undoubtedly in reaction to the amoral calculations of men like Li Yü—warned that there could be no road of compromise between the paths of goodness and profit-seeking. But in the afterword to the chart, Feng stressed the importance of daily self-examination (*tien-chien*) in achieving goodness.[75] More telling, *Groaning Words*, which had, according to Tsou Yüan-piao, provoked controversy in the Capital Newspaper, was later frequently reprinted. Early editions of *Groaning Words* include: one compiled by Lü's disciples, sons and grandsons, in six *chüan*, with a preface of 1593 by Lü K'un; one in three *chüan* with a preface of 1616 and a colophon by Lü's son, Chih-wei. Also known are editions of 1687, 1744, 1796, and 1825, not to mention several undated editions.[76]

Even Liu Tsung-chou, who had criticized Yüan Huang's approach for its association with profit, did not revert completely to an ideal-centered outlook but followed the fact-centered approach in his own quest for sagehood. In drawing up regulations for his family school in 1632, Liu, complain-

72. Lü Wei-ch'i, *Ming-te hsien-sheng wen-chi*, 21:7b.

73. *FSHC*, 6:4a. 74. *FSHC*, 8:4a–8a. 75. *FSHC*, 8:4a–8a.

76. For a list of and a comparison of the contents of the editions of *SYY*, see Keiyu Hikita, "Ryo Kon [Lü K'un] no denki to 'Shingingo' [Shen-yin yü]," *Kenkyū hōkoku*, 11:20–23.

ing that customs and learning had declined,[77] called for the periodic self-examination of errors.[78] More important, Liu wrote an entire work, *Jen p'u* [A Manual for Men], to categorize types of errors and outline a fact-centered approach to self-cultivation. In that work he stated that one should "encourage goodness and correct errors to become a sage."[79] In addition, Liu stressed that this should be done daily.[80]

The practice of the fact-centered method during the late sixteenth century even by prominent scholar-officials like Lü K'un calls for an explanation. To some extent, it facilitated the popularization of sagehood. In particular, it reflected the amalgamation of the three religions and, with its careful accounts of merits and demerits, satisfied a commercial outlook. But the fact-centered method was not exclusively associated with these trends. Some of the most fervent popularizers of sagehood followed the ideal-centered method in their writings; others, who took great care to guard distinctions between the common people and the scholar-officials, adopted the fact-centered method. Lo Ju-fang, for example, advocated the fact-centered method of self-cultivation for the common people in *hsiang-yüeh*, but he reserved the superior ideal-centered method for himself and his audiences in the academies.[81] He actively proselytized sagehood but left behind only writings that conformed to the ideal-centered outlook.

Lü Wei-ch'i was far more preoccupied with social distinctions than Lo Ju-fang, but he avidly recommended the fact-centered method even to his peers. Someone urged Lü Wei-ch'i that common people be admitted to the academy meetings on the grounds that the famous Shao Yung (1011–77) and Wang Ken had also been of common status; but Lü Wei-ch'i unyieldingly directed that "farmers, merchants, and

77. Liu Tsung-chou, *Liu tzu ch'üan-shu*, 25:6b.
78. Ibid., 25:7b.
79. Liu, *Jen p'u*, p. 8a. See also pp. 21b–22a. For a translation of Liu's "Method for the Prosecution of Bad Deeds," ("Sung-kuo fa"), see Pei-yi Wu, "Self-Examination," pp. 26–7. In their appraisal of Liu's *Jen p'u*, the editors of *Ssu-k'u ch'üan-shu tsung-mu* state that many people do not realize that Liu wrote the book "to instruct those who were below average" (93: 26a–b).
80. Liu, *Jen p'u*, 5a.
81. See chapter 2 of this book.

townspeople"—who he feared would only disrupt the gatherings—study instead at the monthly *hsiang-yüeh* meetings.[82] Thus, whatever its popular origins may have been, the fact-centered method was not specifically associated with the popularization of education. It had, by the seventeenth century, gained a life of its own even among those scholar-officials who clearly distinguished themselves from the common people.

To understand the appeal of the fact-centered method and in a related way the lasting attraction of Lü's *Groaning Words*, an examination of the implications of the fact-centered outlook will prove useful. Underlying the fact-centered and ideal-centered methods of self-cultivation were different assumptions about what was worth communicating to others, how wisdom was achieved, and the role of the teacher. Indeed, the very definition of the bonds of social solidarity differed in the two methods.

Those who focused on concrete affairs were painfully conscious of feelings of isolation; they were aware that each person had unique experiences that formed a private sphere that may or may not be shared with others. Lü associated crises (which were the most important of events) with self-reliance, as chapter 7 explained. In addition, his self-scrutiny of errors was often specifically related to his sense of social clumsiness. When Lü in his letter to Tsou Yüan-piao expressed remorse for the way he had behaved when they first became acquainted, Lü explained that he had simply been eager to be accepted. "I had no other [intention]," he confessed meekly, "than the small desire to be accepted by you in a tight and complicated situation."[83] Elsewhere Lü similarly associated regret with social ineptness. "Whenever I entertain," Lü introspected, "I feel great agony. Before each event I am flustered; after the event, I check things off. After checking off things, I suddenly feel regretful."[84] Lü had let minute details about his private anxieties loom large and separate himself from others. In the same spirit, Feng Ts'ung-wu observed that private thoughts were beyond the reach of

82. Lü Wei-ch'i, *Ming-te hsien-sheng wen-chi*, 21:10a.
83. *CWCWC*, 4:49a.
84. *SYY*, 3:424.

others. He stated: "We do not know whether everyone can apprehend the specks of true and false in his heart. . . . Now, in our studies we should not seek [knowledge] from afar but must each silently take inventory (*tien-chien*) of the matters of his own heart (*hsin shih*)."[85]

Not the ideals associated with moral leadership, then, but the sharing of personal experiences became the main basis for community. Chou Ju-teng expressed this sentiment most lucidly by citing Po Chü-i's saying that "the body should not always be healthy and strong; being healthy and strong often creates a mind [that makes distinctions] between the self and others."[86] Lü K'un, thinking along similar lines, claimed that "only men with 'bitter' minds can share illnesses and be sympathetic,"[87] and he expressed in the preface to his *Groaning Words* a deep sense of relief when he learned that a friend, who had "never groaned throughout his whole life," nevertheless shared his feelings of mental anguish. The friend then concluded that everyone must be suffering and therefore suggested: "Our ailments are largely the same. Why not make your record of them public for others?"[88] In his preface to Lü's *Groaning Words*, Lu Lung-ch'i (1630–93) maintained that everyone was ill and that worthies and gentlemen gained eminence not for being healthy but for having insight into their ailments. Most people, Lu Lung-ch'i observed, see only the polished virtues of such worthies as Mencius and fail to realize, therefore, that even the worthies achieved perfection only with great pain.[89] The insistence on the value of illness is significant. Abstract ideals were not held up ceremonially to command respect; rather, even the greatest worthies shared with ordinary people everyday difficulties.

In the ideal-centered method, wisdom was communicated by or received from some authority. The student, accepting the authority of his teacher, made the effort to understand the abstract values to which the teacher pointed. Or emulating such sages as Yao and Shun, or Confucius and the Duke of Chou, the student struggled to achieve the ideals of hu-

85. *FSHC*, 6:4a.
86. Chou Ju-teng, *Tung-yüeh cheng-hsüeh lu*, 11:11b.
87. *CWCWC*, 4:8b.
88. Lü K'un, "Preface," *SYY*, p. 23.
89. Lu Lung-ch'i, "Preface," *SYY*, pp. 18–19.

maneness, loyalty, and sagehood those models represented. The seniority of the teachers and the fine reputations of the sages carried enough power to command the attention of the students and to convince them to make the effort to understand abstract values. In each case, some hierarchical relationship, some distinction between superior and inferior, or between model example and unpolished form, played a role in the transmission of the Way.

Similarly, political power, fame, and wealth served as leverage in prompting the student to wade patiently through a plethora of commentaries towards understanding the abstract ideals of the Classics. The examination system thus socialized those aspiring to be officials into the values of Confucianism. The rewards of office were so great as to lend exceptional power to the Classics. Associating political power and social prestige with the Classics, students struggled to understand the texts and to rise to the level of past worthies. In the minds of many, passing the examinations and enjoying official status were equated with the intellectual and moral authority of the worthies. This Lin Chao-en's teacher understood well when he advised that people would doubt Lin's teachings because he was not an official.[90] And if the most serious Confucian scholars protested strongly that the examination system was an invalid test of morality, their protests only confirm just how strong that association was. Those with a strong sense of self harshly criticized the examinations when they failed; but those who passed usually felt converted, strongly committed to the system of values that justified their social and political standing. To this extent the distinction between the sage-like and the small men seemed to coincide with the real boundary between those who passed and those who failed the civil service examinations.

The fact-centered method diminished the importance of the teacher. Self-cultivation was achieved through the piecemeal evaluation of behavior in specific events; values were defined in terms of critical situations rather than received opinion; and the role of teacher was weak, if present at all. Lü K'un carried out his task of self-cultivation in complete

90. Berling, *Syncretic Religion of Lin Chao-en*, p. 69.

privacy and preferred keeping private records to joining a group. He disparaged as self-deceiving the practice of seeking the aid of friends for mutual correction. Aware that one's sense of shame could certainly discourage frankness, Lü instructed that only "self-prosecution" (*tzu-sung*) would ring true.[91] Lü declared his independence from others in his outline of principles to his *Record of Self-Examination* where he asserted that "one's mind is the stern teacher," and that "studying to govern the mind should be [based on] a contract of which one alone is aware."[92]

Others feared that without the spur of study groups or "beneficial friends" (*i-yu*), they would lose the determination to achieve sagehood. "Friends are necessary for learning," Meng Hua-li insisted, and then explained, "Without set meetings, one's intention will slacken and one will grow tired."[93] Even so, the emphasis on personal experiences undercut the primacy of the master. Meng advised, not that one seek guidance from others, but that one report the results of private self-examination to teachers or schoolmates.[94] Also isolated in spirit was Lü Wei-ch'i. He encouraged camaraderie by founding an academy but did not acknowledge anyone as his teacher. Like Lü K'un, he was destined for the category of "miscellaneous Confucians" in Huang Tsung-hsi's *Records of Ming Philosophers*.[95]

In sum, whether scholar-officials of the fact-centered outlook examined themselves in utter privacy or sought the aid of beneficial friends, moral leaders had faded from their view. An interiorized morality combined with a reliance on external impersonal forms—charts for keeping records of merits and demerits, rules and regulations, and daily routines—had displaced personal hierarchical relations in their self-cultivation and in the communication of values. Although the fact-centered method by no means ruled out a hierarchi-

91. *Hsing-hsin chi*, in *CWCWC*, 3:28a–b. For a discussion of this and other compounds with "self" (*tzu*), see Wu, "Self-Examination," pp. 5, 21.
92. *Hsing-hsin chi*, in *CWCWC*, 3:28a. For an essay, "On 'the mind is a stern teacher,'" see Li T'ing-chi (*chin-shih*, 1583), *Li Wen-chieh chi*, 10:8a–10b.
93. Meng Hua-li, *Meng Yün-p'u*, 4:10b.
94. Meng Hua-li, "Daily Regimen for Beginning Students," *Meng Yün-p'u*, 6:19b. Tr. by Pei-yi Wu, "Self-Examination," p. 23.
95. *MJHA*, 54:14a–b.

cal concept of society, its success did not rest on the leverage of superior over inferior. The dissociation of the concept of hierarchy from the exercise of authority is evident in Lü's use of that concept—discussed in chapter 6—as a value-free paradigm for the exchange of two types of equally important information.

Abstract values, in which men were socialized through the exercise of authority, best suited the definition of community among a bureaucratic elite which had itself passed the civil service examinations. Concrete experiences, and particularly crises, to which even the poorly educated could relate, were the most compelling basis for community in local society. The fact-centered outlook, with its explicit recognition of particularistic experiences provided an apt framework for the cooperation of socially heterogeneous groups—merchant and bureaucrat, well-to-do peasant and gentry.

The fact-centered outlook encouraged writing about statecraft; the ideal-centered outlook encouraged writing about metaphysics. With the fact-centered method, shifting back and forth between writing about self-cultivation and writing about (as opposed to simply carrying out) administrative matters became easier, because the same vocabulary and conceptualization could be applied to both areas. This is shown by three examples.

First, the fact-centered outlook acknowledged more explicitly than the ideal-centered outlook that the official was not only a scholar but also a professional bureaucrat. Just as Lü K'un advised his underlings to review their daily performance of duties by "checking things off," so he checked off lists to cultivate, or discipline, himself.[96]

Second, with the fact-centered outlook, men were both doctors to society and doctors to the mind. Yüan Huang, who came from a family of doctors and who had practiced medicine in his youth, not surprisingly adopted a method of self-cultivation that required the careful scrutiny of objective data in order to effect a cure. Chou Ju-teng, who elsewhere expounded on the hidden benefits of illness, declared that in self-cultivation one should not live dogmatically by fixed

96. *SCL*, 1:1a.

rules. Rather, just as a doctor must match medicines to the symptoms of each illness, so too must one constantly respond to and evaluate new experiences.[97] Similarly illustrating how easily the scholar-turned-doctor could shift from the area of self-cultivation to that of statecraft, the preface to *Yao yen* [Medicinal Words], a book of moral advice by Yao Shun-mu (1543–1627), declared that "no illness is greater than the illness of the mind" and praised Yao as "the Great Doctor Prince who will cure [or, govern] the world."[98]

Along similar lines, Lü K'un wrote *Groaning Words* to cure himself and also conceived of the official as doctor. Lü Wei-ch'i, in a comment which incidentally again underscores the keen sense that each person is distinct, stated: "The approach to learning must suit the person just as medicine is prescribed according to each person's illness." "When, after all," asked Lü Wei-ch'i, "does a doctor ever make out a prescription before the illness?"[99] Kao P'an-lung, who like Lü K'un maintained that the performance of tasks no less than morality should be considered when evaluating officials, instructed those who had illnesses or deficiencies to read Hsüeh Hsüan's *Record of Reading Books*.[100] And Hsüeh Hsüan himself, whose experiential approach foreshadowed Lü K'un's, wrote that reading books is like taking medicine to cure an illness.[101]

Third, with the fact-centered outlook, officials were simultaneously military strategists both in standing guard against the incursion of errors and in defending society against bandits. The distinction between military strategist and scholar was blurred when the general Ch'i Chi-kuang gained a reputation for being scholar, or Confucian; and when the scholar, Lü K'un, outlined plans for city defense.[102] Similarly, Yen

97. Chou Ju-teng, *Tung-yüeh cheng-hsüeh lu*, 2:5b–6a. See also *SCKK*, 6:40b.

98. Wang San-te, "Inscription," in Yao Shun-mu, *Yao Yen*, p. 1. The characterization of *Yao yen* in *DMB* as a "collection of proverbs" is misleading.

99. Lü Wei-ch'i, *Ming-te hsien-sheng wen-chi*, 23:11a.

100. Kao P'an-lung, "Preface," *Tu-shu lu* by Hsüeh Hsüan, p. 1b.

101. Hsüeh Hsüan, *Tu-shu lu*, p. 13a.

102. See discussion in chapter 7. Numerous late Ming officials wrote about problems of local defense. How their military interests related to their other intellectual interests awaits further exploration. For two exam-

Yüan (1635–1704)—who had found inspiration in the writings of Hsüeh Hsüan, kept a diary for his self-criticism, studied medicine, and included two physicians in his list of those who had transmitted the Confucian orthodoxy (*Tao-t'ung*)—believed that military exercise was essential to the training of a scholar.[103] The same congruence is apparent many years later: the great scholar-statesman, Tseng Kuo-fan (1811–72), who successfully turned general to fight the Taiping rebels, examined his mistakes daily in a diary, which he kept from 1839–72 and which bears all the characteristics of a fact-centered outlook.[104]

Among seventeenth-century scholars, the congruence of writing in detail on administrative matters and using the correcting-faults approach to self-cultivation is remarkable. Lu Lung-ch'i, who had praised Lü K'un's *Groaning Words*, kept his own daily record and also edited a detailed administrative guide.[105] Lu Shih-i (1611–72), who had studied with but had not declared himself a disciple of Liu Tsung-chou, concentrated many of his writings on practical matters, and actively organized study societies.[106] There he frequently met a close friend and fellow townsman, Ch'en Hu (1613–75), for "study by promoting goodness and correcting faults" (*ch'ien-shan kai-kuo chih hsüeh*). Ch'en easily moved from statecraft to self-cultivation in his writing. He addressed at length such practical problems as agriculture, water control, and military defense, and also wrote *Sheng-hsüeh ju-men shu* [An Introduction to the Study of Sagehood] to encourage others "to do good and correct their faults."[107] For self-cultivation, Ch'en

---

ples, see Ch'i Piao-chia and Lu Hsiang-sheng, both discussed in Kuhn, *Rebellion and Its Enemies*, pp. 33, 41.

103. Tu Wei-ming, "Yen Yüan," pp. 516–7; 523; 532.

104. Biography of Tseng by Teng Ssu-yü in *ECCP*, 751–55. Hellmut Wilhelm, "The Background of Tseng Kuo-fan's Ideology," *Asiatische Studien* III:3–4 (1949), 90–100.

105. Biography of Lu by Fang Chao-ying in *ECCP*, pp. 547–48. In its emphasis on the importance of moral example, the Sung dynasty administrative guide Lu edited differs from Lü K'un's.

106. Biography of Lu Shih-i by Rufus O. Suter in *ECCP*, 548–49. For interesting examples of daily self-cultivation from the writings of Lu Lung-ch'i, Chang Lü-hsiang, and Lu Shih-i, see Wilhelm, "Chinese Confucianism."

107. Ch'en Hu, *Sheng-hsüeh ju-men shu*, "Preface," 2a; text, 15b–16a. For

advocated the fact-centered method. To his manual on how to study, he appended a sample chart on which the student was to check off whether he had been "reverent," "lazy," and the like.[108] Ch'en further outlined general guidelines for the daily examination of good and bad deeds;[109] and advised the student to take semi-monthly stock of whether one had made progress or regressed and to grade himself accordingly.[110]

Like Lü K'un, Ch'en Hu viewed the world objectively. According to an eighteenth-century preface, Ch'en believed that one should approach learning the way "a doctor cures an illness;"[111] and slipping into the role of doctor, he, like Lü, wrote a medical treatise.[112] But most important, Ch'en's plan for famine relief (which he wrote on returning home after failing the metropolitan examination in 1642) illustrates how the focus on concrete events unfolded new categories and encouraged the display of a broad range of solutions to famine. Just as Lü had analyzed his thoughts in terms of whether they occurred before, during, or after events, so Ch'en organized his material according to the temporal relationship to the event. He wrote the plan while confronting the event (*tang-shih*) but outlined strategies for: (1) preparation against such events in the future—by spreading, for example, information on the art of planting trees; (2) prevention by taking measures against vagrants and urging economy; and (3) social reintegration after the event by encouraging commerce, for example.[113]

Similarly, Wei Hsi (1624–81) could easily shuttle his thoughts back and forth between self-cultivation and practical matters. In self-cultivation, Wei Hsi concentrated on the correc-

---

Ch'en's interest in statecraft, see Wang Ming-sheng (1722–98), "Biography," ibid., 1a–2a.

108. Ibid., 19a. Ch'en records that someone had stated: The scholar's position is low and his power is small; he cannot accomplish good or bad deeds worth recording (ibid., 25a).

109. Ibid., 25a. 110. Ibid., 26b.

111. Wang, "Biography," ibid., 2a.

112. Ch'en Hu, *Chih-ping shuo*. Significantly, Ch'en also drew inspiration from such legalistic thinkers as Shen Pu-hai, Han Fei Tzu and Kuan Tzu, according to Wang, "Biography," in *Sheng-hsüeh ju-men shu*.

113. Wang, "Biography," in Ch'en, *Sheng-hsüeh ju-men shu*, p. 1b. For Lü, see *SYY*, 3:458.

tion of errors, regretted past wrongdoing, and swore to examine himself daily.[114] In serving society, he was entirely pragmatic. Believing that learning should be useful, he rebelled against the highly artificial style of the eight-legged essay. Among his copious writings were a study of historic military campaigns, *Ping chi* [In the Footprints of Armies], and a famous essay on famine relief. This essay, like Ch'en Hu's plan for famine relief, analyzed solutions in terms of the temporal relationship to the event. Accordingly, Wei designed different policies for "before the event"—when one should, for example, improve agricultural conditions and establish granaries—"while confronting the event," and "after the event."[115] With the shift of focus from abstract ideals to concrete data, new categories unfolded to demand more meticulous attention, and the area of statecraft thus filled out. The shift to the fact-centered outlook, with its concentration on merits and demerits, reflects not only the popularization of sagehood but the growing need for a statecraft rhetoric suitable for local government. It is for this second reason that the fact-centered outlook continued into the Ch'ing dynasty, long after the reaction against the followers of Wang Yangming for popularizing sagehood had taken place.

114. Wu, "Self-Examination," pp. 28–34; especially, pp. 29–30.
115. Wei Hsi, *Chiu huang ts'e*.

Conclusion

Lü's crisis mentality, his metaphorical language, his practicality, his didactic writings, his independent spirit, and his bold vernacular style are eye-catching and memorable. But they sparkle in an amorphous area poorly governed by his most self-conscious intellectual activity. Rarely were these features the main subjects of his essays, and never do they form the keystone or supporting structure of a coherent philosophical system. Lü wrote no essays on why he so frequently used the illness metaphor, or why it was important to write about rather than simply to communicate orally his ideas on wall repair. The salient features of Lü's writings thus easily escape the net of questions with which historians most often try to catch intellectual change. Tracing how the meanings of specific phrases changed, interpreting ideas as syntheses of conflicting trends, placing views in an evolving Confucian tradition, and explicating ideas as parts of a philosophical system are all worthy strategies of the intellectual historian. But these strategies would slight Lü's most noteworthy features, which lie in an area poorly defined by his own words, an area which may be labelled "outlook," "mentality," or—because it indicates a particular relationship to the world—"orientation." Finding some method to capture this amorphous area was the main task of this book and has resulted in departures from the custom of most intellectual history both in the treatment of change and in the evaluation of significance.

This study has perceived change only incidentally in terms of the development of Lü's outlook and primarily in terms of contrasts between Lü and others. The contrasts, like pictures of two points in time, suggest that a change has occurred but does not explain how. Most studies of thought concentrate on the process, either by explaining ideas in terms of the biography of a particular thinker or by stressing the transmission and modification of ideas between thinkers. These approaches admirably suit the study of Wang Yang-ming, for example. One can conveniently trace ideas passing from Wang Yang-ming through Wang Ken and Yen Chün on down to Lo Ju-fang. Indeed, the social contacts between teacher and student impart—even if sometimes misleadingly—a comfortable concreteness or reality to the concept that ideas were transmitted. One can also show how ideas grew out of a conscious intellectual struggle; how Wang Yang-ming, for instance, came to terms with Chu Hsi's concept of "the investigation of things" (*ko-wu*) after having struggled with it in frustration. Because Wang engaged in dialogues both with past thinkers and with his own students, and because he and his disciples meticulously recorded those dialogues, the process by which ideas grew out of a conscious intellectual struggle is available to the historian.

Interpreting how Lü's thought grew out of available intellectual traditions would have been downright inappropriate. In boldly declaring, "I am just a me," Lü K'un had refused to affiliate himself with a particular school of thought. In taking the doctrine of the mean as his teacher and measurement tools as his friends, Lü had divorced his ideas from personal relationships through which historians could later trace his ideas. Lü worked within the framework of Confucian values, to be sure, but these he derived by skipping over the Sung Neo-Confucian commentaries and establishing a spiritual bond directly with the early classical philosophers. Claiming a harmony of views with men of the distant past, he broke with his immediate predecessors. Thus an argument for continuity with Confucianism could be made, but it would have little meaning and would entirely obscure the distinctive features of Lü's outlook. Even while working within the general framework of Confucian values, Lü largely based his ideas on his personal experiences—taking his sense perceptions as his guide. Indeed, as Tsou Yüan-piao observed, Lü used the Classics to comment on his experiences.

A search for the intellectual sources of Lü's views would

divert one's attention far away from the salient features of his experiential outlook—his sense of confusion over the vast array of events; his preoccupation with crises as a means of determining what is important; his predilection for keeping lists; and the centrality of concrete events even in his record of self-cultivation. These ingredients and the social implications of Lü's experiential outlook came into sharp focus only through a comparison of how Lü and others patterned their thoughts.

The contrast between Hai and Lü, for example, showed that Lü admitted into his view an objective world that could be grasped only by relying on the senses. Putting the objective world into order called not only for moral integrity but, almost as importantly, the exercise of talent. Laws and institutions were not evils made necessary for the realization of ideals—as Hai Jui believed—but part of the objective world, upon which the talented could build advantageously. Thus Lü defined the official as a doctor who treated social ills with talent as well as virtue and who received a salary for a job well-done. And where Hai fought against greed, Lü, who valued the senses through which objective phenomena were perceived, also capitulated to the self-interest that the senses inevitably stimulate. Lü even went so far as to formulate definitions of community and cooperation that built advantageously upon individual self-interest.

The available materials cannot illuminate the evolution of these ideas or even the process whereby Lü arrived at them. They cannot tell us whether Lü built on, reacted against, or worked obliviously of the harsh statecraft of Hai Jui. But the contrast between Hai, who viewed laws and institutions as a means to impose his ideals on society, and Lü, who believed that laws and institutions were part of an objective world that called for initiative and talent, suggests why self-respecting and humane officials would have found Lü's statecraft more attractive than Hai's rigid, authoritarian approach. And a general late Ming shift to an experiential outlook, that acknowledged a world of objective phenomena and hence the need for talent, also suggests why writings about statecraft gained respectability and attention during the late sixteenth and early seventeenth centuries.

It would also be misleading to try to trace Lü K'un's popular didactic works to the followers of Wang Yang-ming. To be sure, in his use of vernacular language and in his belief that instruction should be simple and entertaining, Lü resembled members of the T'ai-chou school. At the same time, Lü sharply differed from them in his view, shared by many of his contemporaries, that "learned discussions" which had disintegrated into hair-splitting battles among egocentric fame-seekers were an inappropriate way to fulfill one's mission as educator. Interpreting Lü as developing out of or reacting against the T'ai-chou school might explain why he wrote playful songs for illiterate members of his lineage. But, disconcertingly, it might at the same time explain why he shied away from lecturing to the masses. These explanations are simplistic and inadequate. They gloss over how Lü's acknowledgment of the world of objective phenomena stimulated him to write didactic works. This came to light not through a study of the development of ideas but through a contrast between Lü K'un and Lo Ju-fang. The student-teacher relationship had been central to Lo's educational endeavors. In contrast, Lü perceived that didactic works could free educational efforts from personal relations and hence from criticisms that he was gathering a large following. These and numerous other features of Lü's thought were brought to light not through a study of the evolution of Lü's ideas but through contrasts between Lü and other Ming thinkers.

We now turn to the second departure from the practice of most intellectual history—in the evaluation of significance. When concerned with the evolution or unfolding of great ideas, one may appropriately define significance by relying on the templates of past philosophical systems. One can, for example, take as the point of departure what a subject thought about such key terms as "principle," "ether," "the investigation of things," and "intuitive knowledge." But this method would poorly suit Lü K'un whose strengths lie not in carrying out a dialogue with the great thinkers of the past but in bringing order and coherence to his own scrambled and disconnected experiences.

Significance—that is, the capacity of one fact to illuminate another—is also discernible when ideas link up with social and political action. Wang Yang-ming's ideas are patently significant because they had the power to inspire an enormous following and paved the way for—or at least accompanied—the popularization of education. Along similar lines, we look for clues to the Tung-lin movement in the ideas of its leaders Kao P'an-lung and Ku Hsien-ch'eng; and our knowledge that Ho Hsin-yin consorted with fringe social groups and organized his lineage to resist taxes also leads us to look into his writings for clues to social change. In each case the intersection of events and ideas helps us pinpoint significance. Lü's writings neither commanded a cohesive following nor formed the basis for a political movement; his writings simply expressed a view of the world which—as both the frequent republication of his works and the later echoes of his views suggest—was widely shared during the Ch'ing dynasty. But without the affirmation of Lü's ideas by a social movement or a political event, it was difficult to select what was important from the vast array of his writings. That Lü himself was frustrated by the task of imposing order on his numerous disconnected experiences only exacerbates the problem for the historian.

Both to circumvent this problem and to do justice to Lü's experiential outlook, this study took as significant those points where Lü's various concerns intersected. It repeatedly asked which themes clustered together in his writings and what relationship to his world, what orientation, allowed the formation of those particular clusters. What position, for example, allowed Lü to mediate between and give equal voice to military necessity and humaneness—two concerns that frequently intersect in his writings as evident in his amalgamation of the *pao-chia* and *hsiang-yüeh* organizations, in his militant call for wall-building in order to promote a sense of community and to save lives, and in his humane solicitude for the lone soldier? What position allowed Lü to express equally both his preoccupation with the experiences of the senses (which he associated with the bottom of society) and his commitment to Confucian ideals (which he associated with the top)? Or to call in times of crisis both for self-reliance and for cooperation? Such questions revealed the importance of the objective world and the implications of Lü's experiential outlook.

The final chapter, similarly exploring where various concerns overlapped, showed that Lü used the vocabulary of concrete practical concerns even when writing about self-cultivation. In particular, his use of metaphors of illness and battle when discussing both statecraft and self-cultivation suggests that he was groping to capture the convergence of concerns that could not be expressed literally. Lü's concrete language suited not only the daily practical concerns of the masses and an accompanying assumption that most men were mediocre but also the particularistic interests of local society. Even when seventeenth-century thinkers pulled back from the popularizing impulses of the followers of Wang Yang-ming, they found that Lü K'un's outlook continued to express the needs of local government and local interests. There had taken place a reorientation where personal experiences, self-interest, and local concerns had become the center.

Glossary

Chinese terms, names of persons who do not appear as authors in the bibliography, and other proper names.

A-le-ch'ing-a	阿勒清阿
An-ch'ing	安慶
Chai Ch'iu-t'an	翟秋潭
Chan Jo-shui	湛若水
Ch'an	禪
Chang Ch'ang-an	張常安
Chang Chü-cheng	張居正
Chang Tsai	張載
Chang Wei	張位
Ch'ang-an	長安
Chao Nan-hsing	趙南星
Che	浙
chen-hsin	眞心
Ch'en Liang	陳亮
Ch'en Ti	陳第
Cheng Ch'eng-en	鄭承恩
Cheng Kuei-fei	鄭貴妃
Ch'eng Hao	程顥
Ch'eng Ta-yüeh	程大約
Ch'eng Tsu-lo	程祖洛
chi	記
Chi hsien	杞縣
ch'i (material force, ether)	氣

ch'i (mechanism) 器
chia 甲
Chia-ching 嘉靖
chiang-hsüeh 講學
Chiao Hung 焦竑
chiao-t'ai 交泰
Ch'iao Yin 喬胤
chieh 節
Chieh 桀
chieh-chih 節制
chien-ai 兼愛
chien-sheng 監生
ch'ien-shan kai-kuo chih hsüeh 遷善改過之學
Ch'ien Te-hung 錢德洪
Chih-ch'üan (shu-yüan) 芝泉書院
chih liang-chih 至良知
Chin-chiang 晋江
chin-shih 進士
ching-chi shih-hsüeh 經濟實學
ching-shih 經世
chiu-shih 救世
Ch'iu 邱
Ch'iung-shan 瓊山
chou 州
Chou 紂
Chou Hui 周暉
Chou Ssu-chiu 周思久
Chou Tzu-hsün 周咨詢
Chu 朱
chu-ching 主敬
Chu Hsi 朱熹
Chu-hung 袾宏
Chu Shih 朱軾
Ch'un-an 淳安

chung 中
chung-jen 中人
chü-jen 舉人
chüan 卷
chün 均
Fan 范
fan-ch'ieh 反切
Fan Chih-mou 范志懋
Fan Chung-yen 范仲淹
Fang I-chih 方以智
fen 分
fen-yüan 分願
Feng-ch'eng 豐城
feng-liu 風流
Feng Meng-lung 馮夢龍
Feng Yu 馮友
fu 府
Fu Mei 傅梅
Fu Shan 傅山
Han Fei Tzu 韓非子
Han Yü 韓愈
hao 號
Ho Hsin-yin 何心隱
Ho Liang-chün 何良俊
ho-shih lao-jen 和事老人
hsi 悉
hsiang-chia 鄉甲
hsiang-kuan 鄉官
hsiang-min 鄉民
hsiang-pin 鄉賓
hsiang-yüan 鄉愿
Hsiang-yüan 襄垣
hsiang-yüeh 鄉約
hsien 縣

hsin (belief, faith) 信
hsin (mind, heart) 心
Hsin-an 新安
hsin-hsüeh 心學
hsin-shih 心事
Hsin-wu 新吾
hsing 性
Hsing-hsüeh hui 興學會
hsing-ming 形命
Hsing-t'ai 邢臺
hsiu-shen 修身
hsiu-ts'ai 秀才
Hsiung Ping-yüan 熊秉元
hsü (preface) 序
Hsü Chieh 徐階
Hsü Yüeh 徐樾
Hsün Tzu 荀子
Hu Chih 胡直
Hua (Mountain) 華山
Huang Tao-chou 黃道周
Hui-neng 惠能
hui-yü 會話
hun-jan t'ung t'i 渾然同體
Hung Liang-chi 洪亮吉
Hung-tao (shu-yüan) 弘道書院
i 義
i-hsüeh 義學
i-kuan 義館
i-nung min 邑農民
i-yu 益友
Jao-chou 饒州
jen (humaneness) 仁
jen (others) 人
kai-kuo 改過

kan 感
Kan-chou 贛州
Kan-ch'üan 甘泉
K'ang Hai 康海
K'ang-hsi 康熙
ko wu 格物
k'ou 口
ku 孤
Ku Hsien-ch'eng 顧憲成
kuan 關
Kuan Chih-tao 管志道
Kuan Chung 管仲
Kuan-chung (shu-yüan) 關中書院
Kuang-jen hui 廣仁會
kung 公
kung-hsing 躬行
kung-i 公議
kung-sheng 貢生
li (clerk) 吏
li (measure of length) 里
li (principle) 理
li (profit) 利
li (rites, propriety) 禮
li-chia 里甲
Li Ch'ou 李疇
Li-ming hui 立命會
li pu-liao ssu-ko tzu 離不了四個字
Li Ssu 李斯
li-tien 吏典
Li Ts'ai 李材
Li Yü 李漁
Liang Ch'i-ch'ao 梁啓超
liang-chih 良知
Liang Yün-lung 梁雲龍

Lin Chao-en 林兆恩
Lin Tse-hsü 林則徐
Ling-chi (kung) 靈濟宮
Liu I-ching 劉一燝
Lo-an 樂安
Lu Hsiang-shan 陸象山
Lu Lung-ch'i 陸隴其
Lü Chih-wei 呂知畏
Lü Tsu-ch'ien 呂祖謙
Ma-ch'eng 痲城
Ming T'ai-tsu 明太祖
Ming-tao (shu-yüan) 明道書院
mo-ch'i 默契
Mo Tzu 墨子
mou 敏
Nan-ch'eng 南城
Nan-p'ing 南平
Ni Yüan-lu 倪元璐
nien-p'u 年譜
Ning-kuo 寧國
Ning-ling 寧陵
niu yü mu-ch'ien 狃於目前
pai-hsing jih-yung 百姓日用
p'ai 牌
pao-chia 保甲
Pao-ch'ing 寶慶
Pao-ting 保定
Pei Chih-li 北直隸
pien 便
pien-t'ung sui-shih 變通隨時
p'ing 平
Po Chü-i 白居易
shan 善
Shang-ch'iu 商邱

Ming-chih	明職
Nü hsün	女訓
Pao-p'u-tzu	抱扑子
Pien-hsüeh lu	辨學錄
Ping chi	兵跡
"Shan li t'u"	善利圖
"Shan li t'u shuo"	善利圖說
"Shih li shuo"	勢利說
Shu ching	書經
Shui-hu chuan	水滸傳
Ta hsüeh	大學
Tso chuan	左傳
Tso-i tzu-chen	作邑自箴
Tzu-chih lu	自知錄
Tzu-p'ing yao-yü	子平要語
Yang-min	養民
"Yu-wei shu"	憂危疏
Yü-cheng	獄政
Yüan-ju k'ao-lüeh	元儒考略
Yüan shih	元史

Bibliography

Araki Kengo 荒木見悟. *Mindai shisō kenkyū* 明代思想研究. Tokyo: Sōbunsha, 1972.

Atwell, William S. "Notes on Silver, Foreign Trade, and the Late Ming Economy." *Ch'ing-shih wen-t'i* 3.8:1–33 (Dec., 1977).

Balazs, Etienne. *Political Theory and Administrative Reality in Traditional China*. London: School of Oriental and African Studies, 1965.

Berling, Judith A. *The Syncretic Religion of Lin Chao-en*. New York: Columbia University Press, 1980.

Bloom, Irene. "On the 'Abstraction' of Ming Thought: Some Concrete Evidence from the Philosophy of Lo Ch'in-shun." In Wm. Theodore de Bary and Irene Bloom, eds., *Principle and Practicality*, 69–123. New York: Columbia University Press, 1979.

Bol, Peter. "The *Tso-i tzu-chen*: A Twelfth Century Guide for Subprefects." Unpublished paper, Princeton University.

Buck, Pearl, tr., *All Men Are Brothers*. 2 vols. New York: John Day Co., 1968.

Busch, Heinrich. "The Tung-lin Shu-yüan and Its Political and Philosophical Significance." *Monumenta Serica* 14:1–163 (1949–55).

Cartier, Michel. *Une Réforme Locale en Chine au XVIe Siècle: Hai Rui à Chun'an 1558–1562*. Paris: Mouton and Company, 1973.

Chan, Wing-tsit. *A Source Book in Chinese Philosophy*. Princeton: Princeton University Press, 1970.

Chang Chih-kung 張志公. *Ch'uan-t'ung yü-wen chiao-yü ch'u-t'an* 傳統語文教育初探. In *Yü-wen hui pien*, No. 20. Shanghai: Chiao-yü ch'u-pan she, 1962.

Chang Hsüan 張萱. *Hsi-yüan wen-chien lu* 西園聞見錄. 107 *chüan*. Peking: Ho-fo Yen-ching hsüeh-she, 1940.
Chang Lü-hsiang 張履祥. *Yang-yüan hsien-sheng ch'üan-chi* 楊園先生全集. 54 *chüan*. Kiang-su shu-chü edition. 1871.
Chang Shen-yen 張慎言. *Tzu-shui chai wen-ch'ao* 洎水齋文鈔. 3 *chüan*. In *Shan-yu ts'ung-shu* 山右叢書, *ts'e* 73–4. Edited by the Shansi Commission of Documents. Min-kuo edition.
Chang Yüan-pien 張元忭. *Chang Yang-ho wen-hsüan* 張陽和文選. 3 *chüan*. Ts'ung-shu chi-ch'eng edition, No. 2161. Shanghai: Shang-wu, 1935.
Ch'ang-an hsien chih 長安縣志. Edited by Tung Tseng-ch'en 董曾臣 and Chang Ts'ung-hsien 張聰賢. 36 *chüan*. 1815.
Ch'ang-li hsien chih 昌黎縣志. Edited by Ma Hsün 馬恂 and Ho Sung-t'ai 何崧泰. 10 *chüan*. 1866.
Chao Feng-chieh 趙鳳喈. *Chung-kuo fu-nü tsai fa-lü shang chih ti-wei* 中國婦女在法律上之地位. Shanghai: Shang-wu yin-shu kuan, 1929.
Ch'en Hu 陳瑚. *Chih-ping shuo* 治病說. In *Ti hsiang chai ts'ung-shu* 棣香齋叢書, *ts'e* 2. 1833.
———. *Sheng-hsüeh ju-men shu* 聖學入門書. 1 *chüan*. In *Chi-kuo chai ts'ung-shu* 記過齋叢書, *ts'e* 1. 1868.
Ch'en Hung-mou 陳宏〔弘〕謀. *Chiao-nü i-kuei* 教女遺規. 3 *chüan*. In *Wu-chung i-kuei* 五種遺規, vol. 2. Reprint of Ssu-pu pei-yao edition, Taipei: Chung-hua shu-chü, 1960.
———. *Ch'üan Tien i-hsüeh hui chi* 全滇義學彙記. 1738. Preserved in the Library of Congress.
———. *Hsün-su i-kuei* 訓俗遺規. 4 chüan. In *Wu-chung i-kuei*, vol. 1.
———. *Ts'ung-cheng i-kuei* 從政遺規. 2 *chüan*. In *Wu-chung i-kuei*, vols. 1 and 2.
———. *Yang-cheng i-kuei* 養正遺規. 2 *chüan* and supplement. In *Wu-chung i-kuei*, vol. 1.
Ch'en Lung-cheng 陳龍正. *Chi-t'ing ch'üan-shu* 幾亭全書. 64 *chüan*. 1665.
———. *Chi-t'ing wai-shu* 幾亭外書. 9 *chüan*. 1631.
Ch'i Chi-kuang 戚繼光. *Chi-hsiao hsin-shu* 紀效新書. 18 *chüan*. Reprint. Changsha: Shang-wu, 1938.
———. *Lien-ping shih-chi* 練兵實紀. Reprint. Shanghai: Shang-wu, 1937.
Ch'i Piao-chia 祁彪佳. *Ch'i Piao-chia chi* 祁彪佳集. 10 *chüan*. Shanghai: Chung-hua shu-chü, 1960.

Chiang Hsing-yü 蔣星煜. *Hai Jui* 海瑞. Shanghai: Jen-min ch'u-pan-she, 1962.

Ch'ien, Edward T. "Chiao Hung and the Revolt against Ch'eng-Chu Orthodoxy." In Wm. Theodore de Bary et al., eds., *The Unfolding of Neo-Confucianism*, 271–303. New York: Columbia University Press, 1975.

Ch'iung-shan hsien chih 瓊山縣志. Edited by Cheng Wen-ts'ai 鄭文彩. 30 *chüan*. 1857.

Chou Ju-teng 周汝登. *Sheng-hsüeh tsung-chuan* 聖學宗傳. 18 *chüan*. 1605.

———. *Tung-yüeh cheng hsüeh lu* 東越證學錄. 16 *chüan*. Ming-jen wen-chi ts'ung-k'an series, No. 25. 2 vols. Photo reprint of 1605 edition. Taipei: Wen-hai ch'u-pan-she, 1970.

Chou Tso-jen 周作人. *T'an lung chi* 談龍集. Shanghai: K'ai-ming shu-tien, 1928.

Chu Chieh-fan 朱介凡. "Lü K'un ti *Hsiao-erh yü*" 呂坤的小兒語. *Ta-lu tsa-chih* 大陸雜志 19:191–93; 215–20 (1959).

Chu Hsi and Lü Tsu-ch'ien. *Reflections on Things at Hand: The Neo-Confucian Anthology Compiled by Chu Hsi and Lü Tsu-ch'ien*. Translated and edited by Wing-tsit Chan. New York: Columbia University Press, 1967.

Ch'u T'ung-tsu. *Law and Society in Traditional China*. Paris: Mouton, 1961.

———. *Local Government in China Under the Ch'ing*. Stanford: Stanford University Press, 1969.

Chü-chia pi-pei 居家必備. 10 *chüan*. Wan-li edition. Preserved in the Harvard-Yenching Library.

Crawford, Robert B. "Chang Chü-cheng's Legalism." In Wm. Theodore de Bary, ed., *Self and Society in Ming Thought*, 367–414. New York: Columbia University Press, 1970.

———. *The Life and Thought of Chang Chü-cheng, 1525–1582*. Ph.D. dissertation, University of Washington, 1961.

de Bary, Wm. Theodore. "Chinese Despotism and the Confucian Ideal: A Seventeenth-Century View." In John K. Fairbank, ed., *Chinese Thought and Institutions*, 163–203. Chicago: University of Chicago Press, 1957.

——— et al., eds. *Sources of Chinese Tradition*. New York: Columbia University Press, 1960.

———, ed. *Self and Society in Ming Thought*. New York: Columbia University Press, 1970.

———. "Individualism and Humanitarianism in Late Ming Thought." In Wm. Theodore de Bary, ed., *Self and Society in Ming Thought*, 145–248. New York: Columbia University Press, 1970.

——— et al., eds. *The Unfolding of Neo-Confucianism*. New York: Columbia University Press, 1975.

Dimberg, Ronald G. *The Sage and Society: The Life and Thought of Ho Hsin-yin*. Honolulu: University Press of Hawaii, 1974.

Egerton, Clement, tr. *The Golden Lotus*. New York: Grove Press, 1954.

Elvin, Mark. *The Pattern of the Chinese Past*. Stanford: Stanford University Press, 1973.

Feng Ch'i 馮琦. *Pei hai chi* 北海集. 46 *chüan*. Ming-jen wen-chi ts'ung-k'an series, No. 26. 5 vols. Facsimile reproduction of Wan-li edition. Taipei: Wen-hai ch'u-pan-she, 1970.

Feng Ts'ung-wu 馮從吾. *[Feng] Shao-hsü chi*〔馮〕少墟集. 20 *chüan*. Ssu-k'u ch'üan-shu chen-pen, 5th series, vols. 371–3. Photo reprint of Wen Yüan Ko copy. Taipei: Shang-wu, 1974.

Feng Ying-ching 馮應京. *Huang-ming ching-shih shih-yung pien* 皇明經世實用編. 28 *chüan*. Facsimile of Wan-li edition. 5 vols. Taipei: Ch'eng-wen ch'u-pan-she, 1967.

Fu I-ling 傅衣凌. *Ming-Ch'ing shih-tai shang-jen chi shang-yeh tzu-pen* 明清時代商人及商業資本. Peking: Jen-min ch'u-pan-she, 1956.

———. *Ming-tai Chiang-nan shih-min ching-chi shih-t'an* 明代江南市民經濟試探. Shanghai: Jen-min ch'u-pan-she, 1963.

Fung, Yu-lan. *A History of Chinese Philosophy*. Translated by Derk Bodde. 2 vols. Princeton: Princeton University Press, 1952.

Goodrich, L. Carrington and Chaoying Fang, eds. *Dictionary of Ming Biography, 1368–1644*. 2 vols. New York: Columbia University Press, 1976.

Greenblatt, Kristin Yü. "Chu-hung and Lay Buddhism in the Late Ming." In Wm. Theodore de Bary et al., eds., *The Unfolding of Neo-Confucianism*, 93–140. New York: Columbia University Press, 1975.

Grimm, Tilemann. "Ming Education Intendants." In Charles

O. Hucker, ed., *Chinese Government in Ming Times*, 129–147. New York: Columbia University Press, 1969.

———. "Some Remarks on the Suppression of Shu-yüan in Ming China." *Transactions of the International Conference of Orientalists in Japan*, 2:8–17 (1957).

Hai Jui 海瑞. *Hai Jui chi* 海瑞集. Edited by Ch'en I-chung 陳義鍾 . 2 vols. Peking: Chung-hua shu-chü. 1962.

Handlin, Joanna F. "Definitions of Community by Ch'i Chi-kuang and Lü K'un." In Paul A. Cohen and John E. Schrecker, eds., *Reform in Nineteenth-Century China*, 18–25. Cambridge: Harvard University Press, 1976.

———. "Hai Jui and Lo Ju-fang: Alternative Routes to Fame in the Sixteenth Century." New York State Conference on Asian Studies, Buffalo, Oct. 1977.

———. "Lü K'un's New Audience: The Influence of Women's Literacy on Sixteenth-Century Thought." In Margery Wolf and Roxane Witke, eds., *Women in Chinese Society*, 13–38. Stanford: Stanford University Press, 1975.

Hidaka, K. 日高一宇. "Minmatsu no ichi kanryō Ryo Kon [Lü K'un] no taisei hihan to 'Jishōroku' [Shih-cheng lu]" 明末の一官僚呂坤の体制批判と「実政録」. *Kita Kyūshū kōgyō kōtō semmon gakkō kenkyū hōkoku* 北九州工業高等専門学校研究報告 8:97–106 (1975); 9:115–124 (1975).

Hikita Keiyū 疋田啓佑. "Ryo Kon [Lü K'un] no denki to 'Shingingo' [Shen-yin yü]" 呂坤の伝記と「呻吟語」. *Kenkyū hōkoku* 研究報告 10:27–38 (signed 1950); 11:17–30 (signed 1976).

Ho Ping-ti. *The Ladder of Success in Imperial China: Aspects of Social Mobility, 1368–1911*. New York: John Wiley, 1964.

Hou Wai-lu 侯外廬. *Chung-kuo ssu-hsiang t'ung-shih* 中國思想通史. 5 vols. Peking: Jen-min ch'u-pan-she, 1957.

Hsia, C. T. "Time and the Human Condition in the Plays of T'ang Hsien-tsu." In Wm. Theodore de Bary, ed., *Self and Society in Ming Thought*, 249–290. New York: Columbia University Press, 1970.

Hsiao Kung-ch'üan 蕭公權. *Chung-kuo cheng-chih ssu-hsiang shih* 中國政治思想史. 6 vols. Taipei: Chung-hua wen-hua ch'u-pan shih-yeh wei-yüan-hui, 1954.

———. *Rural China, Imperial Control in the Nineteenth Century*. Seattle: University of Washington Press, 1967.

Hsiang-yüan hsien chih 襄垣縣志. 1880.

Hsien-ning hsien chih 咸寧縣志. 1819.
Hsü Fu-yüan 許孚遠. *Ching-ho-t'ang chi* 敬和堂集. 13 *chüan*. Ming edition. Preserved in the Naikaku Bunko.
Hsü Hsüeh-chü 徐學聚. *Kuo-ch'ao tien-hui* 國朝典彙. 200 *chüan*. Facsimile reproduction of 1624 edition. 4 vols. Chung-kuo shih-hsüeh ts'ung-shu series, No. 7. Taipei: Tai-wan hsüeh-sheng shu-chü, 1965.
Hsü I-t'ang. "Social Relief during the Sung Dynasty." In E-tu Zen Sun and John de Francis, ed. and tr., *Chinese Social History*, 207–215. Washington, D.C.: American Council of Learned Societies, 1956.
Hsü Kuang-ch'i 徐光啓. *Hsü Kuang-ch'i chi* 徐光啓集. 12 *chüan*. Edited by Wang Chung-min 王重民. 2 vols. Shanghai: Chung-hua shu-chü, 1963.
———. *Nung-cheng ch'üan-shu* 農政全書. 60 *chüan*. 1639(?). Preserved in the East Asiatic Library, Berkeley.
Hsüeh Hsüan 薛瑄. *Tu shu lu* 讀書錄. 8 *chüan*. In *Chi-kuo-chai ts'ung-shu* 記過齋叢書, *ts'e* 3–6. 1868.
Huang-ming ching-shih wen-pien 皇明經世文編. Edited by Ch'en Tzu-lung 陳子龍, Hsü Fu-yüan 徐孚遠, and Sung Cheng-pi 宋徵璧. 504 *chüan*. 30 vols. Facsimile reproduction of Ch'ung-chen edition. Taipei: Kuo-lien t'u-shu ch'u-pan yu-hsien kung-ssu, 1964.
Huang, Ray. "Ni Yüan-lu: 'Realism' in a Neo-Confucian Scholar-Statesman." In Wm. Theodore de Bary, ed., *Self and Society in Ming Thought*, 415–449. New York: Columbia University Press, 1970.
———. "Fiscal Administration During the Ming Dynasty." In Charles O. Hucker, ed., *Chinese Government in Ming Times*, 73–128. New York: Columbia University Press, 1969.
———. *Taxation and Government Finance in 16th Century Ming China*. Cambridge: Cambridge University Press, 1974.
Huang Tsung-hsi 黃宗羲. *Ming-ju hsüeh-an* 明儒學案. 62 *chüan*. Reprint of Ssu-pu pei-yao edition, 2 vols., Taipei: Chung-hua shu-chü, 1960.
Hucker, Charles O., ed. *Chinese Government in Ming Times*. New York: Columbia University Press, 1969.
———. "Governmental Organization of the Ming Dynasty." *Harvard Journal of Asiatic Studies*, 21:1–66 (1958).
———. "Su-chou and the Agents of Wei Chung-hsien." In

Two Studies on Ming History. Michigan Papers in Chinese Studies, No. 12. Ann Arbor, Michigan, 1971. Reprint.

———. "The Tung-lin Movement of the Late Ming Period." In John K. Fairbank, ed., *Chinese Thought and Institutions*, 132–162. Chicago: University of Chicago Press, 1957.

Hummel, Arthur, ed. *Eminent Chinese of the Ch'ing Period*. 2 vols. Washington, D.C.: United States Government Printing Office, 1943–44.

Irwin, Richard G. *The Evolution of a Chinese Novel: Shui-hu-chuan*. Cambridge: Harvard University Press, 1953.

Jackson, J. H., tr. *The Water Margin*. Shanghai: Commercial Press, 1937.

Jung Chao-tsu 容肇祖. *Ho Hsin-yin chi* 何心隱集. Peking: Chung-hua shu-chü. 1960.

———. *Ming-tai ssu-hsiang shih* 明代思想史. Taipei: K'ai-ming shu-tien, 1962.

Kao P'an-lung 高攀龍. *Kao tzu i-shu* 高子遺書. 12 *chüan*, appendix, 1 *chüan*. 1876.

Keng Ting-hsiang 耿定向. *Keng T'ien-t'ai hsien-sheng wen-chi* 耿天臺先生文集. 20 *chüan*. 4 vols. Ming-jen wen-chi ts'ung-k'an series, No. 20. Photo reprint of 1598 edition. Taipei: Wen-hai ch'u-pan-she, 1970.

Ku Tuan-wen kung nien-p'u 顧端文公年譜. Edited by Ku Shu 顧樞. 2 *chüan*. Appended to Ku Hsien-ch'eng 顧憲成, *Ching-kao ts'ang-kao* 涇皐藏稿.

Ku Yen-wu 顧炎武. *Jih-chih lu* 日知錄. 32 *chüan*. Reprint of Ssu-pu pei yao edition, 4 vols. Taipei: Chung-hua shu-chü, 1961.

Ku Ying-t'ai 顧應泰. *Ming shih chi-shih pen-mo* 明史紀事本末. 80 *chüan*. 2 vols. Taipei: San-min shu-chü, 1969.

Kuhn, Philip A. *Rebellion and Its Enemies in Late Imperial China*. Cambridge: Harvard University Press, 1970.

Legge, James, tr. *The Chinese Classics*. 5 vols. Reprint, Taipei: Book World Company, 1963.
Vol. I. *Confucian Analects, The Great Learning, The Doctrine of the Mean*.
Vol. II. *The Works of Mencius*.

Levenson, Joseph R. *Confucian China and Its Modern Fate: A Trilogy*. Berkeley, Los Angeles, London: University of California Press, 1968.

Li Chih 李贄. *Hsü Ts'ang-shu* 續藏書. 27 *chüan*. Taipei: Taiwan hsüeh-sheng shu-chü, 1974.

———. *Li shih Fen shu Hsü Fen shu* 李氏焚書續焚書. Kyoto: Chūbun shuppansha, 1971.

Li Ch'un-fang 李春芳, ed. [*Hsin-k'o ch'üan-hsiang*] *Hai Kang-feng kung chü-kuan kung-an* 新刻全像海剛峯公居官公案. 4 *chüan*. Nanking, 1606.

Li Shou-k'ung 李守孔. "Ming-tai pai-lien-chiao k'ao-lüeh" 明代白蓮教考略. In Pao Tsun-p'eng 包遵彭 ed., *Ming-tai tsung-chiao* 明代宗教. In *Ming shih lun-ts'ung* 明史論叢. Vol. 10. Taipei: Taiwan hsüeh-sheng shu-chü, 1968.

Li T'ing-chi 李廷機. *Li Wen-chieh chi* 李文節集. 28 *chüan*. 4 vols. Ming-jen wen-chi ts'ung-k'an series, No. 28. Photo reprint of Ch'ung-cheng edition, Taipei: Wen-hai ch'u-pan-she, 1970.

Li Yü. *Twelve Towers*. Retold by Nathan Mao. Hong Kong: The University of Hong Kong, 1975.

Li Yung 李顒. *Erh-ch'ü chi* 二曲集. 46 *chüan*. 1877.

Liang Chang-chü 梁章鉅. *T'ui-an sui-pi* 退庵隨筆. Facsimile reproduction of 1872 edition. Taipei: Kuang-wen shu-chü, 1967.

Liang Ch'i-ch'ao. *Intellectual Trends in the Ch'ing Period*. Translated by Immanuel C. Y. Hsü. Cambridge: Harvard University Press, 1959.

Liang Fang-chung. *The Single-Whip Method of Taxation in China*. Tr., Wang Yü-ch'üan. Cambridge: Harvard University Press, 1956.

Liu, James T. C. *Reform in Sung China*. Cambridge: Harvard University Press, 1959.

Liu Ts'un-yan. "Yüan Huang and His 'Four Admonitions.'" *Journal of the Oriental Society of Australia* 5, (nos. 1 and 2): 108–132 (Dec., 1967).

Liu Tsung-chou 劉宗周. *Liu tzu ch'üan-shu* 劉子全書. 40 *chüan*. 6 vols. Facsimile reproduction of Tao-kuang edition. Taipei: Hua-wen shu-chü, 1968.

———. *Jen p'u* 人譜. Hsüeh-hai lei-pien edition, No. 35. Shanghai, 1920. 1 *chüan*.

Lo Ju-fang 羅汝芳. *Chin-hsi tzu chi* 近溪子集. 9 *chüan*. With *Fu-chi* 附集 (appendix), 2 *chüan*. 1587–1606. Preserved in the Harvard-Yenching Library.

———. *Hsiang-yüeh ch'üan-shu* 鄉約全書. In *Hsü-chiang Lo Chin-hsi hsien-sheng ch'üan-chi* 盱江羅近溪先生全集. *Chüan* 13.
———. *Hsü-chiang Lo Chin-hsi hsien-sheng ch'üan-chi* 盱江羅近溪先生全集. Edited by Liu I-k'un 劉一焜. 13 *chüan*. 1618.
———. *Hsü-t'an chih-ch'üan* 盱壇直詮. Edited by Ts'ao Yin-ju 曹胤儒 and Yang Ch'i-yüan 楊起元. Facsimile reproduction. Taipei: Kuang-wen shu-chü, 1960.
———. *Lo Chin-hsi wen-chi* 羅近溪文集. 5 *chüan*. Preserved in the Naikaku Bunko.
Lo Kuang 羅光. *Hsü Kuang-ch'i chuan* 徐光啓傳. Taipei: Chuan-chi wen-hsüeh ch'u-pan-she, 1970.
Lo, Winston Wan. *The Life and Thought of Yeh Shih*. Gainesville: University Press of Florida, 1974.
Lu Ch'ing-hsien kung nien-p'u 陸清獻公年譜. Compiled by Lu Ch'en-cheng 陸宸徵. 1868.
Lu Lung-ch'i 陸隴其. *San-yü-t'ang jih-chi* 三魚堂日集. 2 *chüan*. In *Ming-Ch'ing shih-liao hui-pien* 明清史料彙編, vol. 7. Taipei: Wen-hai ch'u-pan-she, 1967.
———. *San-yü-t'ang wen-chi, wai chi* 三魚堂文集外集. 12 *chüan* and 6 *chüan*. 1701.
———, ed. *Li-cheng chai-yao* 蒞政摘要. By Hu T'ai-ch'u 胡太初. Ching-ho kuang-jen-t'ang edition, No. 12. 1870.
Lü K'un 呂坤. *Chen k'e* 疹科. In *Lü tzu i-shu* 呂子遺書. *Ts'e* 39. Preserved in the Far Eastern Library, University of Chicago.
———. *Chiao-t'ai yün* 交泰韻. In *Lü tzu i-shu* 呂子遺書. *Ts'e* 46–7. Preserved in the Far Eastern Library, University of Chicago.
———. *Chiu-ming shu* 救命書. In *Ch'ü-wei chai wen chi* 去僞齋文集, 7:34a–53a. In *Lü tzu i-shu* 呂子遺書.
———. [*Hsin-k'e Lü Shu-chien hsien-sheng*] *Chü kuan pi-yao* 新刻呂叔簡先生居官必要. 8 *chüan*. Wan-li edition. Preserved in the Sonkeikaku Bunko, Tokyo.
———. *Ch'ü-wei chai [wen]-chi* 去僞齋文集. 10 *chüan*. In *Lü tzu i-shu* 呂子遺書. *Ts'e* 1-11.
———. *Hao-jen ko* 好人歌. In *Lü shu ssu-chung* 呂書四種. In *Lü tzu i-shu* 呂子遺書. *Ts'e* 24.
———. *Hsing-hsin chi* 省心紀. In *Ch'ü-wei chai wen chi* 去僞齋文集, 3:26b–32b. In *Lü tzu i-shu* 呂子遺書.

———. *Hsü Hsiao-erh yü* 續小兒語. In *Lü shu ssu-chung* 呂書四種. In *Lü tzu i-shu* 呂子遺書. *Ts'e* 24.
———. *Kuei chieh* 閨戒. In *Lü shu ssu-chung* 呂書四種. In *Lü tzu i-shu* 呂子遺書. *Ts'e* 24.
———. *Kuei fan* 閨範. 4 *chüan*. Circa 1613.
———. *Kuei fan t'u-shuo* 閨範圖說. 4 *chüan*. 1590. Preserved in the Harvard-Yenching Library.
———. *Lü tzu chieh-lu* 呂子節錄. 4 *chüan*; supplement, 2 *chüan*. Edited by Ch'en Hung-mou 陳宏謀.
———. *Lü tzu i-shu* 呂子遺書. Edited by Wang Ch'ing-lin 王慶麟 and Su Yü-mei 栗毓美. 1827.
———. *Shen-yin yü* 呻吟語. 6 *chüan*. Preface, 1593. Preserved in the Gest Library, Princeton.
[Lü K'un] Ryo Kon 呂坤. [*Shen-yin yü*] *Shingingo* 呻吟語 Ed., Kōda Rentarō 公田連太郎. Tokyo: Shuppansha, 1956.
———. *Shih-cheng lu chieh-ch'ao* 實政節鈔. Ed., Lin Tse-hsü 林則徐. 10 *chüan*. 1837. Preserved in the Toyō Bunka, Tokyo University.
———. *Shih-cheng lu* 實政錄. In *Lü tzu i-shu* 呂子遺書. *Ts'e* 18–24.
———. *Ssu li i* 四禮疑. Preserved in a composite edition of *Lü tzu i-shu* 呂子遺書, East Asiatic Library, Berkeley.
———. *Ssu li i* 四禮翼. 4 *chüan*. Edited by Chu Shih 朱軾. Ching-ho kuang-jen-t'ang series, *ts'e* 1. 1882.
———. *Ssu li i* 四禮翼. 4 *chüan*. In Chu Shih 朱軾, ed., *Ts'ang shu shih-san chung* 藏書十三種. *Ts'e* 44. 1736.
———. *Tsung-yüeh ko* 宗約歌. In *Lü shu ssu chung* 呂書四種. In *Lü tzu i-shu* 呂子遺書. *Ts'e* 24.
———. *Wu ju* 無如. Preserved in a composite edition of *Lü tzu i-shu* 呂子遺書. *Ts'e* 31. East Asiatic Library, Berkeley.
———. *Yen Hsiao-erh yü* 演小兒語. 1 *chüan*. In *Lü shu ssu chung* 呂書四種. In *Lü tzu i-shu* 呂子遺書. *Ts'e* 24.
Lü Te-sheng 呂得勝. *Hsiao-erh yü* 小兒語. 1 *chüan*. In *Lü shu ssu chung* 呂書四種. In *Lü tzu i-shu* 呂子遺書. *Ts'e* 24.
———. *Nü hsiao-erh yü* 女小兒語. 1 *chüan*. In *Lü shu ssu chung* 呂書四種. In *Lü tzu i-shu* 呂子遺書. *Ts'e* 24.
Lü Wei-ch'i 呂維祺. *Ming-te hsien-sheng wen-chi* 明德先生文集. 26 *chüan*. 1668.
Ma-ch'eng hsien chih 麻城縣志. 1882.
Meng Ch'iu 孟秋. *Meng Wo-chiang hsien-sheng chi* 孟我疆先生集. 7 *chüan*. 1586. Preserved in the Sonkeikaku Bunko.

Meng Feng 孟鳳. *Hsing-chün hsü chih* 行軍須知. 2 *chüan*. 1522.
Meskill, John. "Academies and Politics in the Ming Dynasty." In Charles O. Hucker, ed., *Chinese Government in Ming Times*, 149–74. New York: Columbia University Press, 1969.
———. *Ch'oe Pu's Diary: A Record of Drifting Across the Sea*. Tucson: University of Arizona Press, 1965.
Millinger, James Ferguson. "Ch'i Chi-kuang: Chinese Military Official." Ph.D. dissertation, Yale University, 1968.
Ming shih 明史. Edited by Kuo-fang yen-chiu yüan. 332 *chüan*. 6 vols. Taipei: Lien-ho ch'u-pan chung-hsin, 1970.
Ning-kuo fu chih 寧國府志. 1919.
Ning-ling hsien chih 寧陵縣志. 12 *chüan*. Edited by Wang T'u-ning 王圖寧. 1693.
Nivison, David S. "Protest Against Conventions and Conventions of Protests." In Arthur F. Wright, ed., *The Confucian Persuasion*. Stanford: Stanford University Press, 1960.
———. "The Problem of 'Knowledge' and 'Action' in Chinese Thought since Wang Yang-ming." In Arthur F. Wright, ed., *Studies in Chinese Thought*, 112–145. Chicago: Chicago University Press, 1953.
O'Hara, Albert Richard. *The Position of Woman in Early China*. Taipei: Mei Ya Publications, Inc., 1971.
Ōkubo Hideko 大久保英子. *Min Shinjidai shoin no kenkyū* 明清時代書院の研究. Tokyo: Kokusho kankōkai, 1976.
Okada Takehiko 岡田武彦. *Ō Yōmei to Minmatsu no jugaku* 王陽明と明末の儒学. Tokyo: Kōmeisha, 1970.
Overmyer, Daniel L. *Folk Buddhist Religion: Dissenting Sects in Late Traditional China*. Cambridge: Harvard University Press, 1976.
Parsons, James Bunyan. *Peasant Rebellions of the Late Ming*. Tucson: University of Arizona Press, 1970.
Perkins, Dwight. *Agricultural Development in China, 1368–1968*. Chicago: Aldine, 1969.
Peterson, Willard J. "Fang I-chih: Western Learning and the 'Investigation of Things.'" In Wm. Theodore de Bary et al., eds. *The Unfolding of Neo-Confucianism*, 369–411. New York: Columbia University Press, 1975.
———. *The Bitter Gourd*. New Haven: Yale University Press, 1979.

Rawski, Evelyn Sakakida. *Agricultural Change and the Peasant Economy of South China*. Cambridge: Harvard University Press, 1972.

———. *Education and Popular Literacy in Ch'ing China*. Ann Arbor: University of Michigan Press, 1979.

Sakai Tadao 酒井忠夫. *Chūgoku zensho no kenkyū* 中国善書の研究. Tokyo: Kokusho kankōkai, 1960.

———. "Confucianism and Popular Educational Works." In Wm. Theodore de Bary, ed., *Self and Society in Ming Thought*, 331–366. New York: Columbia University Press, 1970.

Shao-wu fu chih 邵武府志. 1543.

Sheng Lang-hsi 盛朗西. *Chung-kuo shu-yüan chih-tu* 中國書院制度. Shanghai: Chung-hua shu-chü, 1934.

Ssu-k'u ch'üan-shu tsung-mu, ch'in-ting 四庫全書總目欽定. 200 *chüan*. 10 vols. Taipei: I-wen yin-shu-kuan, 1964.

Su Yüan-sheng 蘇源生, ed. *Chi-kuo chai ts'ang shu* 記過齋叢書. T'ung-chih edition.

Sun Ch'i-feng 孫奇逢. *Chung-chou jen-wu k'ao* 中州人物考. In *Sun Hsia-feng ta ch'üan-chi* 孫夏峯大全集. *Ts'e* 30–35. 1845.

———. *Li-hsüeh tsung-chuan* 理學宗傳. In *Sun Hsia-feng ta ch'üan-chi* 孫夏峯大全集. *Ts'e* 15–29. 1845.

Sun P'ei-yang 孫丕揚, Liu Tung-hsing 劉東星, and Lü K'un 呂坤, eds. *Hsün-fang tsung-yüeh* 巡方總約. 1594. Preserved in Toyō Bunka, Tokyo University.

Sung Ying-hsing. *T'ien-kung k'ai-wu, Chinese Technology in the Seventeenth Century*. Translated by E-tu Zen Sun and Shiou-chuan Sun. University Park: The Pennsylvania State University Press, 1966.

Ta Ming hui-tien 大明會典. 228 *chüan*. Photo reprint of 1587 edition, 5 vols. Taipei: Chung-wen shu-chü, 1963.

T'ai-hu hsien chih 太湖縣志. 46 *chüan*. Edited by Chao Chi-yüan 趙繼元. 1872.

T'an Ch'ien 談遷. *Kuo ch'üeh* 國榷. 104 *chüan*. 6 vols. Peking: Ku-chi ch'u-pan-she, 1958.

T'ang Pin 湯斌. *Lo-hsüeh pien* 洛學編. 5 *chüan*. In *T'ang tzu i-shu* 湯子遺書. 1870.

T'ao Hsi-sheng 陶希聖. *Chung-kuo cheng-chih ssu-hsiang shih* 中國政治思想史. Shanghai: Hsin sheng-ming shu-chü, 1932.

———. "Ming-tai mi-lo pai-lien chiao chi ch'i-t'a yao-tsei" 明代彌勒白蓮教及其他「妖賊」. In Pao Ts'un-p'eng 包遵彭 ed., *Ming-tai tsung-chiao* 明代宗教, 5–16. Taipei: Tai-wan hsüeh-sheng shu-chü, 1968.

Taylor, Rodney Leon. *The Cultivation of Sagehood as a Religious Goal in Neo-Confucianism: A Study of Selected Writings of Kao P'an-lung (1562–1626)*. Missoula, Montana: Scholars Press, 1978.

Teng-feng hsien chih 登封縣志. Edited by Chiao Ch'ing-ch'ung 焦欽寵. 10 *chüan*. 1696.

Tsou Yüan-piao 鄒元標. *Yüan-hsüeh chi* 願學集. 8 *chüan*. Ssu-k'u ch'üan-shu chen-pen, 5th. series, vols. 376–7. Photo reprint of Wen Yüan Ko copy. Taipei: Shang-wu, 1974.

Tu, Wei-ming. *Neo-Confucian Thought in Action: Wang Yang-ming's Youth (1472–1509)*. Berkeley, Los Angeles, New York: University of California Press, 1976.

———. "Yen Yüan: From Inner Experience to Lived Concreteness." In Wm. Theodore de Bary et al., eds., *The Unfolding of Neo-Confucianism*, 511–541. New York: Columbia University Press, 1975.

Tung-ch'ang fu chih 東昌縣志. Edited by Hsieh Hsiang-k'ai 謝香開. 50 *chüan*. 1808.

Twitchett, Denis. "The Fan Clan's Charitable Estate, 1050–1760." In David S. Nivison and Arthur F. Wright, eds., *Confucianism in Action*, 97–133. Stanford: Stanford University Press, 1959.

Van Gulik, Robert Hans. *Sexual Life in Ancient China*. Leiden: Brill, 1961.

Wakeman, Frederic, Jr. "The Price of Autonomy: Intellectuals in Ming and Ch'ing Politics." *Daedalus*, 101:35–70 (Spring, 1972).

Waley, Arthur. *The Analects of Confucius*. New York: Modern Library, n.d. First printed, 1938.

Wang Shou-jen 王守仁. *Wang Yang-ming ch'üan-shu* 王陽明全書. 38 *chüan*. Ssu-pu pei-yao edition. Shanghai: Chung-hua shu-chü, 1934.

Wang Lan-yin 王蘭蔭. "Ming-tai chih hsiang-yüeh yü min-chung chiao-yü" 明代之鄉約與民衆教育. *Shih-ta yüeh-k'an* 師大月刊, 21:103–122 (1935).

———. "Ming-tai chih she-hsüeh"明代之社學. *Shih-ta yüeh-k'an* 師大月刊, 21:42–102; 25:63–129 (1935).

Wang Yang-ming. *Instructions for Practical Living and other Neo-Confucian Writings*. Translated and edited by Wing-tsit Chan. New York: Columbia University Press, 1974.

Watt, John R. *The District Magistrate in Late Imperial China*. New York: Columbia University Press, 1972.

Watters, T[homas]. *A Guide to the Tablets in a Temple of Confucius*. Shanghai: American Presbyterian Mission Press, 1879.

Wei Hsi 魏禧. *Chiu huang ts'e* 救荒策. T'sung-shu chi-ch'eng edition, No. 966.

Wei I-ao 魏一鼇. *Pei hsüeh pien* 北學編. 4 *chüan*. 1868.

Wen Chün-t'ien 聞鈞天. *Chung-kuo pao-chia chih-tu k'ao* 中國保甲制度考. Shanghai: Shang-wu, 1935.

Wen Huang 溫璜. *Wen shih mu hsün* 溫氏母訓. Hsüeh-hai lei-pien edition, n.d.

Wiens, Mi Chü. "Cotton Textile Production and Rural Social Transformation in Early Modern China." *Journal of the Institute of Chinese Studies of the Chinese University of Hong Kong*. 7,2:515–534 (1974).

Wilhelm, Hellmut. "Chinese Confucianism on the Eve of the Great Encounter." In Marius B. Jansen, ed., *Changing Attitudes Towards Modernization*, 283–310. Princeton: Princeton University Press.

———. "On Ming Orthodoxy." *Monumenta Serica*, 29:1–26 (1970–71).

Wilhelm, Richard, tr. *The I Ching, or Book of Changes*. Rendered into English by Cary F. Baynes. New York: Pantheon, 1961.

Williamson, H. R. *Wang An Shih: A Chinese Statesman and Educationalist of the Sung Dynasty*. 2 vols. London: Arthur Probsthain, 1935.

Wolff, Ernst. "A Preliminary Study of Hai Jui: His Biography in the Ming-shih." *Journal of the Australian Oriental Society*, 147–161 (1971).

Wu Ch'eng-en. *Monkey*. Translated by Arthur Waley. New York: Grove Press, 1943.

Wu Pei-yi. "Self-Examination and Confession of Sins in Traditional China." *Harvard Journal of Asiatic Studies*, 39, 1:5–38 (1979).

Yamada Y. 山田秀二. "Min Shin jidai no sonraku jichi ni tsuite (1)" 明清時代の村落自治について. *Rekishi gaku kenkyū* 歷史学研究 7:214–230 (1934).

Yang Ch'i-yüan 楊起元. [*Ch'ung-k'o*] *Yang Fu-so hsien-sheng chia ts'ang wen-chi* 重刻楊復所先生家藏文集. 8 *chüan*. Wan-li edition.

Yang, C. K. "Some Characteristics of Chinese Bureaucratic Behavior." In David S. Nivison and Arthur F. Wright, eds., *Confucianism in Action*, 134–164. Stanford: Stanford University Press, 1959.

Yang, Lien-sheng. "Ming Local Administration." In Charles O. Hucker, ed., *Chinese Government in Ming Times*, 1–22. New York: Columbia University Press, 1969.

Yang Tung-ming 楊東明. *Ch'ing so chin yen* 青瑣藎言. 2 *chüan*. 1612. Preserved in the Gest Library, Princeton University.

———. *Lun hsing i yen* 論性臆言. 1 *chüan*. Preserved in the Gest Library, Princeton University.

———. *Shan-chü kung-k'o* 山居功課. 10 *chüan*. 1624.

Yao Shun-mu 姚舜牧. *Yao yen* 藥言. Ts'ung-shu chi-ch'eng edition, No. 976. Changsha: Shang-wu, 1939.

Yen Chung-p'ing 嚴中平. *Chung-kuo mien-fang-chih shih-kao* 中國棉紡織史稿. Peking: K'o-hsüeh ch'u-pan-she, 1963.

Yim Shui-yuen. "Famine Relief Statistics as a Guide to the Population of Sixteenth-Century China: A Case-Study of Honan Province." *Ch'ing-shih wen-t'i*, 3,9:1–30 (Nov., 1978).

Yü-ch'eng hsien chih 虞城縣志. 10 *chüan*. Edited by Hsi Ch'ing-yün 席慶雲. 1895.

Yü, Chün-fang. *The Renewal of Buddhism in China*. New York: Columbia University Press, 1981.

Yü, Kristin. See Greenblatt, Kristin Yü.

Yü, Ying-shih. "Some Preliminary Observations on the Rise of Ch'ing Confucian Intellectualism." *The Tsing Hua Journal of Chinese Studies*. New Series 11,1,2:105–146 (Dec., 1975).

Yüan Hung-tao 袁宏道. *Yüan Chung-lang sui-pi* 袁中郎隨筆. In

Yüan Chung-lang ch'üan-shu 袁中郎全書. Edited by Yang Chia-lo 楊家駱. Taipei: Shih-chieh shu-chü, 1964.

Yuan, Tsing. "Continuities and Discontinuities in Chinese Agriculture, 1550–1700." *Ming Studies*, 7:35–51 (Fall, 1978).

———. "Urban Riots and Disturbances." In Jonathan D. Spence and John E. Wills, Jr., eds., *From Ming to Ch'ing*, 280–320. New Haven: Yale University Press, 1979.

Index

Academies, private (*shu-yüan*), 33–34, 47; construction of, 41, 44, 86; Feng Ts'ung-wu on, 89; ideal-centered method of self-cultivation in, 203; meetings at, 87, 197; proliferation of, 34, 88; proscription of, 52–53, 87; regulations for, 90–92, 98. *See also* Learned discussions; Shou-shan Academy; Tung-lin Academy

Administration: local, 67–69, 78–83, 111–112; writings on, xi, 104–106, 208. *See also* Statecraft; Volunteer efforts

Agriculture, 20, 98, 212; handbooks on, 103, 106, 210

Authority: equated with official status, 206; and fact-centered outlook, 205–208; figures of, 51–52, 118; and ideal-centered outlook, 205–206, 208; for moral leadership, 141; personal experience as source of, 4; reactions to, 56, 118; of Yang Tung-ming, 69, 77. *See also* Teachers

Average men (*chung-jen*), 76, 84, 114, 116, 130, 133, 139, 201

Banditry, xi, 59, 107; and commercialization, 24; and destruction of Yü-ch'eng, 81; and moral suasion, 74; prevention of, xii, 111, 172, 173, 174

Battles, military, 169; metaphors of, 218. *See also* Military concerns

Beggars, self-reliance of, xii, 11, 162–163, 181–182

Beneficial friends (*i-yu*), 76–77, 207

Buddhism, 75, 85, 88, 112, 200; fact-centered method of self-cultivation in, 193; Feng Ts'ung-wu's opposition to, 94, 95, 97; synthesis with Confucianism, 45; and views of Lin Chao-en, 171

Capital newspaper, 13–14, 202

Chai Ch'u-t'an, 43

Chan Jo-shui, 34

Chang Chü-cheng: antagonism to Lo Ju-feng, 43, 45, 53, 88; criticism of learned discussions, 52–53; death of, 65; policies of, 30, 40; and proscription of academies, 52–53, 87

Chang Tsai, 50; *Hsi-ming* [Western Inscription], 49, 153

Chang Wei, 110

Chang Yüan-pien, 15, 45, 77

"Chao liang-hsin" ["A Summons to My Conscience"], by Lü K'un, 174, 187

Chao Nan-hsing, 66

Charitable activities, 10*n*13, 68–73, 107

Ch'en Hu, 210–211; *Sheng-hsüeh ju-men shu* [An Introduction to the Study of Sagehood], 210

Ch'en Hung-mou, 9–10, 115; *Wu-chung i-kuei* [Five Types of Transmitted Guidelines], 10, 107

Ch'en Liang, 104

Ch'en Lung-cheng, 103–104

Ch'en Ti, 4*n*

Cheng (imperial consort), 110

Cheng Ch'eng-en, 110

Ch'eng Hao, 38
Ch'i Chi-kuang, 35, 38, 103, 163; *Chi-hsiao hsin-shu* [New Manual of Effectiveness], 184; manuals on warfare of, 173, 174, 183–184; and regulations, 184–185; reputation as scholar of, 209
Ch'i Piao-chia, 104
"Chia yüeh chieh" ["An Explanation of Family Music"], by Lü K'un, 161, 183
Chiao Hung, 4*n*, 15, 16*n*30, 43, 45
Chiao-t'ai Rhyme-book, by Lü K'un, 155–156
Chien-ai. *See* Universal love
Ch'ien-shan kai-kuo chih hsüeh (study by promoting goodness and correcting faults), 210
Ch'ien Te-hung, 28
Chih-ch'üan Academy, 197
Chih min [Governing the People], 106. *See also Shih-cheng lu*
Children, writings for, xii, 7, 144, 146–147
Ching-chi shih-hsüeh (statecraft and practical learning), 74
Chiu-ming shu [A Book on Saving Lives], by Lü K'un, 172, 174, 177, 178, 181
Chou Ju-teng, 45, 169; on benefits of illness, 169, 170–171, 172, 205; on correcting errors, 201; criticism of, 31*n*78; and self-cultivation, 208–209; on self-scrutiny, 195
Chou Ssu-chiu, 40
Chou Tso-jen, 145*n*6
Chu Hsi, 27, 103, 214; *Chin-ssu lu* [Reflections on Things at Hand], 92–93
Chu-hung, 201; *Tzu-chih lu* [The Record of Self-Examination], 195
Chu Shih, 9
Chung ("the mean" or "middle way"), 123–124
Chung-yung [The Doctrine of the Mean], 155
Chü-kuan pi-yao [Essentials for Officials]. *See Shih-cheng lu*
Ch'üan-shih ko-tien [A Songbook for Exhorting the World], by Lü K'un, 162
Classics: commentaries to, 27; as common culture for scholar-officials, 12–13, 19–20; discussions of, 67; Lü K'un's attitude towards, xi, 192, 214; motives for understanding, 206; as objects of study, 4; and scholar-officials, 13, 16–20; and self-cultivation, 186, 192; Yang Tung-ming on, 76. *See also* Examinations, civil-service; Learning
Clerks, 128–129; contrast to officials, 19, 105, 108, 128–129, 159; and law cases, 61. *See also* Functionaries
Commercialization: and economic equilibrium, 71; and effect on small landowners, 62; and reorientation, 6; of rural areas, x, 20–23, and scholars, 190; and social change, 23–24. *See also* Merchants
Communication: through capital newspaper, 13–14; with common people, 35–36; and coordination (*t'ung*), 142; and oneness of society, 152–153; and paper work, 159–160; two-way, of Lü K'un, 108, 143, 148–149, 151–157. *See also* Printing, spread of; Vernacular language
Community: and abstract values, 208; and debates among scholar-officials, 94; definition of, 5, 6, 215; disintegration of, 57; within families, 91; and humaneness, 46, 51, 90–91; and personal experiences, 205, 208; regulations v. spontaneous group spirit in, 90–92, 123. *See also* Yang Tung-ming
Community schools, 25–26, 68, 70, 158
Confucianism, 53, 77, 213; and academies, 88; in action, 6, 7, 9, 11; and administration, ix, 108; of Ch'i Chi-kuang, 209; fact-centered method of self-cultivation in, 194; of Hai Jui, 119; of Lü K'un, x, 142, 217; socialization of aspirants, 206; synthesis of Buddhism and, 45, 94, 97, 171

Confucius, 4*n*, 8, 76, 89, 96, 98, 131, 145; *Analects* of, 193, 201; on correcting faults, 193; as inspiration for scholar-officials, 16–17, 195; as inspiration for students, 205
Crises: as basis for community, 208; identification of values with, 36; Lü K'un's preoccupation with, xi, 99, 161–185; penchant for, 32; prevention of, 211; responsibility of officials in, 68; and self-reliance, 163, 204, 217; and sense-perceptions, 163. *See also* Experience, personal; Illness; Military concerns

Degree-holders, 58–59. *See also* Examinations, civil-service; *Hsiu-ts'ai*
Didactic works, xii, 26, 103–106, 143–159. *See also* Lü K'un

Education: democratization of, x, 20, 24–28, 30, 46, 48, 74, 86, 89, 111, 148; and fact-centered method of self-cultivation, 204; and ideas of Wang Yang-ming, 217; and intuitive knowledge (*liang-chih*), 74; leaning of scholar-officials towards, 12; moral, 31; promotion of, by local administrators, 111–112, 126, 139–140, 147; v. rules, 126; of women, 147–148. *See also* Classics; Community schools; *Hsiang-yüeh*; Learning
Evidential studies, 3, 4
Examinations, civil-service, 26, 28, 58; call for reform of, 105, 212; competition for, 130; and Confucian values, 206; eight-legged essay in, 17, 212; and personal fame, 112–113; as preparation for office, 17–20, 206
Experience, personal (*t'i-jen*): and adjustment to semi-educated, 7; association with common people of, 154–158; v. classical studies, 5, 76; and correction of faults, 186–187, 194, 197; and crisis mentality, 99, 161–185; importance of, 185; and isolation, 204, 207; late Ming emphasis on, 7; limitations of, 81–83; Lü K'un's emphasis on, x–xi, 108, 183, 188, 192–193, 214–215, 216, 217, 218; sharing of, 205; as source of authority, 4, 28; and student-teacher affiliation, 14–15, 206–207

Famine, xi, 70, 71, 78, 79–81, 173, 181; relief of, 73, 104, 107, 187, 197, 211, 212. *See also* Grain equalization programs; Yü-ch'eng, Honan
Fan-ch'ieh system, 156
Fan Chung-yen, 78, 104, 105; "I-t'ien chi" ["Record of Charitable Fields"], 111
Fan family, 70, 72
Fang I-chih, 3*n*, 14*n*26, 118
Faults, correction of (*kai-kuo*), 10*n*14, 186–212
Feng-hsien yüeh [Surveillance of Officials], 106. *See also Shih-cheng lu*
Feng-liu (romantic) tradition, 71
Feng Ts'ung-wu, 84–99; "Ch'in-chien shuo" ["On Diligence and Frugality"], 94, 96, 97; compared with Lü K'un, 11, 12–13, 15, 126; and correcting faults, 196, 197, 198, 201, 202, 205; criticism of emperors of, 30, 85; fight against self-interest of, 130, 134; friendship with Lü K'un, 16*n*31, 126; friendship with Tsou Yüan-piao, 117; *I-ssu lu* ["Records of Thoughts on Doubtful Points"], 86; *Kuan-hsüeh pien*, 85, 96; and Lo Ju-fang, 53, 84, 67, 121; *Pien-hsüeh lu*, 85; and reliance on regulations, 114; retirement of, 113; "Shan li t'u" ["Chart of Goodness and Profit"], 202; "Shan li t'u shuo" ["Explanation of the Chart of Goodness and Profit"], 86, 130; at Shou-shan Academy, 200; and vernacular fiction, 26; *Yüan-ju k'ao lüeh*, 85, 96
Feng Ying-ching, 77
Feng Yu, 84

Fu Mei, 115
Functionaries (*li*), 19; three types of, 115; and initiative, 137. *See also* Clerks

Grain equalization programs, 68, 69, 78, 103, 104, 111, 212
Great Learning, The. See Ta hsüeh
Groaning Words. See Shen-yin yü

Hai Jui, 54–64; attitude to common people of, 151, 152, 155, 157; and Chang Chü-cheng, 40; as *chin-shih* aspirant, 36, 38–39; compared with Lo Ju-fang, 12, 36, 39–41, 51; compared with Lü K'un, x, 108, 119, 120–126, 127, 134, 136, 138, 185, 215; compared with Yang Tung-ming, 82; criticism of emperors of, 30, 33, 40, 55; fight against self-interest of, 130, 134; handbooks of, 185; and local administration, 21, 35; opposition to compromise of, 123; and redistribution of land, 136; reliance on laws of, 114, 116, 118, 124, 182, 185, 215
Han Fei Tzu, 9*n*11, 97
Han Yü, 56
Hao-jen ko [The Song of the Good Person], by Lü K'un, 145–146
Ho Hsin-yin, 29, 35, 45, 47, 217
Ho Liang-chün, 63
Ho-shih lao-jen (compromisers), 60
Honan, 8, 130. *See also* Hsin-an; Ning-ling; Yü-ch'eng
Hsiang-chia yüeh [Local Sub-Official Personnel], 106. *See also Shih-cheng lu*
Hsiang-yüan (self-righteous hypocrites), 61, 130
Hsiang-yüan, Shansi, 109, 149–150
Hsiang-yüeh (rural lectures), 9*n*11, 47–51; combined with *pao-chia*, 126, 139, 217; and common people, 203–204; handbooks on, 106, 160; and Lo Ju-fang, 59, 157; Lü K'un's instructions to, 198–199; organization of, 85, 103; and self-cultivation, 203
Hsiao-erh yü [Words for Children], by Lü Te-sheng, 144, 146
Hsin-an, Honan, 15*n*29, 67, 196
Hsing-hsin chi [A Record of Self-Examination], by Lü K'un, 187, 189, 190–191, 196, 207
Hsiu-ts'ai ("budding scholars"), 23, 58, 59, 73, 126, 127
Hsiung Ping-yüan, 111
Hsü Chieh, 34, 36, 38, 43, 47, 52, 56, 88
Hsü Fu-yüan, 15*n*29, 16*n*31, 45, 103
Hsü Hsiao-erh yü [A Sequel to Words for Children], by Lü K'un, 144
Hsü Kuang-ch'i, 167; *Nung-cheng ch'üan-shu*, 103
Hsü Yüeh, 37, 38
Hsüeh Hsüan, 195, 210; *Tu-shu lu* [Record of Reading Books], 191, 209
Hsün-fang tsung-yüeh [A General Compact for Regional Inspectors], 106
Hsün Tzu, 98, 114, 126
Hu Chih, 43, 44, 45, 46
Hu Shih, ix
Huang-Ming ching-shih wen-pien [Writings on the Statecraft of the Illustrious Ming Dynasty], 104
Huang Tao-chou, 8
Huang Tsung-hsi, 3*n*, 16*n*31; on lectures of Lo Ju-fang, 42; *Ming-ju hsüeh-an* [Records of Ming Philosophers], 14, 97, 109, 207
Humaneness (*jen*): and Feng Ts'ung-wu, 197; and Hai Jui, 54, 182; Lo Ju-fang's confidence in, 46, 50, 51, 89–90, 98, 182; Lü K'un on, 131–133, 178–179; models of, 205–206
Hung Liang-chi, 10
Hung-tao Academy, 87

I ching, 156, 183*n*86
Idealism: of Classics, 18–19, 167; and commercialization, 23; of Feng Ts'ung-wu, 85–86; of Lo Ju-fang, 51–52; of Lü K'un, 11, 178, 217; realization of, and laws, 215; and self-cultivation, 197, 205–206, 208, 212

Illness, 161–163, 169–170; benefits of, 170–172; metaphor of, x, 213, 218; place of, in conceptual patterns, 163; use of, in giving value to ideas, 171–172; value of, 205. *See also Shen-yin yü*
Independence: contrast to affiliation, 117–118, 120–122; and fact-centered method of self-cultivation, 206–207; of Lü K'un, 213; and "miscellaneous Confucians," 207
Intuitive knowledge (*liang-chih*), 5, 27, 46, 74, 92, 216

Kan-ch'üan school, 15, 16*n*31
K'ang-hsi, 9*n*11, 10–11
Kao P'an-lung, 31*n*78, 90, 116, 167*n*16, 209, 217; on types of officials, 139
Keng Ting-hsiang: death of, 77; and exchange of information, 13–14; as friend of Lo Ju-fang, 39–40, 45, 46–47, 67; and Lin Chao-en, 171; and Lü K'un, 15, 117
Ko-wu ("investigation of things"), 27, 214, 216
Ku Hsien-ch'eng, 15–16, 31, 98–99, 121, 168, 217
Ku Yen-wu, 3*n*, 4*n*, 10*n*14, 14*n*26, 118
Kuan (critical junctures), 168
Kuan Chih-tao, 47
Kuan Chung, 97
Kuan-chung Academy, 86, 89
Kuei chieh [Precepts for Women], by Lü K'un, 143, 147, 148, 149
Kuei-fan t'u-shuo [Illustrated Regulations for the Women's Quarters], by Lü K'un, 110, 113, 143–144, 147–148
Kung-i (public opinion), 62, 151
Kung-kuo ko [A Ledger of Merit and Demerit], 195

Laws: attitude of Hai Jui to, 54–55, 56, 60–64, 118, 124–125, 158, 215; attitude of Lü K'un to, 118, 215; to control greed, 133–134; and feelings of the people, 157–158; v. moral suasion, 105, 108, 113–115, 116, 128; perfected by sages, 75–76; and standardization, 60, 106, 115, 124. *See also* Legalism; Litigation
Learned discussions (*chiang-hsüeh*): benefits for the poor of, 86; debates over value of, 95–96, 98, 120–121, 216; differences among lecturers in, 93–94; Chang Chü-cheng's opposition to, 40, 43, 77; at Ling-chi Temple, 36, 37, 38, 39, 43; of Lo Ju-fang, 42–43, 44, 45–46; loss of significance of, 95, 99; v. practicality, 4*n*2, 75–76, 113; v. "solid learning," 20; of Yang Tung-ming 67, 75, 76, 77
Learning: attitudes towards, 5, 7, 12, 18, 148, 198; emphasis on pleasurable, x, 27; faith (*hsin*) in, 97–98; and morality, 96, 98, 99; objectification of, 4; qualities associated with, 95. *See also* Practical learning
Lecturing: commitment to, of Feng Ts'ung-wu, 84–86; criticism of, 53, 75, 93, 95–96; defense of, by Yang Tung-ming, 75–77; demand for, 46; to establish reputation, 88–89; Feng Ts'ung-wu on, 93, 94–95; at Ling-chi Temple, 36, 37, 38, 39, 40, 43, 47; of Lo Ju-fang, 33, 39; popularization of sagehood through, 74. *See also* Academies, private; Learned discussions; Lo Ju-fang
Legalism, 97–98, 118, 211*n*112. *See also* Hai Jui; Wang An-shih
Li (principle), 27, 141, 216
Li-chia system, 35
Li Chih: analogy between scholars and merchants of, 129, 130, 131; attitude to profit, 130–131, 176; biography of Hai Jui of, 40; compared with Yang Tung-ming, 82; *Hsü Fen shu* [Sequel to a Book to Be Burned], 75; and Lo Ju-fang, 43, 45; preoccupation with illness of, 169, 170
Li Ssu, 98
Li Ts'ai, 66
Li Yung, 10*n*14
Li Yü, 200, 202

Liang Chang-chü, 10*n*14
Liang Ch'i-ch'ao, 3*n*
Liang-chih. See Intuitive knowledge
Lieh nü chuan [Biographies of Model Women], 144
Lin Chao-en, 47, 169, 171–172, 206
Lin Tse-hsü, 107
Literacy, 4, 25–27, 30; spread of, ix, x, xii, 6. *See also* Education
Litigation, 59, 60–61, 63
Liu Tsung-chou, 8, 200, 202–203, 210; *Jen p'u* [A Manual for Men], 203
Liu Tung-hsing, 106
Lo Ju-fang, 12–13, 41–54; as *chin-shih* aspirant, 36–39; compared with Feng Ts'ung-wu, 87, 89, 96; compared with Hai Jui, 39–41, 54, 57, 157; compared with Lü K'un, xi, xii, 12–13, 148–149, 153, 216; compared with Yang Tung-ming, 74, 76–77, 79; and correcting faults, 194; followers of, 67, 74, 121, 170, 195; and humaneness, 89, 90, 194; and oneness of society, 153; opposition of Chang Chü-cheng to, 40, 43; as sage, 33, 35, 36; and self-cultivation, 186, 191, 203; and theme of illness, 37, 169; tracing ideas of, 214; on universal love (*chien-ai*), 88
Lu Hsiang-shan, 38
Lu Lung-ch'i, 9, 31*n*78, 205, 210
Lu Shih-i, 210
Lü Chih-wei (son of Lü K'un), 81, 202
Lü K'un, ix–x, 103–218; on average men, 114; avoidance of lecturing, 216; biography of, 109–113; and bureaucratic paper work, 159–160; canonization of, 8; and collection of information, 160; and commercialization, 23, 130, 131; and conflict of mind and senses, 163–168; control over environment of, 170; correspondence with Yang Tung-ming, 75, 76; crisis mentality of, 213, 215; distrust of human relations of, 116–118; on education, 126; epitaph of, 187–188; fact-centered method of self-cultivation of, 186–189, 202–203, 206–207; and the feelings of the people, 149–158; friends of, 12, 15–16, 196; on greed, 134, 136–137; groping for objective outlook, 123–126, 140–142; humaneness of, 131–133, 178–179, 217; independence of, 15–16, 117, 190, 213, 214; on landlord-tenant relationships, 23–24; list-keeping (*tien-chien*) of, 189–191, 204, 208, 215; long-range view of, 174–185; on the mean, 123–124; medical concerns of, 140, 160, 169; on merits and demerits, 198; and military problems, 173, 174, 187, 209, 217; on official duties, 115; opinion of scholarly debates, 120–121, 151; *pao chia* combined with *hsiang-yüeh*, 49, 126, 139, 217; perspective on society of, 126–129; on power, 122, 134–135; practical learning of, 8, 75, 213; promotion of cotton weaving of, 22; reaction against limited vision of, 163; reaction to Wang Ken, 148; reaction to mother's illness of, 112, 161–162, 163, 169; recognition of, 8–9, 9–11, 107; and redistribution of wealth, 136, 150–151; on regret, 175, 176; search for order through crises, 168–174, 182–183; on self-reliance of poor, 181; sharing of personal experiences, 205; on soldier's life, 178–179; sponsoring of medicine, xii, 187; two-way communication of, 108, 143, 148–149; use of medical metaphor, 140–141, 215; use of music, 161–163; use of regulations, 124, 128, 141–142; vernacular language of, 8, 143, 147–148, 213; "Warning against Ungratefulness," 131; writing style of, 8, 107, 143–144, 213; writings of, xii, 7–11, 36, 99, 143–159, 213, 216, 217
Lü-shih hsiang-yüeh [The *hsiang-yüeh* of Mr. Lü], 47, 50. *See also Hsiang-yüeh*

Lü Shu-chien. *See* Lü K'un
Lü Te-sheng (father of Lü K'un), 111, 144, 146, 149
Lü Tsu-ch'ien: *Chin-ssu lu* [Reflections on Things at Hand], 92–93
Lü-tzu i-shu [Lü's Transmitted Works], 107
Lü Wei-ch'i, 196–198; on correcting errors, 198, 201–202; and fact-centered method of self-cultivation, 203–204; independence of, 207; use of medical metaphor of, 209; on personal experience, 197–198

Markets, proliferation of, x, 20, 22–24, 70. *See also* Commercialization
Medicine: analogy of, 140–141, 208–209, 211, 213; Lü K'un's sponsoring of, xii, 187; treatises on, 104, 106, 160, 211; Yang Tung-ming's sponsoring of, 78–79. *See also* Crises; Illness
Mencius, 18, 50, 59, 205
Meng Ch'iu, 15, 16*n*31, 77, 82, 87, 196
Meng Feng: *Hsing-chün hsü chih* [What the Infantry Should Know], 173
Meng Hua-li, 15, 67, 77, 82, 196, 207; "Preface to the record of Errors for His Three Sons," 201
Merchants, 34, 86, 136
Military concerns: analogy of, 209; defense, 4, 30, 98, 103, 119*n*50, 172, 210; fortification of city walls, 173–174, 177, 178, 182, 217; and sense of crisis, 169, 182; and training of scholars, 210. *See also* Ch'i Chi-kuang; Meng Feng
Min wu [Essentials for the People], 106. *See also Shih-cheng lu*
Ming Chih [Provincial Officials], 106. *See also Shih-cheng lu*
Ming shih [The Official History of the Ming], 109
Ming-ju hsüeh-an. *See* Huang Tsung-hsi
Ming-tao Academy, 47
Mo Tzu, 53*n*90, 95

Neo-Confucianism, 3*n*, 5*n*, 6, 7, 38, 78, 85, 92, 214
Ning-ling, Honan, 109, 110–111, 136, 172–173, 174, 177, 182
Nü hsiao-erh yü [Words for Girls], by Lü Te-sheng, 144
Nü hsün [Instructions for Women], 162

Pao-chia: combined with *hsiang-yüeh*, 48, 124, 126, 139, 217; guides for members of, 104, 160; organization of, 85, 103, 106, 197
Pao-ch'ing Temple, 86, 90, 93
"Plaque for the Temple for the Medicine Sage," by Lü K'un, 169
Po Chü-i, 205
Poor, the: advice to, on saving, 181, care of, 68, 69, 70; difficulties of, 133*n*100; free instruction for, 74; self-reliance of, 108, 163; shaping of policies towards, 157; writings for, xii, 145. *See also* Famine
Practical learning (*shih-hsüeh*): and avoidance of politics, 93; v. classical learning, x, 18–20; praise of Lü K'un for, 8; reorientation towards, 4, 5; of Yang Tung-ming, 74–76, 82
Practicality: in administrative writings, 7, 104–105; of Chang Chü-cheng, 30; of Ch'en Ti, 4*n*2; and lecturing, 75, 93; of Lü K'un, ix, x–xi, 178, 213; of Yang Tung-ming, 67–71, 74–75, 78
Printing, spread of, 6, 35–36
Profit (*li*): attitudes towards, 57, 62, 119–120, 122, 126–127, 129, 130; Lü K'un on, 120, 131–137, 176–177; and political power, 134–135; and self-cultivation, 200; and social discord, 119, 135

Records of Practical Government. *See Shih-cheng lu*
Records of the Ming Philosophers. *See* Huang Tsung-hsi
Regulations: Ch'i Chi-kuang's explanation of, 184–185; Feng Ts'ung-wu on, 90; and Hai Jui,

Regulations (*continued*) 182; Lü K'un's exposition of, 15*n*28; preoccupation with, xi; in self-cultivation, 207
Rural lectures. *See Hsiang-yüeh*

Sagehood: definitions of, 122–124; paths to, 103–218; and power, 134–137
Sages, 33–64; v. common men, 176; death of, 77; and education, 27, 89–90; influence of, 122–123
Scholar-officials, 3–31; distinctions between common people and, 203; as doctors to society, 103–141, 148, 208–209; as doctors to the mind, 208–209; military interests of, 209*n*102; talent in, 137–142
Self-cultivation: combined with service to society, 5, 11, 13, 16, 17, 48; debate on methods of, 196; fact-centered method of, xi, 108–109, 186, 188–189, 190–191, 193–212, 215, 218; ideal-centered method of, 186, 188, 195, 200–201, 202, 203, 208; and lecturing, 75; Lo Ju-fang on, 51; Lu Lung-ch'i's work on, 9*n*11; mechanical use of merits and demerits in, 198–200, 207, 212; outlook of Lü K'un on, xi, 11, 108–109, 169, 174, 218; and scholar-officials, 12; and sharing of experiences, 92; shift to, from statecraft, 210, 211
Self-interest, 57, 218; alternative responses to, 129–137, 215
Self-reliance: Lü K'un's emphasis on, 162–163, 181–183, 204, 217
Sense perceptions: attitude of Hai Jui to, 183; attitude of Lo Ju-fang to, 183; conflict between mind and, 163–168, 170, 172, 183; emphasis on, 185; and Lü K'un, 214, 215
Service to society, 5, 6, 12, 13, 16, 17; and influence of Wang Yang-ming, 28–29. *See also* Administration; Practicality
Shao Yung, 203
Shen Pu-hai, 9*n*11
Shen-tsung, Emperor, 30–31, 105–106
Shen-yin yü [Groaning Words], by Lü K'un, 169, 187–193; criticisms of, 13; editions of, 9–10, 202; and fact-centered outlook, 204, 210; Feng Ts'ung-wu's opinion of, 99; and official as doctor, 209; and sharing of personal experiences, 205
Sheng-yüan. See Hsiu-ts'ai
Shih (power), 130, 138
Shih (tasks, events, duties, affairs), xi, 108, 115, 142, 163–164, 167, 175–176, 188, 211
Shih-cheng lu [Records of Practical Government], by Lü K'un, 11, 106–107, 113, 160, 178, 179, 198
"Shih li shuo" ["Discussion of Power and Profit"], by Lü K'un, 134–135
Shih Meng-lin, 66
Shih-tsung, Emperor, 55
Shou-shan Academy, 16*n*31, 45, 67, 73, 84, 94, 200
Shu ching [Book of History], 52
Shui-hu chuan [The Water Margin], 26, 91
Single Whip method of taxation, 21, 55
Six Classics, 76, 122
Six Imperial Injunctions, 50, 57, 77, 199
Social disharmony, xi, 197; and *hsiu-ts'ai* ("budding scholars"), 58; as result of commercialization, 23–24, 119–120, 131; and riots, 59, 60, 71, 172; and vagrants, 71, 73. *See also* White Lotus sect
Society for Promoting Learning (*Hsing-hsüeh hui*), 73, 74, 78, 83
Society for Sharing Goodness (*T'ung-shan hui*), 69, 71–72
Society for Sharing Pleasure (*T'ung yüeh hui*), 71, 78
Society for Spreading Humaneness (*Kuang-jen hui*), 69, 72, 78, 83
Songs, popular, 11, 42, 74, 92, 144–147, 157, 161
Ssu-li i [Supplement to the Four

Categories of Rituals], by Lü K'un, 9, 146, 155
Statecraft (*ching-shih*), ix, 74, 99; appeal of, 113–126; interest in, in 19th century, 8; late Ming concern with, xi; shift to, from self-cultivation, 209–212; writings on, 4, 5, 104–108, 208, 215, 218
Storytellers, 161, 181
Study societies, 73–75, 210; arguments in, 90–91; benefits of, 207; examination of errors in, 197. *See also* Academies, private
Sun P'ei-yang, 106, 110

Ta hsüeh [The Great Learning], 13, 17, 142, 155
Ta Ming hui-tien [Collected Statutes of the Ming Dynasty], 60
Ta-t'ung, Shensi, 109, 118, 149
Tai Shih-heng, 110
T'ai-chou school, x, 15, 16, 74, 148, 216
T'ai-hua Academy, 87
T'ai-tsu, Emperor, 24–25, 28, 35; *See also* Six Imperial Injunctions
T'an Lun, 37, 38, 40
T'ang Hsien-tsu, 45
T'ang Pin, 8
T'ao Hsing-chih, ix
Taoism, 55, 97, 112, 171, 193, 195
Teachers: affiliation of students and, 14; attitudes towards, 51–52, 56–57, 76, 89, 116, 118; in community schools, 25*n*56; Han Yü's essay on, 56; and "masterless men," 14*n*26, 118; relationship with students of, 8, 59, 149, 205–206, 214, 216; and self-cultivation, 206, 207. *See also* Authority
Teng I-tsan, 77, 153
Tien-chien (checking off lists), 189–191, 202, 204, 205, 208
T'ien-ch'üan Bridge, 28
Ts'ao Yin-ju, 43, 47
Tseng Kuo-fan, 210
Tsou Shan, 44
Tsou Yüan-piao, 13, 14, 15, 16*n*31, 40, 67, 82, 107; and Feng Tsung-wu, 90, 94, 117; and founding of Shou-shan Academy, 45; on learned discussions, 87–88; and Lin Chao-en, 171; and Lü K'un, 187–188, 195–196, 204, 214; on Lü K'un's *Groaning Words*, 192; opinion of Yen Chün, 52
Tsung-yüeh ko [Songs for a Lineage Compact], 131, 145, 146, 147
Tung-lin Academy, 16, 31–32, 99
Tung-lin movement, 12, 36, 121, 217. *See also* Kao P'an-lung; Ku Hsien-ch'eng
Tzu-p'ing yao-yü [The Essentials of Astrology], by Lü K'un, 162

Universal love (*chien-ai*), 53, 88, 95

Vernacular language, ix, 4–5, 7, 184, 185; fiction in, 26; of Lo Ju-feng, 49; of Lü K'un, x, 143–160, 213, 216. *See also* Songs, popular
Volunteer efforts, local, 67–69, 71–72, 73, 74, 78, 83

Wan-li emperor. *See* Shen-tsung, Emperor
Wan-li period, 8, 22, 70
Wang An-shih, 48, 85, 98, 104, 105, 114, 126
Wang Chi, 28, 31*n*78, 45
Wang Chia-p'ing, 118
Wang Ju-hsün, 66
Wang Ken, 28–29, 35, 38, 155; common status of, 37, 46, 203; "Song on the Enjoyment of Learning," 148; tracing ideas of 214
Wang Meng-feng, 67
Wang Na-yen, 69
Wang Shou-jen. *See* Wang Yang-ming
Wang Yang-ming, x, 27–28, 31, 32, 38, 82, 85; followers of, 74, 148, 212, 216, 218; use of *hsiang-yüeh* of, 48–49, 103; intellectual struggles of, 214; and intuitive knowledge, 92; as local administrator, 103; metaphysical discussions of, 195; and *pao-chia* system, 48–49; on private academies, 34; as sage, 33, 39, 40, 45, 51; school of, 15; significance of ideas of, 217

"Warning against Ungratefulness," by Lü K'un, 131
Wei Chung-hsien, 31
Wei Hsi, 211–212; *Ping chi* [In the Footprints of Armies], 212
Wei Yün-chen, 67, 77
White Lotus sect, 23, 24, 60, 119*n*50
Women, writings for, xii, 7, 143–144, 147–148, 162
Wu ju [Disregard Comparisons], by Lü K'un, 132, 146

Yang Ch'i-yüan, 15, 67, 74, 77
Yang Chu, 95
Yang min [Supporting and Instructing the People], 106. *See also Shih-cheng lu*
Yang Tung-kuang, 70
Yang Tung-ming, 65–83; *Ch'ing-so chin-yen*, 81; "Chi-min t'u-shuo shu" ["Illustrated Memorial on the Starving"], 80; commemorative pieces of, 78; and community schools, 25, 68; compared with Lü K'un, xi, 11, 12–13, 15; on correcting faults, 196, 198; *Lun-hsing i-yen* [Personal Opinions on the Nature of Man], 81; narrowness of, 99, 113; "Record of Charitable Fields," 78; "A Record of Grain Distribution," 79; "A Record of Sponsoring Marriages," 80; *Shan-chü kung k'o* [Accomplishments during Retirement], 81; sponsoring of Shou-shan Academy, 16*n*31; and taxation, 21; as teacher, 89
Yang Tung-shu, 70
Yao Shun-mu: *Yao yen* [Medicinal Words], 209
Yeh Shih, 104, 105
Yen Chün, 37, 38, 44, 46, 51–52, 214
Yen Hsiao-erh yü [Acting Out Words for Children], by Lü K'un, 144
Yen Yüan, 210
"Yu-wei shu," by Lü K'un, 110, 119*n*50
Yü-cheng [Prisons], 106. *See also Shih-cheng lu*
Yü-ch'eng, Honan: destruction by bandits in, 81; famine in, 70, 73, 79–81; Feng Ts'ung-wu at, 87; need for charitable efforts in, 70–71; Yang Tung-ming's retirement to, 66–70, 77, 83. *See also* Volunteer efforts; Yang Tung-ming
Yüan Huang, 45, 171, 194–195; approach to self-cultivation of, 200, 202, 208; "Li-ming pien" ["Essay on Establishing One's Destiny"], 195, 201
Yüan Hung-tao, 169
Yüan shih [History of the Yuan Dynasty], 193

Designer:	Randall Goodall
Compositor:	G&S Typesetters
Printer:	Thomson-Shore, Inc.
Binder:	John H. Dekker & Sons
Text:	11/13 Linotron 202 Palatino
Display:	Linotron 202 Palatino